The Whisky Men

The Whisky Men

GAVIN D. SMITH

Birlinn

First published in 2005 by
Birlinn Limited
West Newington House
10 Newington Road
Edinburgh
EH9 1QS

www.birlinn.co.uk

ISBN10: 1 84158 299 9
ISBN13: 978 1 84158 299 3

British Library Cataloguing-in-Publication Data
A catalogue record for this book is available from the British Library

Design by Andrew Sutterby
Printed and bound by Scotprint, East Lothian

For the Whisky Men of Scotland,
Past, Present and Future.
With Grateful Thanks.

I said and said I'd write her down one day
But that's another unaccomplished task.
Look now how thoroughly she's gone and being
The last one of her kind there's none to ask.

It is not by their touch that you recall
The ones you loved but by recorded acts.
If you would beat the coming darkness back
Forego your share of kisses; pile up facts.

ALASDAIR MACLEAN, FROM *WAKING THE DEAD*

CONTENTS

ACKNOWLEDGEMENTS

My sincere thanks most obviously go to everyone who agreed to be interviewed for this book. Without their time, patience, interest and memories it, literally, would not have been possible. I have, however, also been fortunate in obtaining information, support, enthusiasm and practical assistance from many other people. I owe all of them an equal debt of gratitude.

Jennifer Birnie, Irvine Butterfield, Ian Campbell, Liz Cameron, Grant Carmichael, George Christie, Ricky Christie, Des Cummings, 'D', Stuart Duffy, William Delmé-Evans, Neil Ferguson, Peter Gordon, Frank McHardy, Mickey Heads, Christine Jones, Greg Klim, Jimmy Lang, Christine Logan, 'Big Angus' McAffer, Ed McAffer, Bill McBain, Dennis McBain, James and Barbara McEwan, Stuart McHardy, Jim MacKenzie, Ruari MacLeod, Nicholas Morgan, Fiona Murdoch, Archie Ness, Martine Nouet, Richard Paterson, 'Pinky', Donald Renwick, Iain Russell, Andrew Simmons, Drew Sinclair, Donald Smith, Peter Smith, Ruth Smith, Sean Smith, Donald Stirling, Billy Stitchell, Willie Tait, Yvonne Thackeray, Stuart Thomson.

PHOTOGRAPH CREDITS

Irvine Butterfield (pp.136, 139, 150), Grant Carmichael (p.44), Chivas Bros (pp.54, 261, 268, 270), Ricky Christie/Speyside Distillers Co. Ltd (pp.221, 222, 224), Diageo (pp.43, 72, 73, 114, 128, 145, 161, 177, 178, 182, 186, 188, 193, 214, 215, 238, 250, 253, 255), William Grant & Sons Ltd (pp.76, 79), Greg Klim/Boston (p.228), Jimmy Lang (pp.260, 262, 271), Sandy McAdam (pp.29, 195), Jim McEwan (pp.20, 119, 199, 203), Ian Millar (pp.61, 162), Derek Spark (p.95), Eric Stephen (p.91), Whisky Museum, Dufftown (p.248), Whyte & Mackay Distillers Ltd (pp.25, 66, 184).

Introduction

There have probably been more changes in the Scotch whisky industry during the past half century than at any other time in the illustrious history of the spirit. It follows then that most of these changes have occurred during the working lifetimes of distillery staff who are now in senior positions or who have retired.

Very little distilling was carried out during the years of the Second World War, and it was not until 1953 that grain rationing ended. This signalled the start of a period of dramatic growth in the scale of Scotch whisky distillation, with silent distilleries being re-commissioned, new distilleries created from scratch, and working distilleries expanded, often by 'doubling up' the number of stills. According to Moss & Hume (*The Making of Scotch Whisky*) 'this massive investment in the 1960s, without parallel since the late Victorian period, enabled the malt sector to double its output.'

During the post-war years the true 'globalisation' of Scotch whisky began, with increasing foreign investment in the industry and the progressive absorption of smaller distilling enterprises by a handful of increasingly dominant players. Whisky has always been a cyclical business, and during the early 1980s 'bust' followed 'boom', with the closure of a significant number of distilleries and all-round rationalisation.

In very recent times, however, there have been indications that small-scale entrepreneurship in the Scotch whisky industry is alive and well. A number of distilleries that were surplus to the requirements of large companies have been purchased by independent operators, several silent distilleries have been revived by new owners, and a handful of new-build distillery projects are in the pipeline at the time of writing. In the former 'whisky capital' of Campbeltown, on the Kintyre peninsula, Glengyle distillery has been brought back to life after almost 80 years of silence.

If you talk to a number of men who have spent their lives working in the whisky industry, inevitably certain themes recur. These include increased automation, smaller workforces and reduced alcohol consumption.

Distilleries today are much cleaner, more comfortable places in which to work than they were in the days when many of our subjects entered the industry. The days when employees had to break up large lumps of coal to fire the stills and scrub the insides of washbacks with heather besoms seem from a very distant era. Yet they are within the experience of many of the men interviewed for this book. Distillery life may be less hard, but the impression that it is also less fun endures.

Most distilleries ceased operating their own floor maltings during the 1960s, and a more recent trend has been to cease on-site cask filling. Thus, staff are not required to operate maltings, but additionally many distilleries no longer employ warehouse squads to fill and move casks. Spirit is tankered away to central filling facilities, and sometimes returned in casks for distillery maturation.

It is as though the sequence from barley to bottle has been truncated at both ends, and what happens today in a distillery is little more than the 'middle cut' of the whole whisky-making process. It may be cost-effective, but it is difficult not to conclude that much has been lost.

In compiling this book, I have travelled extensively in Scotland, recording the reminiscences and observations of people who have worked in a wide range of locations and an even wider range of roles within the Scotch whisky industry. Many have retired from active involvement in the world of whisky – except perhaps for drinking it – while others are very experienced individuals still employed in the business.

This is their story.

Gavin D. Smith
August 2005

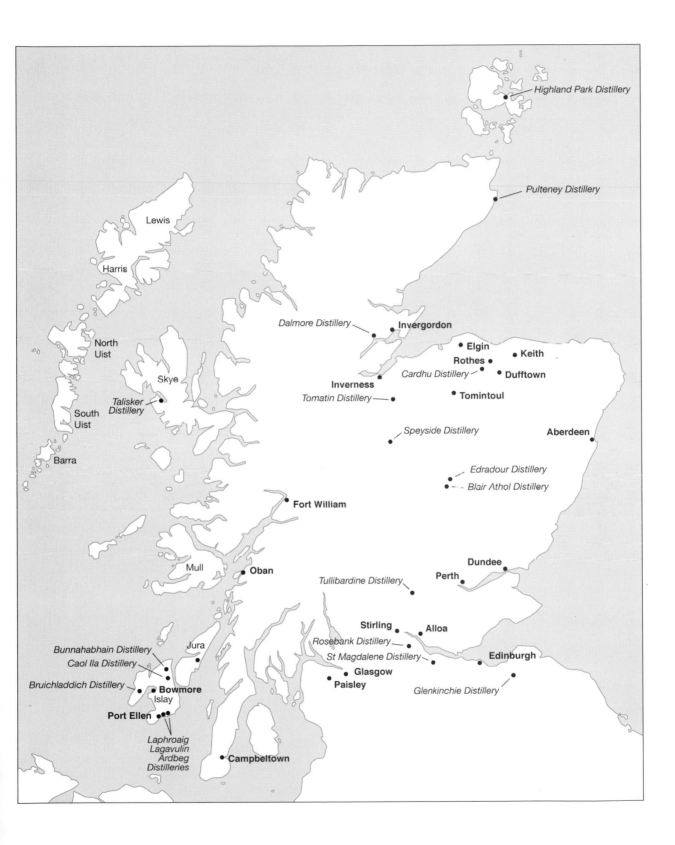

I

The Instigator
WILLIAM DELMÉ-EVANS
Distillery Designer

William Delmé-Evans died in 2003 at the age of 83. Born in Wales, the exotic 'Delmé' came courtesy of a dash of French blood, but the Speyside Grants also figured prominently in his family lineage. He has been described as a latter-day Charles Doig, but while the important role played in the development of the modern whisky industry by the Elgin-based century architect has finally been acknowledged, William Delmé Evans has remained a lesser-known figure.

Yet, during the two decades following the end of the Second World War, Delmé-Evans was at the forefront of Scotland's distilling renaissance, much as Doig had been during the great Speyside expansion of the late nineteenth century.

Delmé-Evans' fame within the distilling industry rests chiefly on three principal projects; the development of Tullibardine distillery in Perthshire, the reconstruction of the long-derelict Jura distillery and the creation of Glenallachie distillery on Speyside.

Tullibardine distillery was subsequently acquired by Whyte & Mackay Distillers Ltd, and was mothballed in 1995. In 2003 Tullibardine was bought by a syndicate of businessmen with extensive experience in the whisky industry, and production restarted during 2004. Jura is a key malt distillery in the Whyte & Mackay portfolio, while Glenallachie, near Aberlour, is now owned by Pernod Ricard, and is a valued ingredient in many of the company's blends.

Interviewed in 2002, William Delmé-Evans reminisced about his life and work within the Scotch whisky industry. Typical of the spirit of a man who took up golf at the age of 70 and could soon beat players with handicaps of less than 12, Delmé-Evans constructed an airstrip on the island of Jura, and then proceeded to

William Delmé-Evans at his drawing board.

obtain a pilot's licence, buying a Cessna 172 in order to minimise the inconvenience of working between his Herefordshire home and the Inner Hebrides.

'It was our intention to produce a Highland-type malt differing from the typically peaty stuff last produced at the turn of the century, he observed. 'I therefore designed the stills to give spirit of a Highland character, and we ordered malt which was only lightly peated. My primary aim was to construct an economic distillery within the space available.'

He also recalled the impact of the arrival of more than 200 construction workers on the peaceful Hebridean island in 1960. 'Eventually there were more than 400 men in total, working on the distillery, building houses and enlarging the nearby hotel. The builders worked seven days a week, but we had some terrible times at the weekends, as most of them were either Celtic or Ranger fans and there were some awful fights on Friday and Saturday nights. Jura was an island with no policemen, and the local doctor had to patch men up after encounters in the hotel bar!' The observations below serve as a fascinating overview of the whisky industry during Delmé-Evans' own lifetime, and are followed by some more personal recollections of his boyhood and career.

'A hundred years ago distilleries were very different from the ones we know today, communications were poor and distilleries were tucked away often in very remote places, although some were in villages, which originally sprang up around the distillery – I think Rothes in Morayshire is a typical case, and where there are now five distilleries.

'In those days the distillery carried out the whole process. They had their own maltings, peat bogs, cooperage and transport. The transport was horsepower in the early days, giving way to steam engines at a later date. The distilling season only lasted for 30 to 40 weeks in the year as that was the time when there was plenty of very cold water for the condensers. Also in the summer months the distillery had to be overhauled, peat had to be cut and dried and then either carted to the distillery or a stack close by. Although the distillery plant was kept very clean during the working season, the period of the silent season was the time to really clean up the whole building and plant, and every item that was paintable was painted: walls, outside of the vessels, pumps and even the big steam engine, which was in any case polished and cleaned during the working season. The coppersmiths and craftsmen would arrive at the distillery and spend many days repairing the plant for the oncoming season's work.

'Maltings consisted of steeping tanks where the barley was soaked before being transferred to the malting floor. On the floor the barley was turned after so many hours according to the temperature of the grain and how it was grown. The maltmen turning the grain used very large wooden shovels, and would flick the grain over to a new part of the floor. When the acrospire had grown to three-quarters of the way up the barley grain, they would know that the sugars had been converted and the growth had to be stopped immediately, the acrospire would have been the first green leaf if allowed to go on. The malt was then put on to a kiln, where down on the ground floor level, there was a basket which burnt coal and peat. The temperature of the drying was critical as at a certain degree of heat the enzymes would be destroyed, and the enzyme diastase is one of the keys to unlocking the change of sugars in the mashing process. The type and amount of peat burned in the kiln gave part of the flavour to the finished product. Highland peats are light and friable whereas the Islay peats are heavy and dark and give off more phenols which collect on the surface of the grain being dried. These days very few, if any, distillery has its own malting, the malt being made by large malting companies, and

The wash still pot being hoisted into the Jura still-house, 1962. William Delmé-Evans measures the deflection on the steel beam, top right.

although the malt would be made to the distiller's specification, he cannot control the type of peat used, but he can specify the amount of phenols in the finished malt.

'The distilling plant has changed very little over the years, the main change is that the stills are now heated by steam coils, or direct gas-fire burners, whereas in the past they were heated by coal fires, and were very difficult to control. The charge to the wash still would have spent yeast suspended in it and this is what made it so difficult to control, as it would froth when nearing the boiling point, there were no sight glasses in those days and the only way a stillman had of knowing how much the still was frothing was by using a "conker". The conker was a wooden ball attached to a long rope from the ceiling of the still house and with it the stillman was able to hit the ball against the funnel of the still – this part of the still is called the bullnose. When the ball hit the bullnose, if it sounded hollow it was alright to continue distillation, but if it sounded hard, the fire either had to be dampened down, or, if the stillman had the nerve, the fire would be covered with black coal so cooling the still down without putting out the fire. If the still did boil over, and it did happen quite a few times, all the boiling hot liquor would siphon through the spirit safe and the still would collapse, like a crumpled paper bag, doing an immense amount of damage which was very costly to repair. The stillmen working the coal-fired stills were highly skilled artists or craftsmen and had nerves of steel.

'The mash tun has not altered very much over the many years, except for the copper and brass dome which is now fitted, more to keep in the steam than anything else, but the cooling of the worts used to be carried out using a "Morton's Cooler", the cooling water flowing inside elongated pipes, sections of the worts flowing on the outside of the pipes in a zig-zag fashion. It was not very hygienic but at least the machine was scrubbed down every week with no ill effects. When the worts had been cooled the yeast was added, various strains of yeast were used. Fresh yeast was used every week, and usually came from the local brewery, and this was mixed with dry yeast from a yeast factory. The yeast and the worts then flowed into the wash-backs (fermenting vessels). The washbacks were made of timber, which was very carefully selected and well matured. The staves of the washbacks were held together with round hoops which had a thread on the end and a tightening block, so that as the vessel required, the hoops could be tightened. In some of the distilleries they still used ordinary hoops as on a cask and those would have to be driven down every few weeks to stop the vessel leaking. Great care was taken over the cleanliness of the washbacks and each week after the week's production men would get inside the vessel and, with long handled scrubbing brushes, scrub the vessel down, until it was absolutely clean. Then the covers would be put on, and the washback would be steamed for an hour or so to kill off the germs and bacteria, and finally after it had cooled down, it was coated with bisulphide of lime. This was left to dry and the covers replaced so that no bacteria would get in to spoil the next week's fermentation. Fermentation is a chain reaction, and the yeast converts the sugar through a chain of chemical reactions before it becomes alcohol.

'The power for running the distillery came from a steam-driven engine which had a huge flywheel. The machines were beautifully kept, with all the brass work and paintwork polished every day. The power from this engine was used to drive the malt mill, the switchgear on the washbacks through a system of pulleys, drive the hoists and a host of other jobs. All the liquor, water, worts and wash, were moved by duplex steam pumps.

'We all know that many hundreds of years ago just about every croft had its own still, and because one crofter produced a better drink than the others he was asked by his neighbours to make them their annual supply of whisky, and so gradually over the years, the crofter became the distiller of today. No one knows exactly why these particular crofters made superior whisky. It could have been the water, the peat, the shape of the stills or perhaps the skill of the man doing the job.

Probably a combination of all three, although the shape of the stills is really more to do with it than anything else.

'Until fairly recently, the 1950s/'60s, most of the distilleries were owned either by individuals or individual families, where the ownership had been in the families for many hundreds of years. The exception was the firm of Scottish Malt Distillers, where quite a few of these old family distilleries combined with about four blenders and they had their outlets in well known brands such as Dewars, Black & White and Johnnie Walker. Going back over many years to the very early days when Scotch was for the first time being exported south of the border, along came the government of the day, "the king", who could not resist serving a heavy excise duty on the liquor, and also making a few new laws to govern distillation, and so the battle of the illicit distiller and the Excise was born. There are some very good true stories about illicit stills, and these have been well documented in various books.

'By the start of the 1800s, the licensed distillers were becoming more respectable, and many of them refurbished their distilleries, and in quite a few cases completely demolished the old buildings and started afresh, but retaining the same-shaped stills and wooden washbacks. Some of the distilleries at this time were enlarged to cope with the increasing demand for Scotch, although as today, trade was very erratic and seemed to go in seven-year cycles, up and down.

'It was about this period that many dozens of small distilleries were built, some very small ones, and at Campbeltown they had twenty such stills, in Perthshire there were ten and so on. However, some of them closed down because their whisky was not to the liking of the blender and the public, or later on, nearer the First World War, the high price of copper and brass enticed the small distiller to sell his plant at quite a large profit. Now there is only one distillery in Campbeltown [currently three in production again], and most of the Perthshire and Fifeshire ones are also closed.

'In the late 1800s the grain distilleries started up, and with them the blending trade. Just about every large grocery, wine shop, large or small brewer, London store and sometimes individual families had their own blend. They did not have large stocks of mature spirit of their own, so they used the "Whisky Broker" to purchase their supplies. The broker would carry very large stocks of all ages of spirit, from various distilleries. He would take fillings, this was the sale given to a sale direct from the distillery to a customer who would supply his own casks, either quarter cask, hogshead or butt. There were very many brokers in Edinburgh and Glasgow and individually they held vast stocks of almost every malt whisky and of every age.

They would, of course, also deal and purchase parcels from any individual who was in need of a sale, so all in all they did a very good job. Many of these brokers were men of great character, and names such as Herbert Ross, Hepburn, Jimmy Barclay, Walker and Boyle were well known in those days. I am not sure, but I do not think there are any whisky brokers left these days. The old ones all lived to a ripe old age, the gallons of whisky that they must have consumed in their lifetime did them no harm – it must have pickled their insides, but they were of course drinking beautiful old malts, watered down by Highland spring water which they used to have brought down every few days from the north.

'There were also large firms of blenders who had their own bottling stores, blending houses and their own name on the bottle, and these people were the backbone of the industry as mostly they would take fillings of upwards of 100 butts a year from a single distillery. Sometimes a broker would lose a cask in his vast stocks and a friend of mine, who has passed on many years ago, was one such broker and when he was in his eighties he found this particular cask in his stock that he had purchased as a young man. The original cask was a butt, 120 gallons at 11.2 over proof, but when it was taken out of bond the maturing and evaporation over the many years had brought the bulk gallons down to 40 at strengths of 5.1 UP [OP is over proof and UP is under proof]. The cask was bottled at the original strength, 5.1 UP, and the whisky therein was 68 years old, it had a beautiful aroma and flavour. Being an old friend of mine this gentleman gave me a bottle which I still have, with a tiny drop left in it, which of course is now just a showpiece.

'During the late 1800s and the start of the 1900s, the railways were extended into the Highlands but of course there was still a large amount of horse drawn traffic. The road over the Grampians was in very bad repair and it was difficult to get to your destination, the journeys were long and tiring. With the railways being extended into the Highlands, it became much easier to get down to the big cities to carry on business. The railways also put sidings into many of the distilleries and this was a very good move as quite a few of the other distilleries would transport their casks to the nearest railhead. I remember Glenlivet transporting their casks on a steam-driven three-wheel wagon to the railhead at Imperial Distillery sidings. Once or twice a week a long train of up to thirty wagons, with an armed guard, would transport the whisky south to Glasgow and Edinburgh to the blending houses. Alas, Dr Beeching after the war ripped up all the railway lines, yet another person who had no knowledge or idea of how the Highlands worked.

'Some of the distilleries were tucked away in very remote glens and others in the open country, but all of them would be near a good source of water supply for cooling the condensers. The water used in the production of spirit was usually from a spring or well, sometimes a very considerable distance from the distillery. The spring water would flow into a large man-made cistern and would be allowed to settle before being drawn off by pipeline down to the distillery for the production water. As the quality of the water had a lot to do with the flavour of the whisky, great care was taken to preserve the purity of this Highland spring water. For most of the Speyside distilleries the water comes out of a granite rock, whereas over on the west coast, the water comes more from schists and graphite rocks. This is just one of the reasons that makes the difference between the Highland distilleries and the west coast distilleries. Also, of course, at Islay you have the thick heavy dark peat which is used to dry the malt in the kilns but on Speyside the peat is much more friable and lighter and does not impart so strong a phenol flavour.

'Distilling at this time was a very exacting job, remembering that there were no chemists, no labs, no gas chromatography, and there were none of the chemicals which are now used to clean and sterilise the plant. It was not until about 1935 that the chemists started to appear in the picture in some force. I think that in this day and age the chemist dictates too much over the production of the distillery. This is a retrograde step as they do not know very much about the history of the trade or the "practice" of making good spirit. All that the chemist seems to want is to show his bosses that he can get more spirit from a ton of barley than the other chap.

'All the distilleries closed down at the beginning of the Second World War in 1939 [there were exceptions], barley being needed for food. The price of Scotch whisky rocketed overnight, so the brokers and blenders became multi-millionaires, at least on paper, but when they were taxed they were back to square one. At that time you were allowed to sell a trading company without attracting tax, so many of the brokers would buy shell companies and would give them an office, office girl, motor car, telephone, etc., and would over the years build up large stocks of whisky in the shell company. Then the company would be sold, giving the broker full profit tax free. The face of the industry changed a little bit during the war as the sons of many of the distillery families were killed and individual distilleries were handed to other members of the family, or sold up.

'After the Second World War was over, restrictions on distilling were in force and only lifted when food rationing was finished, although the distilleries were allowed to start up a limited production before this. By this time there were very small quantities of spirit left in the warehouses, so production was urgently required. A few older distilleries that had been closed down before the war were refurbished and there were three or four new distilleries built.

'By 1948 the industry started to change. Small companies or individual distilleries, that had been in family ownership for generations, were bought up by the blenders, many of whom had made large fortunes during the war. The blenders said that they wanted the distilleries to protect their supplies of malt whisky that they used in their blends but as most blends have at least fifteen or more different malts, in the malt side of their blend, this story did not have much foundation. There is something rather special about owning a malt distillery, and I think that this was the main reason the brokers and blenders wanted to get their hands on the distilleries.

'It was just after the war when the distilleries had started up again that many of them turned over to oil burning. Originally they had oil burners under the stills, which was not very satisfactory. Later the stills were heated by steam coils. The boilers were fired on heavy 3,500-second oil, the steam being used to heat the mashing water as well as for heating the stills for distillation. Some ten years later the price of heavy oil increased dramatically, and it was at this time that one of the biggest mistakes was made. I myself was much against it, and I still am. In order to carry on distilling new whisky at the same price, a way of saving oil was to set the fermenters at a much higher gravity.

'For example, a washback fermenter holding 10,000 gallons after fermentation would have a 10–12 per cent alcohol in the wash whereas by increasing the gravity before fermentation the after-fermentation effect would be to give 15–18 per cent alcohol in the wash. I put this change down to new people coming into the industry, with chemists advising them who had little knowledge of how the distillery plant was designed or how a move like this could change the character and flavour of the whisky. The wash and spirit stills are designed to take a certain charge at a certain strength, but the extra volume of alcohol in the wash [first distillation] using a higher gravity mash, unbalances the charge of the spirit still. In the old days, there were many vessels to collect the distillate from the spirit still, one vessel for the first part of the run called the foreshot, one to collect the spirit run, whisky, another vessel to collect the last part of the run called the feints, yet another one to collect the distillate from the wash still called the low wines. Each week or period the strength of the liquor in each vessel would be taken and the stillman given orders to charge the spirit still with a given amount from each vessel. This allowed a constant amount of higher alcohols and impurities to vaporise and be distilled. However, as distilleries work today there is no real control or consistency. All the products from the stills are put into one tank, so really it is not known the strength of the charge back into the spirit still. Before the increase of gravity in the washbacks took place, calculations had been made so that the distillation balanced out, and it did not matter combining the various parts of the distillation, as it always kept in balance. This is one reason why most of the malt whiskies have lost their wonderful flavours that were present in the whisky produced in the very early days. I put most of this change down to the fact that the young people coming into the trade of distilling have little knowledge of the past, and if the chemist makes a suggestion they think that it is Gospel true. These days all that management wants is to make large profits for their shareholders year after year, with no concern about quality or flavour.

'The change from the old malts and blends that has taken place has been so gradual that it has gone unnoticed by the general public. This was due to old malts being added to the young malts, to make the blend, but now the old malts have gradually been phased out as they finished some years ago, so in these days the young generation of whisky drinkers take it for granted that if the bottle has Single Malt written on it and has an age of 12–20 years it must be good. There is no doubt that it is good, but not nearly as good as that produced fifty or sixty years ago.

'The next step in the industry took place during the 1980s and '90s, when the blenders found themselves being "taken over" by other companies, the biggest racket of them all being Guinness taking over the Distillers Company, and the court cases that followed, with many people being put in jail, but also at this time many other companies were swallowed up by foreign firms owned by Frenchmen, Japanese and Americans. In a way, the Japanese were the best as they tried to conform to Scottish ways of distilling. The Americans had been connected with the distilling industry for a great number of years and most of them understood and followed the Scottish way of doing things. However, the Frenchmen were a law unto themselves, with little regard for the end product. Now, thank goodness, there has been yet another change. The large companies who bought up all the smaller companies find that they have too much malt whisky capacity and are selling off a few of their distilleries to individual small firms.

'Exactly the same pattern of events has happened in the brewing industry. Many of the larger brewery companies have been taken over, leaving brewing in the hands of very few people. Now we have, thanks to the chemists, a standard-flavoured beer. I am not saying that every beer tastes the same, but today if you buy a pint of a certain named beer it is the same in every tin and bottle. Years ago, you would go into a hotel and hear customers saying, "By Jove, this is a very good brew this week," or, perhaps, "Not quite so good as last week," but there was variety. This is probably the reason why so many small breweries have sprung up over the last few years, with good sales of well-flavoured ale. They are by no means a standard flavour.

'You may think that this is just an old man who thinks the past is better than the present, or perhaps that after he has built and designed three distilleries, and been in the industry all his life, he thinks that he knows better than anyone else, but I can assure you that this is not the case. This précis about distilling over my lifetime is just a fraction of my memories of the past, and I hope that the younger generation will learn something of the past and that these few words will be of interest, not only to the young distiller, but to everyone interested in the Scotch whisky industry and Scotland.'

'The earliest recollection I have of brewing was at the age of about seven, when I used to go down to Carmarthenshire to stay with my aunt and uncle for my summer holidays. They lived in a wonderful old Georgian house, which the family had lived in for three generations. The estate consisted of many farms, and the Home Farm of about 50 acres round the house was farmed by my uncle.

'My aunt used to brew two hogsheads of beer every year, which she plied to the tenants on Quarter Day when they came to pay their rent. In those days, all the tenants would use their pony and trap for transport, and at the end of the afternoon they would have to be put in their traps and the pony would be given a good slap on the buttocks and it knew its way home. The beer was very strong. I remember that behind the house there was a long building divided into game larder, larder, dairy, slate pig-salting slabs and a brewhouse. The brewhouse had two large copper vessels, and I remember that on the day of the brewing men would light fires under the coppers to heat up the water for the brew. The water was drawn from their own well and seemed to be of a good quality for making beer. Hops and malt were purchased from a distant relation who had a brewery in Llanelli. The yeast came from a small pub outside St Clears that brewed its own beer once a week.

'My aunt did not use a thermometer, she simply rolled up her sleeve and just touched the water with her elbow. If it was too hot she would order the men to put some cold water into the copper. If it was not hot enough, she would order more fire under the vessel. When the water was at the right temperature, she ordered the malt to be tipped into the copper and the day's brewing had started. After fermentation, the liquid was put into the hogsheads and mixed with a few pounds of raisins and sultanas. The casks were then cork-bunged and left to mature, when a secondary fermentation would take place. The result was a highly intoxicating drink with an excellent flavour. The brew would be used for the farm workers at haymaking time, as well as for the house.

'My next experience was on a holiday to Scotland at the age of about twelve,

The spirit stills, Tullibardine distillery, 2004.

and on this holiday I set foot in my first distillery. I can remember the stills and brewhouse, but as a small boy the impression that has lasted in my mind was the big steam engine with its huge flywheel, and the immaculate condition it was kept in.

'Then, by chance, when I was away at school, the chap in the next bed to mine came from Scotland and we became great friends. His father was an Excise officer in distilleries, and I used to go to Scotland to see them, and so my interest in brewing and distilling was enhanced.

'I trained firstly as an agriculturalist, and then went on to train as a surveyor. It was at this stage that I contracted tuberculosis and was very ill for many years, which gave me plenty of time to study brewing and distilling. It was at this stage of my life that I decided to build an up-to-date gravity flow distillery. When I was almost fully recovered I went to stay with my school friend, and on one of these holidays his father announced that he was going to retire. Knowing my desire to build a distillery, he found an advert in the paper for a disused brewery in the village of Blackford in Perthshire. The well that they drew the water from was still in existence, and I managed to get a sample and send it for analysis. The result came back and I knew the water was almost perfect for distilling. By the end of the week I had purchased the building. By the way, the water from the village is now sold under the name of Highland Spring. With the help of my schoolfriend's father, who kept me right on the Excise requirements, I went ahead and built Tullibardine Distillery. This was in 1947, and by 1949 the distillery was completed and commissioned to production. My very first order came from James Barclay [whisky broker and later managing director of Chivas Brothers Ltd], who was passing by and came in to see me. The distillery went on full production and there was much demand for it but, *Inside Jura stillhouse, 1963.*

William Delmé-Evans' photo montage of Craighouse, Jura, and the old distillery before reconstruction work started, 1958.

foolishly, I sold over half the production to one firm. In 1952 they chopped their order and tried to buy the distillery at a cheap price. This was at a time when my own health was fading a bit. I had been working too hard. After a while, along came the firm Brodie Hepburn, who were whisky brokers, and I obtained a fair and reasonable price for Tullibardine.

'I then went back to my farm in Herefordshire to recuperate, but in 1956 I was contacted by Mr Fletcher and Mr Riley-Smith, who owned estates on the island of Jura. They wanted to revitalise the island. Before World War I there were over 1,000 people, but by 1956 it had dropped to 150. We looked at many ways of bringing some type of industry back to Jura, but in the end we thought it would be better to rebuild the old distillery. The old Jura distillery had closed down in 1913 because the Campbells, who owned the southern estate at that time, decided to double the rent of the distillery buildings. The Ferguson family owned the machinery and ran the distillery. They were the distillers. The Fergusons were old men and when the rent was increased they decided to retire, so the distillery closed down in 1913, the last whisky going out of the warehouse a year later. The Fergusons sold all the plant because with the war coming on the price of copper and gunmetal had rocketed. The Campbells were left with a large building on which they had to pay rates and so, in order to avoid paying them, they removed the roof of the building and this lovely distillery fell into ruin.

'During 1958 I started designing a new distillery which just about trebled

the production capacity of the old one, and by 1963 Jura Distillery was commissioned. Although Jura is west coast, and very close to Islay, the type of malt whisky it produces is completely different and is a fully flavoured, almost a Highland, malt.

Delmé-Evans' photo montage of early construction work on Jura distillery in progress, 21 November 1961.

'No sooner had I opened Jura than Mackinlays, [Mackinlay McPherson Ltd, a subsidiary of Scottish & Newcastle Breweries Ltd], whom I had brought in through Scottish & Newcastle Breweries as an outlet for some of our production and who owned half the shares in the distillery, wanted to build a Highland, Speyside, distillery. I first of all had to find a site, and then design the distillery and the buildings. It was quite a lot of trouble to find the right water, but I did, and I had it piped down from Benrinnes to a site that I had purchased near Aberlour. This was a big chance to put together all the knowledge I had gained over the past few years. By this time, I had worked out the velocities of the vapours being distilled and was able to design the actual stills with all this knowledge behind me. It took me two years to find a site with the right type of water, and another few years to design and build the distillery. My architect was Lothian Barclay, the son of James Barclay. He was a brilliant architect, and together we smoothed out many and various problems. I designed all the plant and the layout of the buildings, and Lothian the actual building. Lothian was my architect for Jura Distillery and I had known him for many years.

'And now here I am back on my farm in Herefordshire, rather an old man. I was lucky enough to marry a Scots girl who was very understanding and gave me a tremendous lot of help in my work. I have had a wonderful life, wrapped up in distilling and agriculture, and I can honestly say that I have enjoyed every minute of it. I think the biggest thrill is to see all your work coming together and eventually commissioning the distillery.'

2

On Malting

By legal definition, Scotch malt whisky can only be made using malted barley, and turning barley into malt is the initial stage in the whisky-making process. As Neil Gunn wrote in *Whisky and Scotland,* 'the distiller's aim is first to ensure that the large mass of starch, held together by proportionately small quantities of albuminous matter, of which all grain is composed, is changed from an insoluble to a soluble condition.'

When Gunn was writing in the mid-1930s this was, indeed, the *distiller*'s aim, as virtually every distillery carried out its own on-site malting of barley. Today, it might be more appropriate to say 'the *maltster*'s aim …', since only a handful of Scottish distilleries now malt their own barley, with the vast majority being processed to individual specifications by commercial malting companies, or in the case of the largest distillers, such as Diageo, in their own dedicated malting plants.

Distillery malting is a labour-intensive process, and an average-sized distillery could employ up to a dozen men in this capacity. The ending of distillery maltings was a significant factor in the creation of smaller workforces (see Chapter 15, 'On Change').

Maltings were centralised partly as labour costs increased, but also because as distillery output expanded during the 1960s distillery-based maltings simply could not produce enough malt to keep pace with the rest of the plant's potential capacity.

During malting, the barley is placed in a 'steep' and mixed with water in order to promote growth in the grain. In traditional floor maltings, the barley is transferred from the steeps onto the malting floor after a period of up to 72 hours.

There it is spread to a depth of 2 to 3 feet, and the barley is known as 'the piece' at this point.

While on the floor, the barley sprouts, and its temperature is controlled by regular turning of the piece using wooden shovels, known as 'shiels', or more recently, machines. This also prevents the rootlets from becoming entangled.

Ruari McLeod, former maltman and mashman at Bruichladdich distillery on Islay, remembers that 'The malt barn that's a shop now, that was the hardest to work here, the back one was quite easy.' But 'up til approximately 24 hours on the floor you had to turn it every four hours, because it was really growing'.

A malting floor at Macallan distillery, Easter Elchies, 1923.

The bed of malt is gradually thinned out over a period of between 8 and 12 days, until it is only 3 or 4 inches deep. The barley is kept at an optimum temperature of around 16 degrees centigrade, and once it has sprouted it is known as 'green' malt.

When germination begins to occur, an enzyme complex called diastase is produced, and it is this which will convert the starch in the grain into fermentable sugars during mashing. Germination must be halted, however, or the fermentable sugars will be consumed by the growing plant. The green malt is transferred to a kiln where the moisture content is reduced, preventing further growth.

There are numerous ways of determining when the optimum germination period has been reached, some scientific, but most practical, and many passed on from generation to generation.

Mickey Heads, manager of Isle of Jura distillery, is an Ileach born and bred, and worked as mashman, stillman and brewer at Laphroaig between 1979 and 1990, when he crossed the Sound of Islay to his present base at Craighouse. Talking of germination in Laphroaig's surviving floor maltings, Mickey says, 'You could tell if the barley was ready because if you rubbed it on the wall it would leave a mark like chalk. Another way was to break the grains open to see the length of the acrospire. When it stretched two-thirds along the grain you knew it was ready.'

Dalmore distillery on the Cromarty Firth in Ross-shire dates from 1839, and manager Drew Sinclair has worked there for almost forty years. 'I mind like yesterday my first day at Dalmore,' he says. 'It was 3 February 1966, and I was 19 years old. My first job was in the old malt barns. The maltmen would take a handful of malt and would split it open to see how far the actual spur was growing up it. We used to take a hundred grains to count them, spread them out, split them open and count. If that spur was three-quarters of the way up that was just about right, you know. So we split the hundred grains, then you'd note in a wee book that, say, 87 grains out of the 100 were right, and that would be pretty good.'

Traditionally, peat was used to fire the kilns in the Highlands and islands, where it was readily available and cheap, while Lowland distilleries would employ coke or anthracite. Today, most malt-drying is accomplished using coal, coke or hot

David Turner tends the peat furnace, Bowmore distillery, 2004.

Jim McEwan (left) and Duncan McGillivray sampling casks, c. 2003.

air, with peat only being used during the first few hours of kilning to achieve the requisite level of 'peatreek'. Maltmen will tell you that after the first dozen hours or so the peatreek stops 'sticking to' the malt anyway, so to kiln with peat for a longer period would be pointless.

Overall, kilning can last up to 45 hours, with the green malt being spread on a perforated metal floor above a furnace. One of the most characteristic of all distillery features is the 'pagoda roof' of the kiln, first developed by Charles Doig during the 1890s. Fans are located in the pagoda roof to draw the smoke up through the drying malt.

Varying degrees of peatiness are imparted to malt, depending on individual specification. Some distilleries, such as Glengoyne, make a virtue of using entirely unpeated malt, and the most heavily peated whiskies traditionally come from the island of Islay. 'Peatiness' is measured as 'parts per million phenols' (ppm).

The degree of peating during malting can have a major influence on the finished spirit. Sample a 'standard' Ardbeg from Islay, for example, and then the unpeated Kildalton expression launched at cask strength in limited quantities in 2004 and the differences are enormous.

The Kildalton was distilled in 1980 as an experiment using unpeated and lightly peated malt. Distillery manager Stuart Thomson explains, 'By removing the peat, the fruity flavours produced by the purifier attached to the still come to the fore, along with the waxiness of the wooden washbacks and more of the grainy flavours of the barley itself.'

In contrast to Ardbeg's experimentation, the Islay distillery of Bruichladdich which traditionally used unpeated or lightly peated malt, is now producing some whisky with higher peating levels.

Bruichladdich's production director is Jim McEwan, an Ileach whose working life began as a 15-year-old apprentice cooper at Bowmore distillery in 1963. He was subsequently appointed warehouse manager, before moving to Glasgow in 1977 as a blender. Jim returned to his native island as distillery manager at Bowmore in 1984, finally embracing the role of global brand ambassador for Morrison Bowmore Distillers Ltd. In 2000 he was recruited by the independent bottling company Murray McDavid Ltd to become part of the team aiming to revive Bruichladdich distillery. A sum of £4.3 million subsequently changed hands for the former JBB (Greater Europe) plc distillery, which had been silent since 1994.

Whisky began to flow again in 2001, and Jim McEwan and the Bruichladdich team, including manager Duncan McGillivray, have subsequently pioneered a number of innovative expressions from this most traditional of distilleries, founded in 1881 on the western shores of Lochindaal. In an attempt to get close to the original style of whisky made a century and more ago, Port Charlotte single malt has been introduced, boasting a peating level of 40 ppm. This compares with the standard 5 ppm, while the distillery's Octomore has a massive level of 80.5 ppm, making it the world's most heavily peated whisky.

Ruari MacLeod and a cask of 13-year-old Bruichladdich in the Bruichladdich distillery shop, 2004.

Jim talked about Bruichladdich and malting in company with Ruari McLeod.

RM: Well, I'll tell you, I started here in 1956.

JM. But you're not an Islay man are you?

RM: No, I belong to Skye.

JM: Just to make that absolutely clear, you can't claim to be one of us, the chosen people! He's a Talisker man, but whatever, he's come here.

RM: I came here first from Skye in 1937 from the agricultural college as a cheese-maker, well, I wasn't fully qualified. And I did nine months with Campbells down in Aoradh, then I went back to Campbeltown, to the creamery in Campbeltown, this was the first time ever in Britain that condensed milk was ever made. It was called 'Fair Laddie', that's what it was called. It was in Campbeltown. Then I went back to the college, but then the war broke out, and I was away for eight years. After I came back I was asked if I'd like to go back into agriculture again, and I said 'yes', and I came over to Islay again. In 1956 I was working for the late Tom Epps down at Aoragh, which is RSPB now. He had no houses for workers, so I was living at Braeside, in a house I was renting, and I was summoned back and forward from Braeside to Aoragh.

 Well, this day I was sent for draff to the distillery here, and I met Mr Rait who was the manager, and he said to me, How would you like to come on the malt-ing floors? I said yes, just like that. That's how I started doing the distilling here. Then in 1960 new houses got built up at the back here, and I applied and got one, and that was it then. [In] 1956, the manager was Mr Watt, and the distillery was owned by Ross & Coulter, and then it became Ross & McCallum after Coulter died. Ross was never here. I started on the malting floors, and they closed in 1961 when Eddie Grant took over.

JM: In 1956, Ruari, and this is really important to me, you were burning peats in the kiln?

RM: I became kilnman after doing two years there. The procedure was that 24 hours of peat only, that's on the green malt, then we changed from that to anthracite'

JM: The same as Bowmore. That proves to me quite conclusively that prior to 1961 Bruichladdich was just as heavily peated as the other Islay malts.

RM: Well, more or less.

JM: Because you don't get the peating done in 24 hours. Because Bowmore is 24, roughly, Laphroaig is 24, the only difference between these distilleries is the volume of peat that they burn in 24 hours.

RM: Aye, that's true.

JM: So when the Grants took over in 1961 they changed the style, closed the malt barns, changed it to unpeated.

RM: Well, when Eddie Grant took over he didn't want any maltings at all. And we had 150 tons of barley left. But he said if we malted it, and this was in June, which was not a very good time to be malting, he would take it over. And that's what we did. We malted it here and he took it over as malted barley.

JM: That's interesting because everybody talks about Bruichladdich being an unpeated malt, but the fact of the matter was that from 1881 until 1961 it was a regular Islay.

RM: Oh yes, yes, yes.

JM: When Grant took it over in 1961 he closed the malt barns, he wanted a lighter style of whisky which was going to be very popular, so he thought, with American consumers.

RM: Aye, that is true, yes.

JM: So the Port Charlotte that I'm making today at 40 parts per million would have been comparable to the Bruichladdich pre 1961.

RM: That is true, yes, but it wouldn't be as heavily peated as Octomore.

JM: No, Octomore is gigantic!

As technical innovations were embraced by the Scotch whisky industry, floor maltings were superseded initially by the Saladin method, sometimes installed in individual distilleries, and later by drum maltings.

Saladin maltings are, essentially, concrete 'troughs', equipped with a series of revolving rakes, in which the barley is steeped. The 'Saladin Box' was developed by the Frenchman Charles Saladin during the 1890s, and became widespread in the brewing industry. However, it was not until after the Second World War that the method was embraced by Scotch whisky distillers. Today, the Edrington Group's Tamdhu distillery, near Knockando in Morayshire, is one of the few that continues to operate Saladin maltings, making malt for its own needs and for its 'sister' distillery of Glenrothes.

Dalmore distillery's floor maltings were converted to a Saladin system in 1956, and the distillery continued to make its own malt until 1981. Drew Sinclair remembers using Saladin boxes when he started in the maltings.

'It took about four to five days for germination to take place. I worked with the Saladin boxes for two to two and a half years. Jim Wilson was the head maltman, and there was a squad of about eight in there.

'We used to wear what we called malt boots, they were canvas shoes, just ankle- length, canvas shoes, with like a twine sole. You couldn't walk on water with them and such like because it would ruin them. You needed Wellington boots for working with the steeps, when its wet, or in the boxes themselves because it was damp in there. When the men came out of the Saladin boxes, there was always the malt fire, they would stand in front of it to get heated up. It was quite drying that.'

Drum maltings, as the name implies, consist of a number of large, revolving drums, each of which may hold between 20 and 50 tons of barley. As the drum revolves, warm air is drawn into it, turning and aerating the grain while germination takes place.

Many drum maltings now perform all the various stages of malting in vessel, often referred to as an SGKV (Steeping, Germination, and Kilning Vessel). In drum maltings, germination times are reduced to around five days – perhaps half those of floor maltings. Although often considered a modern development, a drum malting system was installed at the Rothes distillery of Speyburn as early as 1897.

In 1966 the Distillers Company Ltd constructed a drum malting plant at Burghead on the Moray coast, near Elgin, and greatly expanded the maltings at Muir of Ord, near Inverness. Two years later floor maltings were closed at twenty-nine of the company's distilleries. In 1973 a malting plant was built at Port Ellen on Islay,

and another at Roseisle, near Burghead, which opened in 1980. Port Ellen and Roseisle were unusual among modern drum maltings in that they were equipped to produce peated malt.

Maltmen working in the Saladin maltings, Dalmore distillery, 1950s

Although an essential part of today's Scotch whisky industry, purists will tell you that there are drawbacks to malting on an industrial scale. For example, barley of varying nitrogen levels and moisture contents is mixed together before processing begins, which inevitably results in the compromise of quality for lower unit costs.

Another disadvantage is that the 'piece', as germinating barley is known, is not turned completely from bottom to top as it would be in old-fashioned floor maltings, but merely stirred. During germination this can cause a localised build up of carbon dioxide, leading to over modification, and during kilning the bottom layers of 'green malt' are subjected to very different relative humidities and temperatures to the layers above. This can lead to 'under-cured' malt at the bottom of the kiln and 'case-hardened' malt at the top.

There are currently 14 dedicated malting plants operating in Scotland, while seven distilleries still run their own floor maltings, supplying a percentage of their total malt requirement.

One of them is the Islay distillery of Bowmore, located on the shores of Lochindaal, in the island's principal village. Bowmore is the oldest surviving distillery on Islay, having been established by 1779 by local merchant John Simson. Today it is operated by Morrison Bowmore Distillers Ltd, a subsidiary of the Japanese distilling giant Suntory. Head brewer Ed McAffer has worked at Bowmore for the best part of 40 years.

'I went into the Merchant Navy when I was eighteen,' he says, 'and there was a seamen's strike in 1966. I was home here for about two or three months and I was really needing to get a job. I was on five shillings a week strike pay. So I approached the manager here, and I got a job in August 1966, that's when I started. I was born and brought up in Oa [the Oa peninsula is in south-west Islay], and I just spent about a year away at sea, then I came back home.

'When we were taking what we called the green malt off the floors to put it in the kiln, that was quite a big job in them days because we weren't automated the way we are now with mechanical shovels and whatever. Everything was done by hand, with wooden shovels, you'd put it into a barrow. So you'd go down to the corner and recruit half a dozen of the old worthies, the older guys, retired people, and guys that were out of work. They would get payment and a wee dram, and they'd be in there for half a day doing that job. In them days there's be something like 35 people in the distillery, casuals and full-time, and when you compare that with 10 today that's quite a difference. At the level of production we were doing at that time we couldn't make enough, so malt was being brought in from the mainland as well. That came in the wee coasters.' (See Chapter 13 'On Puffers'.)

Sandy McAdam, formerly of Cardhu distillery, where his father also worked, echoes Ed McAffer's observation about reduced workforces. 'I've got a photo of my father at the warehouse at Cardhu, taken in the late '30s, at the loading bank outside, putting whisky onto a lorry, and there's about fifty staff there at that time. It illustrates the amount of people who worked there back then.'

Cardhu stands close to the northern banks of the River Spey, and is operated by the world's leading drinks company, Diageo. Distilling on the site has its origins in an illicit operation run by Helen and John Cumming, believed to have begun in 1811.

Sandy McAdam's recollections of working in the Cardhu malt barns makes it clear just what hard, uncomfortable, physical work this was.

'The first job in a morning, at six o'clock, was getting in and stripping a kiln.

Malt drums, Speyburn distillery, 1923/24.

After the malt's been kilned you have to shovel the malt into the conveyors and away to the malt bins. That was dirty, dusty work, and there were no such things as respirators in those days. You'd hold a hankie over your face as you came out, and you'd be black. And there were no showers for the men. It was about 1948 or '49 before they got any showers.

'Even when I was in the malt barns in the middle '50s, the only shower we had at Cardhu you had to light a stove and heat your water before you could use it. We used to use hot water out of the supply that boiled the copper for the mashing. You'd take a pailful out of that and wash yourself. Even in the houses, it wasn't until the late '40s that there were baths in the houses. When I was going to school the toilets were a special, separate outside building. There was a coal shed and a toilet for each house.

'The work in the malt barns was very hard. You'd be in with the malt, then you'd to strip the kiln, or turn the malt. It was very hot work, too, but there was always the dram for dirty jobs, which helped. [The year] 1968 was the time they closed all the maltings at the distilleries, and then the malt came from the big plant they built at Burghead up on the Moray Firth.'

Dennis McBain is a coppersmith for William Grant & Sons Ltd in Dufftown, the malt whisky 'capital' of Speyside, where six distilleries are currently in production. In his early years with the company, Dennis took his turn on the malt floor, and his recollections of the job confirm those of Sandy McAdam in respect of hard work.

'My father worked for Grants at Glenfiddich, and two of my brothers, so it was a real family thing. I started off in the Speyside Cooperage down the road at Craigellachie, serving my time to become a cooper, but it wasn't the job I thought it was, and I enquired about getting a job at Glenfiddich. That was in October 1958, and I was sixteen years old.

'The old brewer knew my father, and told me that he didn't have a job, but he'd keep me in mind. Then a job came along; he started me off in the malt barns. The Glenfiddich maltings were where the reception area is now.

'When the maltings stopped at Glenfiddich around 1964 there were seven people employed there, and they were found other jobs, helping in the bottling hall and things like that. Working in the maltings was very dry, dusty work, especially up in the kiln where you had to turn the malt to get it dried off. That was a dirty, dirty job, and the protective clothing they have for jobs like that now just wasn't on the go then.'

Malt was a demanding mistress, too. Neil Ferguson of Caol Ila on Islay notes that 'Even when I was here and floor malting was going on, that was a seven days a week job, you worked Saturday forenoon and Sunday forenoon, because malting is a continuous sort of thing, so the work had to be done. And sometimes in the summertime, the malt that was on the floors would grow very rapidly with the heat, and half a day on the Sunday was not enough, you had to keep turning it, so somebody had to go out on overtime and turn it again. You were quite happy to do that, you got double time for it.'

One of the distilleries still operating floor maltings is William Grant's Balvenie, the 'sister' distillery to Glenfiddich. The first spirit flowed from the Balvenie stills on 1 May 1893, after fifteen months of construction and a cost of £2,000.

Most of the Balvenie make has always been used for blending, and is a major

component of Grant's Family Reserve blend, but it has also achieved considerable success as a single malt since being seriously marketed from the early 1970s.

Dennis McBain says, 'Balvenie maltings are pretty much as they were when I started, proper traditional maltings with solid iron steeps. They take the barley in off the fields from the same place, and there's the same dust. About the only difference is that where we had to throw the malt – or turn it – by hand, they have machinery now to do that, and it's still one of the hardest jobs in the distillery nowadays. Coopers have a hard, physical job as well, of course. Balvenie is getting more modernised now, but it fell behind Glenfiddich in terms of modernisation for a time.'

Despite its insistence on traditional methods, Bowmore has updated the business of distillery malting to good effect.

According to Ed McAffer, 'The floors were smaller in the old days, there only were two floors, because our maltings as they are at the moment are three levels, and on each of these levels there are fourteen tonnes [of malt]. But in the '60s when I started, the top level was a barley loft, where we stored all the barley, and the other two levels just had ten tonnes on them because you turned it by hand. Nowadays you can fill the floor from wall to wall and one man can turn it with a machine. That 20 tonnes that they were making in them days, there would be half a dozen men

Cardow (Cardhu) distillery, mid-1930s. Innes James, Excise officer, holds the dipping rod, with Sandy McAdam's father to his immediate right.

involved in the operation, seven days of the week, and now there's just three guys do the same job.

'At the moment the level of production that we're doing, 75 per cent of the malt we use is our own. We steep 42 tonnes of barley a week, and we make 39/40 tonnes of malt from that. We bring the rest from the mainland, it comes by road straight from the maltings right into our own maltings. We take our malt from Simpson's maltings down at Berwick-on-Tweed. Our barley comes from the Borders area as well, it's top quality Optic that we use all the time. It gives us a high spirit yield.

'We can source the grain nowadays, with the way things are, right back to the origin, right back to the very seed, the field it was planted in, and the fertilisers that were used to grow it. The grain is grown, harvested, stored, and then we bring it over and store it here and malt it. We order say, for a figure, 2,000 tonnes for this year, and that will have been put in last year, it will be the crop from the previous year. The supplier will know exactly where it comes from, it's traceable all the way back.'

Balvenie maltings 2004, showing kiln and pagoda head.

Jura's Mickey Heads notes, 'In the old days, the quality of malt fluctuated a lot. You didn't have constant storage facilities like we do now, keeping it at a regulated temperature and moisture level, and you get much higher yields and better conversion rates from modern barley varieties.'

Dr Harry Riffkin heads the Fife-based firm of Tatlock & Thomson, analytical and consulting chemists, which specialises in advising the Scotch whisky industry. Harry agrees that modern malting varieties of barley brought huge increases of yields. 'For a long time Golden Promise [introduced in 1966] was the favourite, then

Ed McAffer works up a thirst turning barley on the Bowmore malting floor.

Triumph came into favour. In the mid-1980s you were getting something like 390 litres of alcohol per ton of barley, but that had improved from around 330/340 litres. Triumph took yields up to 410, and it's now possible to get 420 litres from modern varieties given a good growing season'.

Today, most Scotch whisky distillers use British barley whenever possible, though a percentage of imported barley is also utilised. In *Harpers Wine & Spirit Gazette* for 18 June 1948, 'Caledonia' wrote: 'For many years barley from Canada, Australia, Denmark, and other countries has been used to supplement the home crop. No foreign barley, however, beats good home grain from the Laichs of Moray and Banff either in quality or quantity of spirit produce.'

The writer was able to state that 'many of the classic whisky makes, especially those in Spey and Glenlivet districts are distilled from local barley exclusively. This necessarily tends to preserve the traditional character of the whisky. Some barley samples have more husk than others; a high proportion of husk increases the aldehydes and gives a coarse character to the whisky.'

Jim McEwan's first contact with the world of Scotch whisky came via the maltings at Bowmore distillery.

'My early recollections of work, when I was a little kid going to Bowmore school, on a Monday and a Wednesday, that's the days they loaded the kilns, going up School Street in Bowmore, I would always smell the pipe smoke, because the boys were at the thick black twist, the whisky on the breath because at six o'clock in the morning the first big dram was poured, and they also wore semmit [vest] and drawers, and they didn't have showers in these days, so you had the smell of green malt, human sweat, whisky breath and pipe smoke.

'Because the roof was so low it just used to come out through the window, and on my way to school I was like a dog in a butcher's shop, you know, it would pull me towards the window. And I'd be looking in the window and old John McNair and Sandy McArthur and Angus McNiven would say, "Where you going today Jim?" "Oh, I'm going to school." "Och, forget the school today, come in here, there's a brush." I'd be brushing all day, and they would give me ninepence. Ninepence was exactly the right money to get you into the local pictures in Bowmore.

'But when I was at home, my mother would look at me, knowing full well by the smell that was off me, the alcohol, the tobacco, the green malt and the human sweat, I had never been near the school. So she was always saying to me, "What did you do at school today, Jim?" "Aw, history," or "English," I'd say. "Come here a minute," she'd say. She'd get hold of me, she'd sniff and then wallop! "No supper for you tonight," up the stairs with a thick ear. What I liked about the old malt barns really was the hand-turning. All the shovels up at the same time, and all down at the same time.'

Neil Gunn made the point, still just as valid today as it was in the 1930s, that malt 'determines not only the quantity of alcohol that may result from its fermentation but the quality of the ultimate distillate itself'.

Writing about Scotia distillery in Campbeltown, *The Wine and Spirit Trade Record* for 14 April 1924 observed: 'The fuel is peat, followed by coke, and the whole malting process is carried out with scrupulous care, on the principle that the Whisky cannot go wrong if the malt is right. That is the motto of Mr Hardie, the manager, who dealt with malt for forty years before he came to Campbeltown from the north-east of Scotland.'

When the work of the maltings is done, the malt is 'dressed' to remove rootlets and other impurities, then ground in a mill into a rough floury meal – known as grist – ready for the brewing phase of whisky-making to begin.

3

On Brewing

In the context of whisky-making, 'brewing' consists of the processes of mashing and fermentation. According to David Daiches (*Scotch Whisky*), 'the characteristic smell that hangs around a distillery is compounded of many factors, but the pungent smell of the mashing is central'.

Until distillation, the business of making whisky is very similar to that of making beer, and much of the vocabulary is common to both. It is during brewing that alcohol is first created.

The 'brewer' in a distillery was a very important figure, the equivalent to what modern business-speak would probably term a 'line manager'. The title and the roll are both now much less common than they used to be.

Archie Ness was brewer at Craigellachie Distillery, near Dufftown, in the heart of Speyside. He explains the traditional role of the brewer:

'After I came off the mashing I learnt the stills and all the other work, and in 1975 I was asked if I was interested in a brewer's job. It was an offer I couldn't refuse. If they thought I was fit for a brewer's job, then I'd better take it.

'When I started as brewer at Craigellachie we were still dramming [see Chapter 8, 'On Dramming'], and as well as dramming, the brewer's main duties included doing the fillings, which was three days a week, you had to check out the malt as it came in, all the paperwork and that, and you were kept quite busy. You were supervising all the stages, in charge of everything from the malt, the coal, ordering it and that. Everything from the start right through to the spirit coming out of the stills and being filled, it was all the brewer's responsibility. If there was anything wrong, the men always came to the brewer first. If you couldn't sort it out you went to the management.'

Unlike many distillery workers on Speyside, Archie did not come from a distilling family. 'I was working in the timber trade with my father,' he recalls. 'That was in the time of the travelling sawmills. I left school when I was fifteen, started work up at Glenfiddich Lodge, where my father was at the time, then we moved on to Aberlour, Fochabers, and at Craigellachie, where we lived. I did that for seven years, then I had a falling out with my father, and I went to Craigellachie distillery to see if there was any work.

'The manager told me that there was nothing at the time, but then the inspector came out of his office and said, "The man lives local, why not take his name, you never know what might come up." A month after that I got a message to say I was to go down to the distillery, and there was a job as a mashman. I started on 15 October 1962. I started on night shift, and that was my first time inside the distillery. I didn't know what I was going to.

'I was twenty-two. When I started on night shift, I learnt the job off another mashman whose job I was taking over really. In those days it was Sunday night and Monday night on nightshift, then you came off on Tuesday. Wednesday you worked all day in the filling store and the cooperage, Thursday morning you went out work-

Craigellachie distillery, 2003.

ing in the filling store, and then it would be back to the mashing. You worked till 12 o'clock and then you came back on Thursday night at 10 o'clock till six in the morning, and Friday till six on Saturday morning, and that was your week.

'I learnt the job from this man who was part English, part Scottish, and I could hardly understand a word he said. He wouldn't let you do things on your own, let you open and shut valves, he was always there doing it, which wasn't a good way of learning. You're trying to memorise it all, and if you're not doing it yourself it's much harder. I got a small book and was noting it all down, so that I could remember, because you only had the one week learning, and the following Sunday morning you were on your own six till two, apart from the tun room man, who only had four or five years to go till retiring, and you'd the stillman next door.

'On the Friday night, when I'd finished the mashing, I went to get my notes out of the desk, and they'd gone. I said to the mashman, "What's happened to my notes?" and he said, "You don't need them, I tore them up and put them in the bin." He said, "You've got it all up here," pointing to his head. That weekend my stomach was full of butterflies, because there I was, on my own, to start off. I managed to remember enough to keep me going, and in between times I could ask the brewer things when he came in, and that's how I picked up the mashing.'

The purpose of mashing is to extract fermentable sugars by mixing the grist with hot water, and Archie Ness explains in detail, from a practical point of view, how that is achieved.

'The mashing is what happens after the malting side of it, when you start mixing the malt with water. Your mash in those days had what we called four waters. You'd heat the mash tun with hot water, to warm it up, then you'd drain that off, and then you'd start off with your malt and your water, at a certain temperature, and mix that up, then turn that with the mixing rakes, twice round, then that was left to sit for one hour. Then you drained off the sweet liquor, which we called worts, from the mashtun through the underback and back to the cooler to cool it to a certain temperature, then on to the washback upstairs.

'It took approximately three hours to drain, then you'd add a second water to mix with the grist already in the mash tun. That followed the same procedure with a slightly higher temperature. The first and second waters went into the washback, where it was left to ferment. Then you put on a third water at a hotter temperature, and that took all the goodness out of the residue of grist left in the mash tun, and returned to the heating tank and was used in your next mash, so there was no waste. Then your fourth water was what we called the pumping water, and that was when you pumped the draff from the mash tun. You pumped the draff from the mash tun up into a tank upstairs.

The mashtun, Convalmore
distillery, Dufftown, 1922. As
was customary at the time,
the mashtun was made of cast
iron and open-topped.
Convalmore was closed by
owners DCL in 1985 and is
currently used by William
Grant & Sons Ltd for ware-
housing purposes.

'You had four chaps. The stillman came through, the tun room man, the maltman and myself. You had four rummaging sticks, long poles, and you'd take a position around the room, and you just pumped when you felt it get sticky. You couldn't put on too much water or you'd overflow the tank upstairs, and that took twenty minutes to empty.

'You could put on your water too hot, which would kill off your malt, you had to watch the temperatures, that was the main thing. You had to keep a check on all your valves to make sure they were closed when they should be.'

Modern mashing techniques have been developed from processes common in the brewing industry. The 'lauter' tun – named from the German word for 'clarifying' – has more efficient mixing and drainage systems than the traditional mash tun.

This greater efficiency leads to a higher extraction of sugars during the fermentation stage, and maximum extraction is the ultimate aim in most modern distilleries. Traditionally, mash tuns were constructed of iron, with domed, copper tops, though today most are made from stainless steel.

Of Craigellachie, Archie Ness says, '[Now] they have a big, new mash tun in what used to be the malt kiln. It's all computerised, and one man goes in and presses the buttons, and the computer does his mashing. It's all timed and that. Now you only have one mashman and one stillman, before we had a tun room man as well.

'The mash tun used to be between the mill room and the stillhouse when I was there, and you hadn't much room to move around in there. They decided to update because the old mash tun dated from 1965, and was starting to need repairs. Now you can do a mash in five hours, where it took us eight hours. It speeds up the process. Nowadays, they keep the stirrers going all the time, and the second water is actually going on before the first water is off. In our day we drained everything. You speed up the whole process of distilling by making more wort.'

After the wort has been drawn off from the mashtun, the spent grains which are left in the tun are known as draff. Although starch and sugars have been extracted, there is still a high protein content, and draff makes ideal cattle feed.

According to Grant Carmichael, formerly United Distillers & Vintners (UDV) general manager on the island of Islay, 'Islay is still famous for the quality of its beef cattle, a lot of that due to the wonderful feeding they get from the distillery draff. Very, very high quality cattle.'

Unlike Archie Ness, Bill McBain did come from a distilling family, and spent most of his working life at the Dufftown distillery of Mortlach. The Glenfiddich coppersmith, Bill, is one of his brothers. Ultimately a stillman, Bill recalls his early years at Mortlach.

'There were three mashmen, two tun room boys, a boilerman, and we had to "throw" the mash tun, that is shovel the draff out of it by hand. You'd to put on clogs, and a lot of the boys didn't like the clogs because they were awful slippy on the brass plates. At that time you got a dram for jobs like throwing the mash tun, and if you'd done a dirty job before that you'd already had a dram before that, and I've seen some of the boys fall down the hole. They didn't stay there long mind, because the thing was hot. You just went in with a pair of trousers and your clogs on, nothing else. This was to shovel the draff down the three holes in the mash tun.'

Ruari MacLeod was a notably long-serving mashman at Bruichladdich distillery, and in conversation with Jim McEwan, he recalls his days mashing the Laddie.

'At first when I came here I worked in the maltings, then I went from the maltings to the mash house, from the mash house to the stillhouse, but then I went back for two or three months to the mash again. And every time they wanted a new stillman the manager always had a wee talk and said, "Oh no, I think you'd better just stay at the mashing," so I was there till I retired.

'I enjoyed it because my ambition was to be even better than any of the rest. I used to go round the distilleries, find out what they were doing, and when I retired one of our directors said to me, "How would you like to do the whisky trail, part of your retirement present?" We were up at Macallan distillery, and the manager was doing a guided tour, although I didn't know he was the manager, he didn't look like a manager to me. They were mashing, and I just moved away from the party I was with, went over to the mashman and started talking to him. What temperature they were doing, everything they were doing, and later the manager came across and said to me, "Oh, were you not interested at all in the making of the whisky?" "No," I said, "for the simple reason I've only just been about 50 years making whisky." "Oh, where've you been?" he says. "At Bruichladdich distillery." "Oh aye," he says, "who's the manager there now?" I said, "Mr Allan." "Oh, I know him very well," he says, and we started talking, and that was it. That's how you get caught out. Yes, you go to find out what other people are doing. I still do to the present time. I always want to find what temperatures they're running the stills at, what temperature they have for the mashing, and it does help you at the job.

'The most important thing you need to make good whisky is a good mashman. And a mashman that the manager relies on. If you can't rely on the mashman doing a good job, well it's not easy to get rid of them, but you can eventually. The mashman is more important than the stillman.'

JM: That's a mashman talking. If you asked me the same question I would say a cooper.

RM: What I'm wondering about, say, the likes of Jura when I was there for a while, you have no control on the mashing in. The temperature's already there and you press a button, and that's it. The manager came in and said, 'Oh, we're going up two degrees,' and I said, 'Why?' He says, 'We're going up two degrees and that's it.' So I said, 'Fine.' I left him like that. The other two mashmen, when they came in, I just told them, 'That's it in the book there,' but I did not change. I still stood at 155 [degrees Fahrenheit], I think it was, for a fortnight. There was more whisky coming off the vats I'd filled than there was coming off the rest of them. Because it was far too hot, the new temperature. What they were producing actually was porridge. Do you agree with me on that, Jim?

JM: Aye, well the mashing temperatures are essential. If your temperature's not right you've not got the sugar to dissolve and you produce glue.

RM: At the present time that's all set, all automated, and you have no control of it. It's a lot easier for any mashman today, it's a lot easier, and they can't make a mistake.

In Harpers Wine & Spirit Gazette for 18 June 1948, 'Caledonia' noted that 'Variations in the methods of mashing and fermenting account to a certain extent for the difference in the character of the various malts. It is the brewing stage that determines the quantity of fusel oils and volatile acids in the finished spirit. Suitable mash tun temperatures are essential for the conversion of the starch in the grain into maltose and dextrin. Yet I have known Highland distillers to mash at temperatures varying from 140 degs to 155 degs F., and each was convinced that an alteration by a single degree would endanger the quality of the whisky.'

Grant Carmichael remembers that 'A wonderful cure for a cold was what they called the "bra-lish". I have no idea how you spell the word, which was the sweet wort, coming from the mash tun. It's very, very sweet and hot, it's like a toddy, although, of course, there's no spirit in it. It's very sweet and sugary and malty. If you had a cold a dram of clear spirit put into a cup of this stuff, bra-lish, was guaranteed to cure the cold.'

Once mashing is completed, the wort is pumped to the washbacks where fermentation takes place, and Professor G.H. Palmer of Heriot Watt University wrote in 1999 that fermentation 'is one of the most important stages in the production of whisky'.

During fermentation a variety of flavour compounds are obtained from the wort, in addition to large quantities of ethanol, or alcohol. These flavour compounds, or congeners, include esters, aldehydes, higher alcohols and acids. It is the esters which contribute significantly to fruity and flowery aromas in the finished spirit.

In the washbacks yeast is added to the wort to induce fermentation, with the temperature being maintained at a level between 20 and 32 degrees in order for the yeast to remain active. It is important, however, not to allow the temperature to rise too high, or fermentation will take place too rapidly, and the spirit ultimately produced will be adversely affected, since the coarse acids, aldehydes and alcohols that will give harshness to the ultimate spirit are created at higher temperatures.

The end product of fermentation is wash — which consists of water, yeast and alcohol at around 5 or 6 per cent volume. Ed McAffer, chief brewer at Bowmore distillery, explains, 'You have a tun room full of fermenting wash, and when it ferments out after 48 hours, in effect you've got a big 40,000 litres tank of "super lager" lying there, without the gas in.'

The washbacks are often 20 feet tall, though some are even larger, and a medium-sized distillery is likely to have 6 or 8 washbacks. Somewhat confusingly, they are located in the tun room, which is not the place where the mash tun is situated, as you might expect.

Washbacks were traditionally made from Oregon pine, oak or larch, though stainless steel has replaced wood in many distilleries, not least because it is much easier to keep clean. Before training as a coppersmith, Dennis McBain had to take his turn at less skilful jobs at Glenfiddich.

The washbacks, Argyll distillery, Campbeltown 1922. Argyll was established in 1844 and closed within a few months of this photograph being taken.

'In the tun rooms, the wooden washbacks have a steam hose in now, and various methods of cleaning them out, but at that day they had the heather besom on the end of a long wooden poll, about a 16 foot pole, and the chap had to go down a ladder into the bottom of the washback, and scrub it with the besom, just work his way down from the top. That was a really hard job. They were still doing that when I came here, so it's not back in the Dark Ages!'

Bill McBain recalls, 'There were five of us brothers at the distilling in all.

Newly-installed traditional wooded washbacks, Glengyle distillery, Campbeltown 2004.

My second oldest brother started work at Mortlach and I went to Parkmore Limes [the limeworks at Parkmore, Dufftown] when I left the school at fifteen. I was there for two years, then I left and went to Mortlach distillery. Three of my brothers were all there at one time or another. Dennis went to Glenfiddich, Gordon was at Balvenie for a time, Alistair was at Glenfiddich, and he left Glenfiddich to go to Mortlach.

'Five brothers were all helping to make whisky at that time of day. My father worked at Glenfiddich for a time too, but he was actually the last of us all to go into the whisky industry, he'd worked at Parkmore Limes before that. Parkmore Limes and the stills were the two big employers in Dufftown in those days.' Recalling how he started work as a tun room man, Bill says:

'One day there was a trainee manager who was working in the tun room because there was somebody off work not well, and he didn't like it, so he came down and said, "Would you like a job in the tun room?" I said I was maybe not fit for it, but he said, "Give it a try, and if you're not fit for it I'll give you your old job back again." But I wasn't keen so nothing came of it, and then a few months later another boy left, and the same thing happened, the trainee manager had to fall into his place again. Back down he came again to me, and this time I said I'd give it a try.

'The washbacks — the hardest bit was standing in the middle with a great long shaft with a heather besom stuck on it. You started at the top and worked down, swinging it from side to side, and it was rough on the muscles. You'd do it in four "strips", then you washed out the bottom, and then you limed it after that. There was a bucket of it, we called it "head lime". It came in chunks, like rock, pure white, and you put a bit into a pail, and you put water into it, and it bubbled up. Then you lowered it down to the bottom of the back, and the boy at the top held the hose and filled it up with water, and then you used the heather besom with it. You started liming at the top, spreading it right round the back, and you'd just keep dipping the besom into the pail.

'Then we had a sweeping brush which we used to brush the lime down the drain after we'd spread it over the floor. You started at the outside and worked in' til you came to the centre where the ladder was, then you climbed back up the ladder and out. When it was dry it was pure white, bonnie to see. Sometimes the back would get "stuck" as we used to say, it stopped fermenting, which meant that the back wasn't clean or there was something dirty about it and it stopped the work of the yeast.

'The tun room man always had a job to do, because you didn't finish work till seven, and after five o'clock one of you stayed up in the tun room for the switching [the 'switcher' is a revolving blade in the mash tun which cuts the head from the fermenting wash to prevent it overflowing], and the other boy, he went down and he kept the steam in the boiler going. The boiler boy had sometimes to come up and start the steam engine. The steam engine did more or less everything at that time. It drove the mill, it took in the barley and the malt because it drove all the elevators, it drove the stirring gear in the mash tuns and all that.'

Today, a mixture of cultured yeast and brewer's yeast is usually used in fermentation. In the absence of oxygen, the yeast absorbs part of the sugar as 'food'. The zymase enzymes, maltose and other sugars in the wort are broken down into ethyl alcohol and carbon dioxide.

Writing in *Harpers Wine & Spirit Gazette* (18 June 1948), 'Caledonia' noted that 'Distillery ferments depend largely on the quality of yeast. A rousing fermentation gives a larger quantity of spirit, while a slow, gentle ferment produces a more saintly spirit. In quick ferments are created the coarse alcohols, acids, and pungent aldehydes which catch a man's throat when, years afterwards, he takes a glass of "Scotch".'

Modern yeasts are less volatile than the older varieties, so truly dramatic fermentations are rare. Neil Gunn wrote (*Whisky & Scotland*) during the 1930s: 'I have seen men in past days, stripped to the waist, with long birch sticks laying

Mortlach distillery entrance, 1953.

into the ebullient yeast-froth for dear life in a battle in which they were not always completely victorious. With the automatic switchers going full speed, I have heard one of these backs rock and roar in a perfect reproduction of a really dirty night at sea.'

Drew Sinclair recalls at Dalmore using soap in the washbacks. 'It was curd soap, obviously not scented. We had switchers in the washbacks, blades, and there were two speeds, a low speed and a high speed. Now even on high speed you would see these washbacks shaking, just bouncing away like that at times. Really, really fierce. And they would start bouncing the lids off. That was when you put the soap in. And the soap just knocked it back. Very often it would come

Grant Carmichael

over the top, but in those days there was always somebody around, there was a tun room man on the job, you see, to deal with it.'

Grant Carmichael was born in Edinburgh, and his early work experiences were in a number of Lowland distilleries owned by the giant Distillers Company Ltd.

'When I started in the distilleries, at Glenkinchie and Linlithgow, Lowland distilleries, each distillery had its own lorry, and every week the lorry driver and a man went off round the breweries to collect liquid yeast. The bulk of the yeast we used then was liquid, actually a mixture of dried yeast and brewer's yeast. The dried yeast started fermentation quickly, and the brewer's yeast, which had been heated previously, finished the fermentation well. Nobody uses liquid yeast any more. Brewer's yeast is still used, but it has always been compressed now.

'They used to go to Fowler's brewery in Prestonpans, and that was a very nice one to go to, just a small brewery, and they produced "Wee Heavy", which was a lovely, very strong ale. In Edinburgh they used to go to McEwan's at Fountainbridge, to Calder's, Younger's, and I think to Steel, Coulson & Co. and there was a strict rota of who was to accompany the driver. Because when you accompanied the driver you got a sample at every one of these breweries that you went to, so woe betide anybody who jumped the queue and took somebody else's turn. The driver would have his beer, too, of course.

'Much later, when I was on Islay, we used to take yeast in liquid form from the mainland, though nowadays the breweries all compress their yeast, and the different distilleries would all take their turn at sending a lorry down to the pier to pick up the yeast when it came in, and then drop it off at the various distilleries around the island. That sort of thing. Women would come in when they knew the yeast had just arrived at the distilleries, and would come get a handful, just a few ounces, for making bread.'

According to Drew Sinclair, 'We used to use DCL yeast plus brewers yeast. The brewers yeast came in from Burton-on-Trent by rail, in "hoggies", with bungs in. Sometimes, in hot weather, when we unloaded them and lined them up beside the track, the fermentation inside these casks meant they would just go "whoosh!" It sprayed right out, and hit the top of the trees, went right up away in the air.

'We used to get the dried brewers yeast from the same place, and we used to collect it from Invergordon station, too. Again, in hot weather, the bags would be leaking. But many years ago they stopped bringing it in, because what was happening was if they had an infection at their brewery, we were just taking it up to the distillery then. So they decided to stop that and do it with strictly cultured yeast.'

Modernisation and automation of equipment and processes has inevitably embraced the brewing stage of whisky-making, just as it has malting and distilling.

'You've cut down fermentation times in the washbacks these days,' Archie Ness notes. When I started it was 48 hours fermentation, now it's down to 32 hours in most places. All of this means that you've got more "raw material" ready for the stills, but you can only work as fast as they can, you can't bypass the stills.'

Not everyone agrees that the fastest and most efficient way of fermenting the wort is necessarily the best, however.

Drew Sinclair

Dr Harry Riffkin, of analytical and consulting chemists Tatlock & Thomson, believes that advances in distillery production efficiency during the past few decades have frequently come at the expense of spirit character. He has never been interested in increasing output for its own sake, and says bluntly, 'The object of making malt whisky is to make a quality product. If you want to make a lot of alcohol cheaply, do it in a grain distillery.'

One of Riffkin's examples of how increased production has led to flavour loss concerns fermentation. 'Scotch whisky fermentation is not a sterile process,' he explains. 'What happens is that the yeast predominates during the first 36 to 48 hours, producing most of the alcohol, and so often fermentation is stopped then in the interests of maximization of throughput. However, if you leave it for longer – upwards of 96 hours – lactic acid bacteria develop, which give you desirable complex flavours. If the lactic acid fermentation is allowed to optimize, you will get fruit flavours like pear-drops, banana and apple aromas. These are all chemical esters, and all add to the complexity of the new make.'

Broadly in agreement with Riffkin is Alan Rutherford, a former Scotch Whisky Production Director for UDV, and now Visiting Professor of Distilling at the International Centre for Brewing & Distilling at Heriot Watt University in Edinburgh.

He says, 'Gravities in the washbacks have increased, from the high 1040s up to 1058 or even 1060 in some cases. You get more throughput that way and it's also more energy-efficient. Improved yeasts have led to improved fermentation, too.'

Not every distiller has abandoned the older ways, however. Frank McHardy is manager of the iconic Springbank distillery in the old distilling capital of Campbeltown, on the remote Kintyre peninsula in Argyllshire. It is reckoned that distilling has taken place on more than 30 sites in the town, and during its Victorian heyday no fewer than 23 distilleries were operating simultaneously. Today there are just 3. Frank McHardy has been in the whisky business for 42 years, and first came to Springbank in 1977. Having spent time on the other side of the Irish Sea, at Bushmills distillery in County Antrim, he is once again making whisky in Campbeltown.

Springbank continues to use traditional methods wherever possible, and features wooden washbacks. Frank notes, 'When we collect worts in our washback we ensure that the original gravity is kept low at between 1047 to 1050. This recreates how things were done years ago when you would seldom find original gravities of 1057 to 1058. The low original gravities mean that the alcohol content in the wash is also low at around 4 to 4.5 per cent.'

Alan Rutherford points out, 'In theory, fermentation is pretty complete after about 48 hours, so why not stop then, you might argue. But you can't because it often changes the spirit character. Short, 44- to 48-hour, fermentations make a nutty, spicy character. If the character of your spirit is heavy, sulphury, meaty, then it's no good cutting back fermentation times from around 100 hours, because it will alter the spirit character significantly. The old distiller knew that from experience, but so does your young Heriot Watt graduate, due to science.'

So much for the technical stuff, but ask most distillery workers to talk about the fermentation stage of whisky-making, and they will initially tell you about wash drinking. This is, after all, the stuff that Ed McAffer describes as 'superlager'. It seems to have been an accepted feature of distillery life all over Scotland, and William Grant & Sons' malt distilleries manager Ian Millar remembers instances of wash drinking at Blair Athol distillery, in Pitlochry, Perthshire, not far from his birthplace of Aberfeldy.

Ian started work at Blair Athol at the age of nineteen. 'One of the guys, Sandy, was on day shift, starting at 7 a.m. He had had a few jugs of 'Joe' (fermented wash), topped up by a big sook out of the warehouse dramming beaker at 5 o'clock, then a couple of pints on the way home just to finish off. He arrived home at 6 p.m. and promptly fell asleep. He woke up an hour later, looked at his watch, and immediately panicked. He leapt up, belted down the road to work, dashed in, and apologised profusely to the mashman for being slightly late. It was only then that it dawned on him that it was 7 p.m. and not 7 a.m.

'Drinking Joe was fairly commonplace, three or four of the shift process guys were regulars at it. One of them was a stillman, and he was witnessed by the office cleaner exiting the stillhouse with his trousers at his ankles, backfiring gas and liquid all the way across the courtyard to the toilet block. This happened quite often if you took the Joe too early, as it would continue fermenting – or even speed up – inside your body.'

Jim McEwan agrees. 'If you picked a washback which was still fermenting

you got the most horrendous cases of diarrhoea. These guys made Linford Christie look like a slowcoach, you know.'

Springbank distillery, Campbeltown, 2004.

Speyside had its share of wash drinkers too, as Sandy McAdam confirms. 'I worked for a while at Imperial [at Carron, close to Dailuaine] when it reopened in 1955. One chap worked for the contractors, the builders, and he was away for the Joe. This day he went up to the tun room for a drop, and he met the exciseman just as he was going in. So he was quick thinking, and turned to the exciseman and said, "I was just looking for the toilet." The fact was he was building the toilet at the time. Obviously the exciseman didn't believe him, he knew just what was going on.'

Wash drinking may have been widespread, but on Jim McEwan's native island of Islay the practice seems to have been elevated to something like an art form. Remarkably, given Ian and Jim's recollections of its possible effects, it was often considered a desirable hangover cure!

'Port Ellen distillery was full of characters, recalls Grant Carmichael. 'The wash, or the "Joe" as they call it on Speyside, "kuch-an" as it's called on Islay, was freely available, the tun rooms were open. Port Ellen Laphroaig, Lagavulin, in fact all the distilleries, and Bowmore in particular, the ones that were in the villages, you forever had to be watching the tun room, as people would forever be sneaking into the tun room for a jug of the stuff. This was just people coming in off the street. You had to chase them for their lives.

'And then security became tighter, places are much more secure than they were, and people now don't do that. There's none of the old characters left now who would come and drink wash, not that I know of. But this was an accepted thing. When James [Jim McEwan] was at Bowmore, all the wash drinking was going on, and when it was dramming time, people would appear from the village, all the characters.'

Jim McEwan says, 'I remember the manager Jimmy McCall saying to me ... I used to open up the cooperage on a Saturday morning, get the fires going for the coopers, and Jimmy McCall would say to me, "Right, you're the first man in in the morning." I was only a boy, and he'd say, "Right, keep your eye out for these bloody wash drinkers," and he'd give me a torch. So I'd come in and open the doors, go through the whole distillery, open the tun room door, and I remember Fat Sam ... my first day on duty, I went into the tun room, and Fat Sam was called Fat Sam because he had a huge stomach, and I could hear talking, and they were singing Gaelic songs, and I'm really scared, I'm shining the torch, and shouting, "Who's there?" And this voice comes ... Fat Sam pushes himself in against the wall, of course there's the door, all I can see is his stomach, this appendage, and he says, "There's nobody here Jim, carry on, carry on." Seventeen years of age and a guy that size, I'm not going to argue. So I kept walking.'

Bowmore's current head brewer, Ed McAffer, echoes Grant and Jim's stories about wash-drinking at Bowmore:

'At the weekend the distillery shut down, but you left behind a tun room full of fermenting wash. No matter how secure you thought your tun room was, the local worthies would somehow find their way in, and you'd maybe come in on the Sunday night, whenever you would start, there would be a bucket with a bit of string tied on it, obviously evidence that they'd been in and used it.

'The old manager Mr Macaulay, he used to say there was one guy, I won't mention his name, but where a rat could get in he could get in! There was always a way to get in, by climbing away up and in windows that you'd left open for ventilation never thinking anyone could find their way in through them, but they'd get in about there. They'd come in during the night, and if you were on nightshift you had to be ever vigilant round about, chasing them out. When we were young guys it was a daunting thought, we used to go about in pairs on the nightshift if we thought that

BRUICHLADDICH, ISLE OF ISLAY, FROM THE EAST. B.6573.

there was somebody about. These guys were hardy, you know, and we were just young. But once you got older and got to know them you just chased them. They thought they could take advantage because we were just young and new at the jobs. They just came in to look for it. "We're just going to help ourselves." "No you're not," sort of style.'

Talking with Ruari MacLeod, Jim McEwan declared, 'Mashmen were the worst drunks of the lot, because they would drink the bloody wash. They were wash drinkers, mashmen.'

'Well, all the days I was working here, and I had two or three working with me, they never touched wash,' replied Ruari solemnly. 'You had people coming round about, people coming in at night to turn the floors and that, to give you a hand turning the floors, and the manager came down and gave them a dram. And of course, after the manager went away, up to the washbacks and have some of the wash. And of course some of the maltmen as well, during the day. I never tried it, well, not yet.'

Bruichladdich distillery (right, with chimney, pier on the left), 1950s.

JM: Well, you're not bloody trying it now! Wash drinking was very common.

RM: On the island they called it *kuch-an*, that's the Gaelic for wash.

JM: Even in Bowmore, the boys at the corner, the local likely lads, would watch the manager going in at ten o'clock, he would change the shift, he'd give the men their dram, and he'd drive past in his car, and they'd all wave to him. As soon as his car was outside they'd be up the road and into the washbacks. And they became connoisseurs. They could stand at the corner in Bowmore on a Tuesday night, and it would be, 'Well, Donald, which one will it be tonight?' 'Oh, well number five will still be switching, but number six will be finished.' 'Right, number six it is.' They were like wine aficionados, they were connoisseurs. It was a big, big thing, drinking wash.

RM: Yes, yes it was. I mind once I came in at six in the morning, and I was mashman at that time. And I heard talking. And there were three locals, at six in the morning. And one of them got up, and he said, 'Oh there's a lot left yet.' Seven or eight thousand gallons of it ... A lot left yet! At that time of the morning. That was them in all night.

JM: Maltmen drank wash a lot. The first time I was given a bottle with string on the neck I learnt a very valuable lesson. It was Angus McNiven at Bowmore, Old Angus. I was just in the distillery one week, and Angus gave me a bottle with string round the neck. And he said to me in Gaelic, 'Go and fill this bottle.'

Now I never realised the significance of the string around the neck, so I went to the tap and filled it with water. And I took it back up to the malt barns, and there's the boys shovelling away. A lemonade bottle. And I handed the bottle to Angus, and as I handed the bottle to Angus I knew I had done something very, very wrong, but I didn't know what it was. But my sixth sense said run, run, run, so as I handed the bottle to Angus, and he took one look at the bottle, and he looked at me, and he must have thought this guy is taking the piss out of me, giving me water. The fact of the matter is it was my first week. I started running and this lemonade bottle came flying past my ear, and smashed. And from that day onwards, if someone gave me a bottle with string on it I would go to the washback and fill it with wash.

I've seen as many as twelve round a washback on a Sunday morning in Bowmore, just standing there drinking it, the odd dead rat floating by, take it out and carry on drinking. It was a wonderful thing, wash drinking.

RM: You had to pick one that was fully fermented. They were very good at it. They'd ask you, 'Which is the next one you're going to pump?' Number one or number two, whichever it was. That's it, that's the one they'd go to. I don't know what effects it had on them, but it made no difference anyway. But it didn't do them any harm, that's the honest truth.

4
On Distilling

The process of distillation undoubtedly embraces a greater range of variables than any other stage of malt whisky-making. Along with maturation, distillation has the largest single influence on the business of turning a field of barley into whisky in a bottle.

Today, science has explained most of the mysteries of distilling, and Alan Rutherford, Visiting Professor of Distilling at the International Centre for Brewing & Distilling at Heriot Watt University in Edinburgh, points out that 'The scientist can think of ideas that assist the business goals of making distilleries more efficient. But the scientist can also argue *against* increases in efficiency too, at times. As a scientist I was able to argue why they couldn't do certain things for extra efficiency. For example, you can't drive stills for seven days because of the copper chemistry of pot stills. You need to let air in at least once a week to allow the copper to rejuvenate.

'The chap who had been in the stillhouse for thirty years would know that, though he wouldn't know why, and he would therefore have found it harder to argue against it than the scientist. The industry is far better equipped now to tell the business world what can be done and what can't be done to make good spirit.'

Happily, however, myths and legends linger. The likes of Linkwood manager Roderick Mackenzie, who refused to have spiders' webs removed from the Elgin distillery's stillhouse in case it adversely affected the spirit, are rare today. There is still, however, a sense that having managed to produce a fine spirit by a complex interaction of ingredients, equipment and procedures, only a foolish person would tamper with the precarious winning formula for the sake of it.

Neil Ferguson was a stillman at Caol Ila on Islay when the distillery was completely rebuilt in 1972–73, having started work there in 1969. It is interesting to note that while the Distillers Company Ltd which owned Caol Ila was keen to make it larger, more modern, and more efficient, they were careful not to do anything which would alter the distinctive style of single malt made there.

'I don't think there would be a great difference between the whisky made in the old distillery and the whisky made in the new one,' declares Neil. 'When they rebuilt the distillery they made exact copies of the old stills, as exactly as they could, using the very latest computer technology at the time. They made them identical in every possible detail.'

Essentially, what happens during malt-whisky distillation is that the liquid wash is heated in a copper pot still to a point at which the alcohol becomes vapour. This vapour rises up the still and passes through the 'lyne arm' or 'lye pipe' into the cooling plant, where it is condensed back into liquid form. Traditionally, the cooling plant was a coiled copper tube, known as a worm, immersed in a large 'tub' of continuously running cold water, though many distilleries are now equipped with modern condensers.

The first distillation takes place in the wash still, and it increases the strength of the wash from around 7 or 8 per cent to what are known as 'low wines' of between 21 and 28 per cent. This initial distillation will usually last between 5 and 6 hours, and continues until all the alcohol has been driven off.

When distillation has ended, the wash still will contain some 40 per cent of low wines and around 60 per cent of 'pot ale'– the waste liquid, which is now often processed into cattle feed, being mixed with draff into pellet form or evaporated to form pot ale syrup. The low wines are pumped into the low wines charger, and ultimately into the spirit still, where the second distillation takes place.

Here the alcohol content of the low wines is significantly raised, with the spirit being run from the condenser into the spirit safe, where it is tested by thermometer and hydrometer, with the spirit being directed through a swivelling spout. The spirit safe is sealed by lock, and at no point can the stillman analyse it by nose or taste.

The early part of the distillation is the lighter alcohols, the foreshots, which are too volatile, and are run off into the feints receiver to be re-distilled with the next batch of low wines. The foreshots run usually lasts from 15 to 30 minutes, with the strength dropping from around 85 per cent volume to 75 per cent volume.

Traditionally, the stillman tests for the presence of foreshots by mixing some spirit with distilled water in the spirit safe. While the sample is milky, foreshots are present, but when it is clear the stillman will direct the spirit entering the spirit safe into the spirit receiver and collect the 'middle cut' or 'heart of the run.'

Mortlach was the first distillery to be constructed in Dufftown, reputedly being established in 1824. Bill McBain worked there for more than forty years, most of them spent as stillman. According to him, 'When your spirit starts to come off we usually ran it for twenty minutes to half an hour. That was your foreshot, to clean it. Now you tested it with water.

'There's different ways you can try it. One way is to fill your sample glass in the spirit safe half way up with spirit, then top it up with water. You get a reading off that, something like 15 to 20 under proof, and if it's clear it's alright. But if you try it after quarter of an hour and it needs half an hour to clear it's blue and it'll stay blue. That's not spirit, that's feints; feints are blue. What we call "clearic", pure whisky just made, if you put just a sip of water in, it's alright, but if you put in too much water it's blue as anything. It's no good that way.

'Another way of doing it is to run whisky up into your sample glass and run

Stillman checking the strength of spirit at the spirit safe, Glenlivet distillery, 1980s.

the water at the same time till it comes up to the top, and you shut that off and leave it to settle. Sometimes it's clear and sometimes it's blue, and if it's blue it's not time to go onto spirit, you've to wait. You were supposed to do that every time a still came in [i.e. was distilling into the spirit safe], I've seen us do it twice or three times a shift.

'If everything was going right it would be going into the safe alright without testing it, and you'd give it half an hour to run the foreshots. It was usually about two hours and twenty minutes you'd run the spirit then you'd knock it off after that. It depended on the strength. The stronger the spirit came in the better it was and the longer it took to drive it off.'

Retired Islay stillman 'Big Angus' McAffer from Lagavulin echoes Bill McBain's experience of testing for foreshots with water.

'You had a water test. When you put the water in if it was turning blue you knew it wasn't just right. So you had to leave it for half an hour on the feints before putting it onto spirits. Then you'd test it again, and when everything was clear you'd take that as spirit. At that time you were running for four and a half hours, sometimes five hours, that's how long they were on spirit.'

In many distilleries today, such practical tests as described by Bill and Big Angus have been abandoned in favour of a computerised, timed run, which takes no account of the potability of the spirit at any specific point, but requires less skill and initiative from the stillman.

The 'middle cut', or the 'heart of the run' which is collected in the spirit receiver, can account for up to 40 per cent of the spirit distillation, though in many cases it can be as little as 15 per cent, depending on the style of spirit desired.

The 'cut points' at which the stillman begins to collect the heart of the run and then stops collecting it are crucial to the style of whisky produced. If a 'heavier', more full-bodied style is required, the initial cut point will be later than that for a lighter-bodied whisky.

The new spirit run lasts for between two and a half and three hours, with strength falling from around 72 per cent to as low as 60 per cent, depending on the final cutting point of the individual distillery.

As the stills get progressively hotter, the heavier alcohols in the low wines start to vaporise, and these are known as the feints. A small amount of the fusel oil in the feints is beneficial to the spirit's character, and for a full-bodied whisky the stillman will wait to cut at a comparatively low strength.

Usually he cuts when the strength of the distillate has fallen to around 63 per cent volume. Some 35 per cent of the total run is comprised of feints, and they are re-distilled along with the foreshots and the next batch of low wines. Spent lees — essentially deoxygenated water — are all that remains in the spirit still when distillation is complete.

Along with cut points, temperature is another important distillation variable. If the stills are run too hot and fiery, unpalatable spirit may result, as it will not have benefited from a gentle reflux. Reflux is the condensing of spirit vapour on the swan neck of the still; the condensate subsequently running back down into the still for further distillation. If the spirit is driven off too quickly because of a high temperature it will be heavier, due to less copper contact. Bill McBain says, 'If you run spirit too quick it's not so good as the spirit that you run slow. We ran it down there at Mortlach watching the temperatures, being careful, but there were a lot of stills that they ran not worrying about the temperature, and that's what's happening nowadays. It doesn't matter to them as long as it's spirit. It's running hotter than we used to run it.

'With the coal fires, when we were on the spirit [i.e. collecting the middle cut] we opened the doors and hosed it down, to make the flames die down, and the whisky was just running nicely into the safe. You had enough fire in below the still to run the whisky at that steady speed all the time. About half way through sometimes the coal started to burn up again.

'Once you were off spirit you filled up with coal, shut the doors and "drove it off" as we say, to empty the still. When they went on to steam that was the doors gone, and you controlled it with steam valves and that, but it wasn't quality it was quantity they were needing. You need a good stillman to get good whisky, if he knows how to run it well then that's it.

'In the wintertime, for example, in very cold weather, the spirit would slow down, and you'd maybe give it a bit more heat to get it going. Inside the still whisky is in the top, and if you put too much steam on it's just like boiling a pan, it comes from the bottom up. If you put too much steam on and push it too hard it starts to mix with the spirit and then when it's run off you'll smell or taste the feints. I've tasted feints in it myself; that means I was running it too quick.'

One of the most tangible factors affecting the character of spirit produced during distillation is the size and shape of the pot stills themselves. Tall stills — most notably like those at Glenmorangie, modelled on the original gin stills installed when the distillery was built in 1843 — give lighter character as a general rule. This is because only the lighter alcohols are able to ascend the still and pass over the lyne arm into the condenser. With shorter, squatter stills, such as those at Macallan, heavier alcohols are able to pass over into the condenser, producing a heavier, oilier style of spirit.

There is a common belief that the best whisky is made in small stills, and distilleries such as Glenfiddich and Macallan on Speyside are good examples of establishments which have increased their output significantly over the years by installing more stills of the same size and design as the originals rather than commissioning larger ones. Glenfiddich boasts no fewer than 28 stills, while 21 operate at Macallan.

'A big still never makes good whisky,' declares Bill McBain. 'If you get a wee or a sizeable spirit still and a sizeable wash still you'll make a lot better whisky than in the big ones. At Mortlach every still had a "dip", and you didn't fill above the dip level. Maybe a couple of inches was fair enough, but not six or eight inches. You'd just fill them to a certain level. They were never filled up. We filled them up to the man door and that was it. They tried it for a few weeks filling them higher in one pair of stills, but they didn't carry on with it. We just had the man door open, and when you saw the froth coming out and the liquid you shut your man door and then you shut your valve off. You knew it was as full as you wanted it. It took twenty

Worm tubs at Glenfiddich, 1923.

minutes to half an hour to charge, depending on the size of your spirit still.'

If still size and shape are the most obvious influences on spirit style, then there are also much less apparent ones, such as the type of condenser in operation. Modern condensers consist of a series of copper pipes through which cold water is passed within a copper jacket. The alcohol vapour condenses on the pipes when it enters the jacket. Far less water is used than in worm tubs, and because of the greater contact with copper, the spirit from a modern condenser is likely to be lighter in character than that from a worm because one effect of copper contact on the distillate is a chemical reaction which takes some of the 'body' out of the spirit.

The whisky produced using worm tubs is heavier in body because it has comparatively little copper contact, and old distillery workers insisted they could tell whether spirit had been distilled during summer or winter, as the copper has even less effect when the water in the worm tubs is extremely cold. Winter spirit, they claimed, was detectibly heavier.

Donald Stirling is operations manager at Diageo's Dalwhinnie distillery, which stands close to the Perth – Inverness road at 1,164 feet above sea level, making it the highest distillery in Scotland. 'The fact that our water tends to be very cold is good for the Dalwhinnie character of whisky,' he remarks. 'It's very important to condense the vapour quickly.'

Dalwhinnie is one of the distilleries which retain worm tubs, and Donald points out that they are not kept simply because they are traditional, but because they play a vital part in maintaining the distinctive character of Dalwhinnie single malt whisky.

'The character of Dalwhinnie tends to be quite sulphury,' he says, 'and to get that you really want as little contact with all the copper as possible. You don't want air to get in because that rejuvenates the copper and kills off the sulphur character, so we drive the stills from Sunday night right through, flat out, drive them to exhaustion — that way we keep the character.

'The worm tubs are ideal for that character because if you have a modern condenser instead it has multiple copper tubes, too much copper contact for us, but the vapour comes off the top of the stills into the worm tubs and is condensed quickly. The coldness of the water is an important factor, because it helps condense the vapour quickly, giving less copper contact.'

Although the principles remain the same, the business of distillation has been the subject of a significant amount of change during the last half century. Coal-fired stills have all but disappeared, and today stills which are heated directly have a flame which is provided either by oil or gas. The majority of stills are, however, indirectly heated, using steam coils and pans. It is usual for the wash stills to be equipped with 'kettles' as they are generally known – cylinders which fill with steam, while spirit stills tend to be heated using coils.

Oil-firing makes the bases of the stills brittle in a way that gas does not, and as a general rule, the more gentle heating obtained by indirect firing increases the life of the stills considerably (see Chapter 5, 'The Coppersmith').

A still of between 2,000 and 4,000 gallons capacity, including condenser, will cost at least £60,000, and the life expectancy of the still would be between 10 and 15 years, though stills are usually replaced in sections rather than in their entirety.

There are perils with ageing stills, as Jura distillery manager Mickey Heads notes. 'I've seen stills "panting" at times, either when the copper is wearing very thin, or if they've been overcharged. The still will move and throb, and eventually it could collapse. Believe me, it's not something you want to see!'

Bill McBain says that the wash stills lasted less long than the spirit stills, 'because at that time of day you had a rummager inside, which went round and round. It was wee links of copper, and it went round the sides and round the bottom because with the wash, with the heat in below, it would have stuck to the copper and burnt otherwise. At Mortlach we had two stills were burnt in the bottom, and by God you tasted it in the whisky when it came off. You could taste it in the new make.

'One day when we got our dram in the stillhouse we said to the brewer, "That dram's singed." So he went and got the manager and they went into the filling store and took a sample out, and yes, it was singed. This was back in the '50s, and despite that it was filled.

'With the heat and the rummagers inside you needed to replace your stills quite often, but the wash stills were a fair thickness, and the spirit stills were thinner. It wasn't so hard on them, you see, you'd no rummagers in them, it was only low wines and feints that was in them. You'd just the fire in below. Whereas in the wash stills the "ale" was awful sticky and sometimes you got yeast in it too, and sometimes draff, and if anything got stuck on the copper it always got bigger and it burnt it. We started opening the man doors, and every time you charged it with wash we looked in with a torch to see there were no black bits on the still before we started charging again.

'There was a manager at Mortlach who didn't like the fact that you lost some spirit through having the man doors open, but you lost it through the air cran valve anyway when it was open, but you only lost a sip really. They complained about losing spirit out of the air cran and the man doors and all the rest of it, but when you went into the filling store – another job you did from time to time when you were working in the tun room, you went to the filling as well – if a hose didn't shut off you'd have such a mess, you'd be wiping spirit off the floor, and nobody worried about that.'

Direct firing – whether with coal, gas or oil – is hotter than steam heating, and 'toasts' the distillate, giving, it is argued, a different flavour profile to the same wash. Old stillmen will tell you that the whisky produced using direct firing was heavier, possessed of more 'guts' than that made using indirect firing.

Grant Carmichael of Islay says, 'The old Caol Ila whisky was a bit more toffee-flavoured than that from the new distillery. This was largely due to the fact that it was a coal-fired wash still. In a coal-fired wash still you tend to get stickiness, although you have your chains that go round, you still get a certain stickiness. Not so consistent in quality, obviously not, because steam distillation produces a much finer spirit, so the old one was a wee bit more complex, because you get different flavours coming out at different times.'

The difference between whisky made using coal-fired stills and steam-heated stills was not always obvious, however. Bill McBain remembers that in 1963 Mortlach was knocked down to the ground. 'Everything was completely flattened. They stopped distilling in July 1963 and started up again in July of 1964. Before the rebuilding we had the wee stillhouse and the big stillhouse. There was number one spirit still and one and two wash stills in the wee stillhouse, they were wee ones like the 'Fiddich ones. The big wash still, along with two and three spirit stills, was in the big stillhouse.

'Then after they rebuilt it they had the six stills all in a row, instead of two stillhouses they made just the one, which had the three pairs in it. There were still two stillmen on at that time, and that was when I started as a stillman, after the rebuilding. I was a stillman there until I retired.

'It was still working on coal after they rebuilt it, and in 1970 they went on to steam. The manager who was there when they rebuilt it went on to become an inspector, and the first distillation of whisky with steam, he and the brewer had a glass of whisky made with steam and a glass of whisky made with coal, to taste it and see which way made the best whisky. The inspector had a mind to say that the coal was a far better whisky, but he picked the wrong one, he picked the one made with steam.'

Former Craigellachie distillery manager Sandy McAdam says, 'I think you get a better control with the steam than you did with the coal, and you get a better

Opposite:

Bill McBain tending a fire, Mortlach stillhouse, following the distillery reconstruction, c. 1964/65.

whisky. If you were running spirit with a coal fire it depended partly on the quality of your coal. That made a big difference. Some coal could be really good and the next could have like slate in it which gave you a lot of problems. If your fire went down or anything, you hadn't the same control when you were running the spirit as you had with steam. Even if you were very experienced, bad coal could affect what you were doing. With steam once it's set you have no fluctuation, and for running spirit that consistency is what you need. A slow, easy run.'

Not everyone agrees, however. 'The coal fires were a better experience than the steam, because you had more work, you got a certain way of running them,' says Bill McBain. 'If you were a good stillman, by the time you'd finished the run and it came down to zero [0 per cent abv] you went and there was just a wee fire in your box, when you'd finished you just had ashes to rake out, but if you weren't good you

A 'man door' on an Isle of Jura distillery still.

were raking out fire, coal and everything. I've seen some of the boys down there filling ashes into a barrow, and going outside and the flames come shooting up out of it, because there was coal in it. It saved you work if you could get it just right and burn all the coal off, you just had maybe a barrow-full of ashes to get out if you were doing the job right. It was about experience. I think we made better Mortlach than they do today. There's a lot of chemicals in the malt now, whereas years ago there wasn't nearly so many chemicals.'

According to Lagavulin's 'Big Angus' McAffer, 'The whisky we made tasted different, it wasn't so "forced"' the way it is today. Nice and smooth and easy to take it was. When you were putting a spirit still on spirit you damped the fire with a shovelful of dross so it was only trickling, and there was no trace of feints, it was running more slowly than it is now. They are doing more mashing now, and more distilling, so they've got to push on. Less feints in the spirit then.'

There is no doubt that in the days of coal-fired stills a high degree of skill was required on the part of the operators in order to produce really good spirit. The stillman was more highly paid than the maltmen, mashmen, or tun room men. As Drew Sinclair of Dalmore observes, 'The stillman was always the best paid man, he was the top man.'

Writing in the 1930s, Neil Gunn observed: 'The stillman's job is one of great responsibility, for negligence on his part may not only wreck the still, but, what can hardly be detected at the time, ruin the flavour of the final spirit. Considering his comparatively small wage, his faithfulness to his task is surely a tribute to the Highland worker.'

In *Harpers Wine & Spirit Gazette* of 18 June 1948 'Caledonia' wrote: 'It is the Highland still-man who, in the last analysis, has the final say in determining the character of the whisky. The precise moment in the distilling process when the feints or impure spirits are separated from the whisky which is run into the spirit receiver is at the discretion of this high functionary. Very carefully with his sampling beads he keeps testing the whisky "run" until, reduced with water to some 30 degs under proof, the spirit remains clear in the glass. At the close of distillation he has only to run some of the feints for a short time into the spirit receiver to give the whole a pungent, feinty, objectionable flavour, more readily detected on the palate ten years later than there and then in the crystal distillate.

'The great still-man, like the great poet, is born, not made. Of whisky chemistry he knows little, but works according to methods handed down by tradition from father to son since the smuggling days.'

The work associated with coal-fired stills was dirty and labour intensive. Bill McBain remembers beginning work at Mortlach. 'I was seventeen ... I started shovelling coal from the railway wagons into the stillhouse. They had a siding of their own, and a guard who was employed by the railway, and he came in with the full wagons of malt and coal, and then he hooked them onto the train when they were empty, and he went away down to the station. They took a lot of whisky out by train too at that time of day. There's nothing left at Mortlach now to show the railway was ever there.

'I shovelled coal there about six months, and it was hard work. Sometimes the lumps of coal were so big that you couldn't lift them, you rolled them out of the wagon onto the platform, and down into the stillhouse.

'Down at the coal drags, taking in the coal it was very noisy. We always said that was the reason most of us boys are deaf – with the rumbling of the drags and the noise of the coal being moved. It went on till we got the manager down to the stillhouse and the reading that they got when they checked it was below the safety level. Over that level they would have had to do something about it, but it was down below, so nothing was done.'

After working in the malt barns at Cardhu, Sandy McAdam went on to be fireman for the stills.

'You had a stillman and a fireman in those days. It was a hard job, but the still-men were pretty good, they used to give you a hand. You were shovelling coal from the start of your shift. That was before there were even mechanical stokers in the stills, so you were shovelling tons of coal into the fire and then clearing it all out when it was finished.

'I think the first big change in the industry was going from coal-fired stills to steam. That was a big, big change. DCL started rebuilding distilleries from the 1960s onwards, doubling up a lot of the stills, and they did away with the hand-firing of stills and went on to conveyors, for taking the coal in. The coal was dumped outside and fed into the stillhouse on conveyors, and the stills had mechanical stokers fitted, which cut out a lot of work. You still had ashes to pull out, but it was nothing like so bad.

'The problem you had with the mechanical stokers was that if it was a frosty night or there was snow they could freeze up, the incoming conveyors would freeze up, and you had to go out and chip ice off them, or heat them, and they'd break more readily with the frost, and you'd have to get engineers in. If it froze or broke down you had to go back to shovelling coal by hand until you got it going again. Then oil-fired boilers came in and that was all a thing of the past. The boiler gave you the steam for the stills.'

Bill McBain makes a very valid point about the different levels of skill and hands-on involvement required now compared to when he was a stillman.

'You felt that you were responsible for making that whisky, you felt that you were an important part of it. At this time of day a stillman hasn't got the experience that we had. When we were doing it we were *seeing* what was happening, and we were doing it. Nowadays it's the computer that does it, and all they are doing is filling a still, boiling it, driving the whisky off, and they're all in the one place. We had to go and poke the fires, clean out the clinkers and ashes, and fill them up with coal again.'

Chatting with Ruari MacLeod, Jim McEwan stresses that, 'There's more consistency these days. When you go back to your time and my time, sometimes the stillman would be absolutely drunk. And the fires would go out. And then he'd wake up, and on would go a big fire, and he'd try to make up the time he lost when the fires went down, and she was off the boil.

'Occasionally when I'm nosing older whiskies I find a dram that's really feinty, a lot of feints in it, it's very oily, very greasy, like mutton fat, and I look at the cask and it's a good American refill or a sherry, and I know the fault does not lie in the casks. It lay with the man 25 years ago, because he had six drams a day, because he had coal fires, because he had to heat the stills, and that doesn't happen now, because computers are running it, and they never change. Everything is pre-set. The foreshots are pre-set, the middle cut is pre-set, the feints are pre-set, everything is balanced.

'One man can sit there, he can unload the lorry of malt, one man can sit there, "Oh there's a malt lorry." That's it, hoppers open, conveyor started, goes to the bin, the milling's done, okay, it's time for the mill to come in automatically, once one milling's done it's in the grist bin, another one comes forward automatically, and so it goes on.

'So if you're asking me, Ruari, if things are better today, I'd say there is less chance of a bad batch, whereas 25, 30 years ago there was every chance that maybe a bad batch was coming through the odd occasion because the man had drunk too much. But having said that, I think the quality of distillation in these days was better. It was slower distillation, there wasn't the same pressure, distilleries have expanded incredibly, the capacity, that's why all the malt barns closed. Previously, a distillery's production was governed by the size of the malt barns, and then when commercial maltings came in, the malt barns closed, because the distilleries went for bigger mash tuns and more stills.

'I think historically the quality of the spirit when it was well-made was far, far better in some cases than what we are getting today, because it was a "touch" thing. When you were getting the middle cut you added the water, you watched it

Dalmore distillery fire,
1964.

cloud in a glass, when the cloud cleared it was there. I've been in distilleries and I've said to guys, "How do you find the middle cut?" "Ah well, we just dip the vat, and when we've got fourteen inches in the vat, in the feints receiver, it's time to switch to the middle cut." And that's not the way to do it. You'd do it traditionally on the nosing.'

Ed McAffer of Bowmore distillery doesn't think automation would affect the character of the whisky too much. 'In the stillhouse the stillman's got to be on the ball to take the spirit off, so from that respect it might affect it if the stillman isn't actually, physically there. If he is there, to put the spirit on to run, to take it off at the right time and the right temperature and the right speed, and he doesn't hash it and bash it, just takes off the nice, pure spirit, with no impurities in it, the rest of it then is up to the cask, of course. The quality of the new spirit going in has got to be just right, it doesn't matter what the cask does, if it's harsh going into the cask, the best cask in the world won't put it right.'

In extreme cases, the stillman could do a lot worse than just produce a batch of poor whisky. Drew Sinclair recalls the fire of April 1964, which badly damaged Dalmore's 'No. 2' stillhouse and the tun room. Production was halted for nearly a month as a result. 'The stillman just left the vent open at the top,' says Drew. 'Because it was open fires then, it was a coal fire, and he left his charging valve open and the vent valve open and the wash just poured out, down on the fire and it set alight. That was in the wee stillhouse.'

Controlling stills was a fine art, occasionally even requiring the addition of soap, which had much the same effect in a still as it had in a washback (see Chapter 3, 'On Brewing'). Former Bruichladdich distillery manager Ian Allan notes, 'There was always a soap box on stills when I started. It stopped your still frothing right up. Just a slice of a piece of unscented soap went in. With modern steam heating and "sight glasses" in the still you can see it bubbling up now, and it's easier to control with the steam than it was with coal or gas.'

Bill McBain explains that, 'In the old days they had wooden knockers up on the still necks, before they started putting sight glasses on. They were on ropes, and I just used to haul one in and let it go, and it hit the neck of the still. You'd get an empty sound until it started frothing up, then it got duller and duller, and then that was the time to open the doors up and hose the fire down to let it come back down again. They must have been made of hard wood because they lasted for years. Any other wood, with the weight of it and the heat, it would have cracked.

'It would be 1964 that we did away with the knockers and got sight glasses at Mortlach. Some stills have got two glasses, one above the other. A lot of managers didn't like to see the wash boiling in the glass if they came in, because they used to say that was what the pot of the still was for.'

One distillery where 'knockers' survived when most distilleries had installed sight glasses was Tomatin, situated some 16 miles south of Inverness. Founded in 1897, Tomatin is now in the ownership of a consortium comprising the Japanese distillers Takara Shuzo and Okura & Co.

Stuart Duffy started working at Tomatin in 1967, 'Before they'd extended it a lot. It was twelve stills then and the one mash tun, with twelve washbacks. But then after five years I left, I came down to Aberlour, to Glenallachie distillery, and they came and poached me back to Tomatin. By that time it was upgraded to 23 stills, 2 mash tuns, and 24 washbacks, I think it was.

Tomatin Highland Malt Scotch Whisky bottle, featuring the distillery, c. 1920s.

'Tomatin's not a pretty distillery, but the stillhouse was well worked out, that was two lines of stills right down, one big still house, but even then they had no sight glasses in their stills, even with that amount of stills. The stillman spoke about "walking the line", and he just hit the ball against the stills.

'They didn't have the sight glasses because it was so much packed into the stillhouse that the chargers were all up on top, you couldn't see the top of your stills, so it was just a smack with the ball and keep walking to the next one, and if it was up in the top you had to go and turn down the steam. If it wasn't up, you turned up the steam and you just kept walking.

'Their stills were automatic charging and discharging at Tomatin. You just pressed a re-charge sequence and it went through the sequence and your steam came on. One of the stills when I was there, they had a trial, it was actually a wash still, it was settling itself, automatically, just with a couple of diaphragms. Everything was kind of botched together at Tomatin, it was trial and error, but the ideas were good.'

Tomatin may have been innovative in some ways, but the distilleries of Islay were not slow to move with the times, either. 'Big Angus' McAffer recalls the changes that took place in terms of distillation at Lagavulin, on the south-west shores of the island, during his long spell of service at the distillery.

'I started here in 1957, and I still keep coming back, to keep up with what's going on. I stay in Port Ellen now, but I was brought up on a wee croft close to here, and we went to Port Ellen in 1948. It was a distilling family, most of us were in the distilleries. My Uncle Archie was there, and his father, they worked here. My Uncle Archie was the cooper. His dad was the head maltman here. My great-great-grandfather used to work in the farm across the road. At that time the distillery and the farm were all one. It all belonged to Peter Mackie.

'I was nine years working the boilers and that, and then I went to the stillhouse in 1964,' he says. 'Jack Wilson was the manager then. He put me in there because he was short of a man. I was there stoking anyway, and I knew the dips [the levels of filling within the stills] and I knew everything, so when this man went off sick he put he in there. I was there until I retired, that would be seven years ago. I liked working in the still house, it was the stokers then, and then they got the steam, the oil, it was far easier then.'

Now operated by Diageo, Lagavulin was founded in 1816 by John Johnston, and was acquired by James L. Mackie & Co. in 1867. Peter Mackie was the nephew of James, and learnt the art of distilling at Lagavulin, acting as sales agent for the nearby Laphroaig distillery until 1907. However, after an argument over distillery

water rights with the Johnston family of Laphroaig he set out to make as close a copy of their single malt as possible.

In order to achieve this, he created a new distillery alongside Lagavulin, christened Malt Mill. Malt Mill operated its own kiln with open fires, a pair of washbacks, and a pair of stills closely modelled on those at Laphroaig. It did, however, share the Lagavulin mash tun. Malt Mill was dismantled in the early 1960s, though the distinctive Laphroaig-type stills continued to be used in the main Lagavulin stillhouse until 1969, when they were replaced by a pair of more typical Lagavulin design. At this time the four stills were converted from coal to steam heating.

'In my early days here we had a waterwheel between the Malt Mill and Lagavulin, and another water wheel down below,' says Big Angus. 'When the power went off anytime the water wheels were put to go. The same with the tun room. It was the belts that were working the switchers. When the power went off they had to go on to the water wheels. They were a back up. All that went away just like that

'Big Angus' McAffer in the Lagavulin stillhouse.

when they did all the rebuilding work around 1963.

'The still house is a lot bigger than it used to be. There's two wash and two spirit stills now. There was just the one wash and spirit, coal-fired, for Lagavulin, and one wash and spirit for the Malt Mill. Really just the one still house, different compartments, just next door.

'It was a good dram, the Malt Mill. I don't know if there's any about yet, but I doubt it. That closed a way back when they rebuilt the stillhouse. There was a wash still and a spirit still, that was all. And they were a different shape and everything to the Lagavulin stills. And it was peat-fired, there was no anthracite. There was anthracite used down here, but across the road in the Malt Mill it was all peat.

'The mashman would run the Malt Mill stills, when the mashing was finished he was going into the still house. Once the distilling was finished in the Malt Mill he went back to mashing. When they did the rebuilding they went on to the mechanical stokers, still coal then, small coal, and then they went on to oil later.

'The exciseman was the boss in those days. Even the fire doors on the stills were locked at the weekend. You couldn't start them until he came down with the keys and opened the doors on Sunday. Two to ten would be the first shift on Sunday.

'Many's the time I was giving the stillman a hand to clean the stills on that two to ten on a Sunday. The exciseman opened the doors, and then you started up, and you started the mashing then too. He had the keys for everything, he was the boss alright. At that time you were often on twelve hour shifts. I've seen me doing three weeks night shift, twelve hours.'

Cleaning stills was often about more than coal fires, however, as Drew Sinclair notes of Dalmore. 'In the old days they used to put linseed oil on the stills to shine them up, and believe it or not they used to clean them with pot ale first. The stills were pretty dark when I came here, but later we started to clean them up, using steel wool, and then we would varnish them.'

Neil Ferguson has happy memories of working the stills at Caol Ila, on the east coast of Islay. The distillery was established in 1846, though today's modern buildings bear little resemblance to their Victorian forebears.

'One day I was working in the stillhouse,' says Neil, 'and the fumes were coming off, and they were fairly powerful, and I looked out of the end window of the stillhouse and I saw a dog running along the roof of the warehouse. I looked again a few seconds later and a man was following it. I thought, "These fumes are pretty powerful!" Then I realised that I'd got the roof of the warehouse exactly lined up with the hillside behind, and they were actually walking on that, but for a moment or two it had me worried.'

Stills tend to be operated in pairs, with equal numbers of wash and spirit stills. It is not uncommon, however, for distilleries to be equipped with more spirit stills than wash stills in order to cope with the amount of low wines produced in the wash stills. William Grant's Balvenie distillery in Dufftown has four wash and five spirit stills, while the neighbouring Kininvie stillhouse operates three wash and six spirit stills.

On the other side of Dufftown, Mortlach distillery operated a particularly idiosyncratic method of distillation.

'At Mortlach there was one still that ran spirit every third charge, it was the wee one,' says Bill McBain. 'The other spirit stills were running spirit every run. The wee one distilled the stuff that was too weak and it built up the strength and made a spirit of its own. It was more or less the strongest of the lot.

'There was a manager there who said that he wouldn't fill casks unless he had one run out of that wee still. Whether it made a difference I don't know, but he had to get at least one still run from it into the filling. He thought it made it better.'

Stuart Duffy worked as a stillman and latterly as supervisor at Mortlach prior to his retirement.

'The way the stills were set up, you'd a stronger spirit coming off, the end spirit coming off, because you'd number one spirit still which was boosting the strength all the time. You only took spirit off number one every third run, so you were boiling it and it was getting stronger. We called it the 'Wee Witch'. It was the manager before always called it the Wee Witch because she kept on brewing and brewing.

'When I was there I kind of tried to push this Wee Witch thing, because if I hadn't have pushed it it would have been forgotten about, it would just have went away, because none of the young ones ever knew anything about it.

'John Winton, he was inspector, and one day he was in the stillhouse when I was there on the stills, and he explained to me why he called it the wee witch. He'd been manager there and then he was inspector for the SMD. He was back in this day and he started telling me about this still, number one spirit, which he called the "Wee Witch".

'They said it wasn't Mortlach unless you had a run of spirit in each filling off number one spirit still. You always tried to make sure that there was a run of number one in each filling.

'It would be coming off up the 70s [percentage abv.] in strength, compared to 68 generally. It was that bit stronger. You always filled at 63.5. It was in the 70s in the filling store, before you started reducing, whereas some distilleries your spirit's only 66 maybe when you start reducing.

'Old' Mortlach stillhouse,
1950s.

'The likes of Bill [McBain], he was there before Mortlach was done up the first time, and he was there when there were two stillhouses. There's a lot fewer people working there now, and they're all young and new, and none of them kens any history of Mortlach.'

Let's give the last word on traditional distilling to Bill McBain. 'The stillman's job is crucial, he can make whisky that's undrinkable or he can make whisky that's very, very good. And every still is different in a way, even though they are all really very similar.'

5

The Coppersmith

DENNIS McBAIN

'My father worked for Grants at Glenfiddich, and two of my brothers, so it was a real family thing. I started off in the Speyside Cooperage down the road at Craigellachie, serving my time to become a cooper, but it wasn't the job I thought it was, and I enquired about getting a job at Glenfiddich. That was in October 1958, and I was sixteen years old.'

'The old brewer knew my father, and told me that he didn't have a job, but he'd keep me in mind. Then a job came along; he started me off in the malt barns. The Glenfiddich maltings were where the reception area is now.

'I was in the malt barns for nine months to a year, when a job cropped up in the maintenance department. Around that time a chap named Willie McLauchlin took a job at Glenfiddich, and he was a fully qualified coppersmith. He'd actually served his time in London, and had been working for a local coppersmith, and Willie Grant's took him on to look after all the copper stills.

'Again the old brewer came to me and asked me if I'd like to go and help him, so I served six years under Willie and became a coppersmith. We actually built up a squad and manufactured our own stills, worms and condensers, and it was only when the company expanded a bit and some of the lads left that we weren't able to manufacture the things quickly enough, that it stopped.

'They'd never done this before, it just began around 1976 after they'd taken on an engineer and then Willie McLauchlin. That was when the maintenance side of the business started up, they hadn't had a maintenance department before that. We carried on making smaller items like condensers, and Willie retired, so it was just me and the lads.

*Dennis McBain welding an
entry pipe for a still. The
'chain link' in the foreground
is a rummager, intended to
prevent unfermented matter
and yeast from sticking to
the bottom of coal-fired
wash stills.*

'It's very heavy work. It's one of the few trades that modern technology hasn't
helped that much, except that when I started all the joints in the stills were riveted.
Then they took on the oxy-acetylene welding, which was a great boost. The stills
were easier to make and much less hard, physical work. Forsyth's now make our
stills, just down in Rothes, and it's very, very similar to when I started doing it. The
actual method is the same.

'I'm often asked the question, "Why copper?" I don't know when they started
making stills out of copper, but copper is an ideal material for manipulating into the
shapes, and it's a good conductor of heat, and it also acts as a catalyst to take the sulphur out in the wash still. These people long ago knew what they were about.

'All the copper comes in flat sheets, and it's heated to soften it and manipu-
late it into the shape that you want, and then you give it a bit hammer, which closes all the molecules and hardens the copper and helps it keep its shape. With a bit of
overtime you'd make a new still from scratch in three weeks to a month.

'Glenfiddich has small spirit stills. Macallan has slightly smaller, I think, but
Glenfiddich stills have a distinctive shape to them. When they expanded they got
more stills of the same size and shape rather than bigger stills, because they obviously didn't want to change anything to do with the spirit. They've stayed the same shape
and just been replaced like for like. At Glenfiddich they've got 15 in one still house
and 13 in the other, so 28 in total. It sounds a lot but it's because they're so small.

'Quite often the question is asked why do different distilleries make different whisky? The shape of the stills is obviously one of the main reasons, along with the water and possibly the type of heating. They had external heating at Glenfiddich, it was always coal, but due to environmental issues we're now putting all of the stills onto gas.

'I think it does make a difference to the spirit because it's an inner heat as oppose to an outer heat, but it wouldn't be a difference the people drinking the whisky would notice I wouldn't think, not by the time you've had your maturation in the casks. That's another thing to take into consideration, of course. Different distilleries use different amounts of sherry butts for their mixtures, and they are allowed to mature for different lengths of time. When you think of all the different things that distilleries do you couldn't possibly have the same type of whisky.

'Today, I'm responsible for maintenance work at Balvenie as well as Glenfiddich, and also at Kininvie. Kininvie was built in 1990, and is just behind Balvenie. The stillhouse is on its own, but there are two mash tuns – one is Balvenie, one Kininvie. And two tun rooms, you have to have that for Customs & Excise. The malt bins are all together, but are marked as Balvenie and Kininvie.

'All three distilleries, Glenfiddich, Balvenie and Kininvie, have different shapes of stills. Apart from the two older wash stills at Balvenie, the other two wash stills and the five spirit stills are the same shape, heads, height and everything, and they are the biggest in the three distilleries. Kininvie's wash stills are similar in size to Balvenie, but the spirit stills are smaller than the Balvenie ones, but bigger than the Glenfiddich ones. We have three different sizes of spirit stills and three different sizes of wash stills.

'We use the same water, or at least water from the same area, we use the same malt, but we have three different whiskies, so I'm more or less convinced that the size of the stills is the factor that makes the difference, and in particular the height of the stills. The height is important, where the vapours go over, that's very important. The shape and the height of the stills has quite a bearing on the spirit that you'll get off them. Which is why you don't change the shape of the stills. The last thing you want to do is change the product if it's selling well.

'I enjoyed the coppersmithing work. It was very interesting, and then we moved into multi-skilling, whereby you'd learn a bit of everything and fill in where you were needed. I still look after all the copper side of the distillery, and general engineering. We've just had an apprentice finishing his time recently, which is good, because it's a long time since we've had an apprentice at Glenfiddich, in the engineering line, anyway. Hopefully, by the time I retire in three and a bit years he'll have learnt everything he needs to and be able to take over.

'Obviously copper wears out and I replace pipes and do running repairs. The sample cocks on the sample safes need quite a bit of work off and on, because they're continually being used, and overall there's still quite a bit of copper work for me to do with the three distilleries to cover.

'I look after the filling store, the automatic filling heads and all the other moving parts, as you'd say. On the warehousing side there are pumps to look after, and the Solera system [whereby a range of fifteen-year-old Glenfiddichs from different types of cask are married before bottling in Solera butts which are never allowed to empty] creates more work. We're into coming out with different types of whisky, the rum finish and so forth, and it always involves a bit of extra pipe work and little innovations on the filling side. I do all the small copper work, everything apart from stills and condensers, and I work on things like the rummagers inside the wash stills.

'Some of the spirit at Glenfiddich is tankered away to Glasgow, but a lot is filled on site, when it's going to be bottled as single malt. We're the only distillery in Scotland that does everything from beginning to end, from the barley in the field to the bottles.

'Everybody was on coal at one time, and they went onto different means of heating the stills, gas, oil, whatever, and Glenfiddich is one of the last to switch from coal. Glendronach over at Huntly is still on coal. Coal is competitive pricewise, which is maybe why we stayed with it for longer than a lot of people.

'Depending on whether you're building a still for coal or steam, there's a big difference in the thickness. At Glenfiddich, when we were on coal, the bottoms of the stills were 16 mm thick, in order to cope with the weight of the stills and the heat. And the flue plates in the sides were 10 mm thick, and the shoulders 4 mm thick, with the head 3 or 4 mm thick.

'With the steam stills you can get away with 6 mm because they are supported, they sit on a base with the steam coils inside, unlike the coal ones. They don't have to withstand the abrasiveness of the coal fire, the dust and that. There's an inner wear with the coal, but there's also an outside wear from it.

'When you build a still you start of with the flat bottom, just like a round table, and it's domed, purely for strength, and it's turned up at the edges so you can fit the flue plates on. The flue plates are the bits that you don't see, that fit into the brickwork. You have the bottom, then you have four sections of copper sheets to form the circle, then you have the shoulder, which again is formed from flat sheets which you put together in the form of a cone, then soften them, hammer them out to form the globe-type shape. They are made up, then they are welded onto the flue plates. The head is rolled and shaped and beaten out and hammered to hold that

shape rigid and give it strength. It can be riveted onto the shoulders of the still or welded. We rivet our heads onto spirit stills because the heads will outlive two or three copper "pots". It saves you the expense of having to replace a head that's not really worn out. You just take the rivets out and put it back onto the new pot. Otherwise it's all welding now.

'A wooden mallet and a hammer is more or less the total of the coppersmith's tools. The mallet is used because it is softer on the copper, and then you have to shape it, and then it has to be hammered, so you don't want big dents in it which you'd get if you didn't use a mallet. If you used a metal hammer you'd stretch the copper and thin it, so you do it in such a way that you're not thinning the copper. You could press them out on a machine, but it would take the easiest route and you'd end up with very thin copper.

'I was down at Forsyth's last week because they're making a still for us just now, and it's still the same old ways as it was forty-odd years ago, you can't do it with a PC. It's still very much a craftsman's job, and very labour intensive. That's one of the reasons lots of the young lads don't want to go into it, they'd rather go into the electrical side and that.

'But the money is quite good at it, and they're very busy in the summertime when all the distilleries shut down and they work longer hours then, so the money over the year is good, and that's an attraction. Forsyth's have taken on a lot of apprentices over the years. They like to take on young lads and train them rather than take on coppersmiths, which is good for the trade.

'I still enjoy my work, they're a good bunch of lads, by and large, and they're a good company to work for. They're not the biggest or the best payers, but there are other things, like a non-contributory pension, that have to be taken into consideration. We're well looked after.

'The wash stills in the old days, they each just had a rope with a lead ball on it, which the stillman swung against the head of the still to let him know whether or not it was boiling up in the head, because you didn't want it to boil right over. He knew by the noise of the ball if it was boiling up or not. It's a duller sound when they're frothing, and you'd know to open the doors, and if it was too vicious they'd open the doors and hose the fire to dampen it down quickly.

'One of the first jobs I did when I was serving my time with Willie McLauchlin was to put in what we call the sight glasses, so that the stillman could actually see the liquid boiling up. We fitted those into the original stills. You could argue there was a lot more skill involved in distilling then, based on people's individual knowledge and experience.'

Opposite:
Distillery copper work in Forsyth's yard, Rothes, 2000.

6

On Maturation

Neil Gunn declared that 'Probably the most desirable flavours in whisky are produced on the malt-kiln and in the cask,' and Frank McHardy of Springbank in Campbeltown insists 'Seventy-five per cent of the flavour of the whisky you're going to get from the cask.'

However, Ed McAffer of Bowmore makes the vital point that 'The quality of the new spirit going in has got to be just right, it doesn't matter what the cask does, if it's harsh going into the cask, the best cask in the world won't put it right.'

It is clear then that the cask is far more than a container. Just how it was first discovered that whisky kept in a wooden barrel improved with age is anyone's guess. Perhaps an illegal distiller or smuggler hid some casks and only got the chance to retrieve them some considerable time later. The increased smoothness and sophistication of the spirit would have been immediately apparent.

In *Harpers Wine & Spirit Gazette* for 18 June 1948, 'Caledonia' observed that 'the maturing of whisky is a natural, slow process, during which the pungent taste of the new spirit gradually disappears, giving place to a mellowness and delicious ethereal aroma'.

By law, Scotch whisky must be matured for a minimum period of three years in oak casks not exceeding 700 litres in capacity, and the importance of the wood into which spirit is filled has increased since the chemistry of maturation first began to be fully understood from the 1970s onwards.

Most distillers now operate rigorous wood management programmes, working on the principle that while, as Ed McAffer says, good wood cannot make bad spirit good, bad wood can make good spirit totally undrinkable.

Oak is semi-porous, so there is an element of interaction between the wood itself and the external atmosphere, which helps to remove harsh notes and increases the complexity of the spirit during maturation. Some of the higher alcohols slowly change into esters and other compounds with delicate, pleasing aromas.

The spirit takes colour from the wood, which has invariably had a previous content – usually either sherry or bourbon – as well as character components from the previous filling.

Writing in 1948, 'Caledonia' noted, 'Sherries are the ideal casks for maturing whisky. During recent years, however, they have grown scarce … A re-fill sherry, with the wine-like bouquet not too pronounced, is indeed the perfect malt whisky.'

These days, only a tiny proportion of casks used for Scotch whisky maturation are made from European oak, and have previously held sherry. More than 95 per cent are American oak, and were formerly filled with bourbon.

Springbank's Frank McHardy recalls that most of the distilleries in Campbeltown had a cooper.

'When I came to Springbank initially in 1977 we used to use the coopers from Glen Scotia distillery. They had two at that time. So we actually employed them on an ad hoc, part time basis to prepare casks. Casks now are such good quality that very few coopers are required. I've been in this game long enough, 41 years now, and I can carry out simple repairs to a cask. I mean most people can use a driver, to harden them up. We can't take ends out, or put casks together, but we can repair them.

'One thing we do here at Springbank is inspect our casks. We have a scheme whereby each month, while we don't inspect every cask, we wander round the warehouses with a torch and look down the stows for any obvious signs of leakage. Not like some people, who fill the warehouse, lock the door, go away and only come back when the casks are ready to be removed.'

The 'angels' share' of spirit evaporation as it is known is reckoned to be around 2 per cent of bulk per year, which, in practical terms, means that the company of William Grant & Sons Ltd loses around 2.4 million litres per year in Dufftown alone.

Maturation is an expensive business, not only because of the loss of bulk, but because the valuable spirit is doing nothing to earn its keep during all those years of seclusion.

The degree of bulk lost depends on prevailing humidity and temperature levels, with whisky in a comparatively damp warehouse losing strength but maintaining bulk. This is considered to be better for optimum maturation than dry warehouses where strength is less affected but bulk falls.

Whisky matured on an island like Islay might be expected to lose more strength than on Speyside, where the drier east coast atmosphere would lead to greater loss of bulk.

The size of cask also affects maturation, as, in theory at least, the smaller the casks, the more quickly the spirit in it matures, as the percentage of loss through transference, absorption and exposure to heat and damp is greater than in a larger cask.

'Caledonia' observed, 'These changes [which take place during maturation] are influenced by various factors such as the strength at which the spirit is warehoused, the vapour pressure inside the cask, and the size of the cask, whether quarter-cask, butt or hogshead.'

Whisky also matures differently in different types of warehouse. Modern racked warehouses, which hold casks in stacks up to twelve high, tend to be prone to greater seasonal variations of temperature than old-fashioned 'dunnage' warehouses, built of stone, with cinder or earth floors, and with casks stacked just three high.

Maturation will also take place more quickly in casks stacked near the top of racked warehouses, as this is the warmest area. It may seem that such differences are mere nuances, detectable to only the greatest noses and palates, but this is not the case. Put two samples of whisky filled into two casks on the same day but with one stored on the floor and the other twelve racks up, in front of any whisky drinker, and the difference will be obvious.

Many casks are now 'palletised' for ease of handling – that is, stored on their ends on wooden pallets, up to six high. It has been suggested that casks stored at the centre of a palletised warehouse might require six months of additional maturation as there is less air circulation and therefore comparatively less evaporation.

Most experts, while acknowledging the practical and economic necessity of modern racked and palletised warehousing facilities, insist that their personal preference remains for old-fashioned, damp, stone-walled dunnage warehouses, and a number of the people responsible for bringing fine and rare single malts to the market insist on keeping their best casks in dunnage conditions.

Frank McHardy

'Warehouses with not more than two floors, with an equable temperature, proper ventilation, and atmosphere not too dry are ideal for the flavouring of whisky,' according to 'Caledonia'. 'Modern concrete floors are not favoured by experienced distillers,' he concludes.

Master distillers and blenders will also insist that their prime single malts are kept at the distillery where they were produced, thus maintaining the integrity of the locale, of the 'micro-climate'.

There is a strong body of opinion which insists it is just a romantic notion that whisky matured in Campbeltown, for example, will be affected by the prevailing salt sea breezes during maturation.

As yet, science has no definitive answers regarding the relationship between maturation and location, principally because of the impossibility of objectively comparing casks. Were samples of identical spirit filled into 'neutral' containers such as stainless steel and some matured in Campbeltown and some in central Scotland, then it might be possible to conclude that changes during maturation were attributable to local conditions, though there would always be warehouse variables to take into account, too. No two warehouses are ever precisely the same, just as no two casks are. Such speculation is pointless anyway, since whisky filled into a neutral container made of something like stainless steel simply would not mature at all.

Traditional dunnage warehouse, Balvenie distillery, 2005.

Frank McHardy has no doubts that location does influence maturation, saying, 'There's something in Springbank which is salty like in taste, whatever it is. That comes during maturation. You don't get it in the new spirit. I mean it's only three and a half miles to the Atlantic out there, you've got the prevailing winds coming in. I mean all our buildings are full of salt, the windows get all grimy and have to be cleaned. It's all salt. And when I seize up in the middle of the golf course, it's the salt!'

Jim McEwan agrees. 'I think it's very important that we're maturing the whisky here on the island [Islay]. If you look at the old metal railings on the steps of the malt barns, see how the metal's flaking, and if you look at the cars on Islay, they only last half as long as they do in other places, so the salt must do something to the whisky when it's maturing.'

Speaking about Craigellachie distillery, Sandy McAdam says, 'No maltings, and not even any warehousing now. They were centralising everything down at Menstrie [in Clackmannanshire] latterly, and the new make was tankered down to Menstrie. I don't know if it's a good idea putting everything down there. What about the old idea that whisky was matured where it was made? Does that change it?'

Archie Ness declares, 'Whisky was stored in the warehouses at the distillery, where it matures, with the air giving it the flavour, and all the rest, and you're putting it all down south, to a different area, with different water to reduce it with. I think it must change the whisky.'

'You get the best whisky out of an old sherry cask, lying in a damp warehouse,' insists Sandy McAdam. 'Just earth floors and maybe the gutters leaking and rain coming in a bit. I still maintain that that atmosphere gives you the best dram in the end. If you bring an Islay malt over to the mainland to mature, you must lose something, with the different air. You don't have the same climate, the salt and all that.'

Grant Carmichael has equally clear views on the subject regarding Islay.

'Now, of course, most distilleries tanker the stuff out,' he says. 'A lot goes out in tankers. In fact Mundells, the local contractor, have two tankers, I think. They tanker stuff away for Diageo, it goes away to Cambus [Diageo's facility in Clackmannanshire], and it's put into casks there. All of Caol Ila's production is matured over there. It still has to be matured in oak for three years to call it whisky. Regardless of where it's done, it's got to mature in Scotland. Thank God these rules and regulations are still there or it would be going all over the place.

'The warehouses at Lagavulin, and at Port Ellen, are kept full of Lagavulin, and the rest goes off the island. If you mature it on the island you'll get a more mellow whisky at the end of the day. Mature it on the dry east coast of the mainland, for example, a much drier climate than here, you'll get a greater evaporation, so the volume comes down, but the strength remains high, so it can be quite sharp, whereas on Islay you don't lose the same in evaporation because of the damp, salty air, and the salty air helps, let's be honest. It's breathing in some moisture surrounding these warehouses down by the shore, and this is what gives all these south coast distilleries their saltiness. It's from the air.'

Caol Ila's Neil Ferguson recalls, 'In the old days any spare time you had at all you were sent over to the warehouse to help out over there, stacking barrels, taking barrels up, rolling barrels around. It was a lot more labour-intensive that way. The warehouse is still in use, there's actually quite a lot of whisky in there.

A lot of it, I think, goes into some of the more expensive blends such as Johnnie Walker Blue Label. A lot of our whisky here goes to Johnnie Walker. Johnnie Walker takes a tremendous amount, always has done. A lot of Caol Ila goes for normal Red Label and Black Label and so on, but also for the more expensive ones. And quite a lot of the specialist bottlers like Gordon & MacPhail, people like that, they also ask for whisky to be matured here.'

Like Grant Carmichael, he reckons the character of the whisky that goes into the bottle is definitely influenced by where it is matured.

'I think it affects the character of the whisky, certainly. Personally, I would prefer to drink the whisky that's spent 15 years down here, or 10 years, rather than whisky that's been over in the Central Belt. I think most people would prefer that it had been matured down here. The likes of Bruichladdich, their stuff is all matured on the premises, it's even bottled on the premises. That's a very big selling point.

'Diageo only bottles something in the region of 2 per cent of their overall production of Caol Ila as a single malt. Production here is tremendous. Surely they could mature that 2 per cent here? The warehouse is there. Tanker away the other 98 per cent, yes. All the filling machinery was down there in any case, but they took it all out. Because there was only one warehouse, casks were always taken to the mainland to mature anyway, it's not something new.

'The warehouse at Caol Ila is the only bit that survived the distillery rebuild, and if you leave the windows open in the warehouse the sea air gets in between the slatted floors. The angels' share has been absorbed by the floorboards and the walls over more than a century. It smells fantastic. You can't get away from the sea here. We *are* an island. Every distillery is situated beside the sea for ease of transportation, and they virtually all have their own piers. The water and the very air seem to have a different effect on the whisky, especially the casks that are matured here. A combination of the water and the peat.'

Ed McAffer says, 'We've got something in the region of 25,000 casks on site at Bowmore; 50 to 60 per cent of what we make is kept here. Our old dunnage warehouses are all filled up with the sherry-type casks, we fill them here. Some tankers go away, because it's obviously all to do with space, that gets filled on the mainland, and then they store it there, but it will all go into top quality casks.

'I'd like to think it definitely does have a difference, however. You can tell the difference from warehouse to warehouse here. We've got two warehouses that are outside the village, there's a low warehouse and there's a big, high, racking warehouse, and you can tell the difference between the low warehouse, which we call number five, and

Caol Ila distillery, 1950s.

number six, between the whiskies coming out from there. The old warehouse down in the distillery here, number one, is different again from those. To me, the whisky that comes out of the low number five warehouse has a dry and sulphury smell off it, it's got a dusty smell off it. I always thought that about spirit that comes out of there.

'Number six, the majority of casks are not as sweet generally as the whisky down in the old warehouse. That's the best maturing warehouse, especially for the 17-year-old. It really changes it into a smashing dram after 17 years of lying in there. It could be the sea air that's in it, the locality of it being right next door to the sea. The wind is coming through the wee windows, it's breathing that all the time.

'At the moment we're just sending away one tank a month, and the rest we fill into cask and store here. They'll mature it eight, ten, whatever years, and then they'll sample the spirit, and maybe decide to use some of it in different blends, but the majority of it, the good stuff, will be kept for the single malts, all the different expressions. I mean, we do it into bourbon barrels, and it stays in the bourbon barrels for eight, ten years, and then they'll take it out and put it into sherry casks or port casks, and finish it off for a couple of years in there. That's all done on the mainland, ours is the initial filling, and its left here for the length of time they want it to mature, and then they'll take it away and do whatever they want to do with it.'

The influence of location on maturation would appear to be well illustrated by the case of Dalwhinnie distillery, situated over 1,000 feet above sea level, and vulnerable to wild weather in winter.

'We have around 1,500 casks maturing on site,' notes operations manager Donald Stirling. 'This is Dalwhinnie, which will be bottled as single malt. In the warehouses at other distilleries there is quite a lot of evaporation from casks, but our level of evaporation is less because it is a harsh climate. We have quite high humidity levels, so Dalwhinnie takes a while longer to mature than some similar whiskies.'

Eric Stephen lives in Dufftown. 'I'm warehouse team leader for William Grant & Sons, been here 41 years past. I started in 1962. I've been here 41 years, and my daughter used to work in the Customs & Excise at Glenfiddich, she was a Customs & Excise administrator. My father was cattleman at Balvenie Mains for a while, and he had a son served his time here as a cooper.

'My first job was when the stills were coal fired the coal used to come in in wagons, and I was a young chap, 18 years old, and I had to empty out the coal wagons. I was at that 4 or 5 months, and then I went in the warehouse, and I've been there ever since.

'At that time of day there were no fork-lifts, just a table and "skid", and we had to lift all the casks manually. Push them all manually. There was no easy way. The warehouses were mainly traditional dunnage warehouses [with earth floors]. It was 1963 when the first racked warehouses were built up here, and that was a big step. They're about six high up there, and with dunnage you could only get three high, any more and the weight would crush the bottom casks. So it doubled the capacity in the same floorspace.

'Them days, casks were dispatched on a Tuesday, and when the exciseman used to go around on a Monday you had to dip all the casks for dispatch, dry dip and wet dip [to check quantity and strength]. Then the lorry would turn up on Tuesday morning, so you had all the casks to push out onto loading banks for that. We put away quite a lot by railway then, as well, so the railway wagons used to come in and you had to load them. And if any casks were leaking down the railway we had to go down and repair them.

'Even with the bottling in them days you only shoved in about six casks a week. Six casks for a whole week. That was the Glenfiddich single malt. Last week we emptied 118 tonnes at 2,000 litres a tonne, so work it out for yourself! That's what they're bottling now. Then it was just single malt, but you've got Balvenie now, as well, and Double Wood and Single Barrel Balvenie, Glenfiddich Havana, Caoran and Solera. In those days it was just the one.

'We used to do a re-vatting in the summertime. That was taking in all your different parcels of 8-year-old to do a vatting. All the painters, coppersmiths and everyone came to give you a hand pushing casks to dump it all into a big vat and then fill it back into casks again. That was the stuff for their bottling.

'We still do the same thing today. All the same ages are vatted just to marry it off, so that all the casks are uniform ready for bottling. All put into the vat and married together, then sit in the warehouse for maybe a couple of months before going into the bottling hall. The stuff that went out by road and rail was customers' casks, your Johnnie Walker, your Dewars, Bells of Perth and all that. Whoever was buying it for blending. There were quite a lot of customers' casks here, stored in our warehouses. Dewars and so on. We have very few for customers now, to save paying the rent they have them in their own big bonds down south. They buy it as new spirit and take it away off site in tankers.

'We did our own blending here, and then when Girvan [Grants' grain distillery and warehousing complex on the Ayrshire coast] opened in 1963 we put quite a lot of stuff down to Girvan for blending too, for your Grants blend. Before that the blending was done here. The blend was put together here and it was bottled down in Paisley.

'If some of the old-timers wakened up now and saw the far end of the site, all your big palletised warehouses, the maturing tuns in number eight here, they'd be mesmerised. There's about 50,000 casks in one warehouse. At the last count we had 770,000 casks on site.

'We've got 45 warehouses in total. That's here and along at Convalmore too [the former distillery, closed in 1985, and subsequently bought by Grants for its warehousing capacity]. There's just the warehousing there now, and it's mostly dunnage, though we've palletised one of the old ones. We've taken the two storey floors out and put in a concrete base.

'With palletisation one man can keep the filling line going. He loads the cask onto his trailer, goes down to the warehouse, unloads, records all his numbers, does his paperwork and all that. One man. If we were storing in dunnage, or even vats, you've got a three man team or even a four man team.

'In the old days we used to have a squad tapping as well. Two men going round every week and checking every cask for leaking. If they found any leaking they repaired them or patched them. Now they just fill the warehouse, shut the door and leave it. If you find an empty cask the excise just waive the duty and that's it.

'I've eleven people working for me now. Going back six or seven years I had about fifteen. It's got less and less. And there's more work because we're handling all

these different finishes as well. We're doing bodega sherry and such like. There's a lot of extra paperwork, keeping track of it all, keeping numbers correct and so on. They bottle Solera and Havana on site, and 18-year-old and Balvenie Single Barrel on site.

'At one time of day it was all just Glenfiddich and Balvenie you had on site, but now you've got Burnside, Wardhead and Aldunie. Burnside is 99 per cent Balvenie and one percent Glenfiddich, Wardhead is 99 per cent Glenfiddich and 1 per cent Balvenie. Your Aldunie is 99 per cent Kininvie and 1 per cent Balvenie. It's done like that so that when you sell casks to customers they can't sell it using our distillery names. Kininvie goes for blending just now, they haven't decided what to do with it yet. They'll maybe keep it as a fifteen-year-old single malt you see, I don't know.'

Staying in Dufftown, Stuart Duffy describes the filling regime during his latter years with what was then United Distillers plc, now Diageo.

'The warehouse squad was based at Dufftown, and they just came in whenever there was a filling. Three times a week at Mortlach. It's still maturing on site,

Eric Stephen (left) and warehouse colleagues, Glenfiddich distillery, 1961/62. The squad had just finished unloading casks from the flat-back lorry into the bonded warehouse to the rear — now the Glenfiddich shop. The hut to the right was used by Customs and Excise staff.

but now the filling is finished there, it's all taken away to Auchroisk distillery [at Mulben, near Keith] to get filled now, tankered away. There's a big filling store, where they take it in in tanker from a few distilleries, and they fill it there. It goes away from the distillery, the whole thing, it's just down to a place where they're producing whisky and that's it. It's not the same.

    'Probably some of it'll come back to Dufftown or Mortlach to be matured. In fact, just before I left, they took whisky, tankered whisky from Skye across and filled it at Auchroisk, and they dropped it right back to Skye, and they sent a warehouse-man across from Dufftown to warehouse it in Skye. The reason was they didn't have the men to fill it and warehouse it at Talisker, but the cost must have been horrendous. They'd have been better sending their squad across to just do the job there.'

7

The Cooper

DEREK SPARK

'Born and bred Dufftown, born 1942. Folk speak about the good old times, well I'm not sure if they were good or not. Quite hard for us, being brought up then, there wasn't a lot of money at that time. That in itself is quite a change to what the youngsters have now. Left the school at fifteen. Before I left I went looking for a job, and I went to Mr Taylor at the Speyside Cooperage. Dougie's father [Douglas Taylor is Managing Director of the Speyside Cooperage] stayed in Dufftown, in Balvenie Street, and I went to him and asked if there was any jobs. And he says, "Oh aye, ma loon, when can you start?" sort of thing. The tattie [potato picking] holidays were coming up, and he says, "Come down then, and if you go back to school once you're finished, if you pass the tests I set you, then you can start." So I went to him and worked the tattie holidays, and I started with him I think it was the end of October 1957.'

'Used to get up to leave Dufftown for seven o'clock, and I wasn't at home again in Dufftown till seven o'clock at night. Very small pay then. I was getting top line £3 5s 8d. I was five months at Taylors, and there was a job came up locally, one of the apprentices had left to go to London to stay with his parents down there.

'I was just an apprentice, and I actually dropped in pay when I went to the firm, Joseph Brown's cooperage, because I hadn't the same hours. I didn't start till eight o'clock, and I finished at five o'clock there, you see. I was down to about £2 3s and something, and by the time I went home and paid my mother some digs money, there wasn't much left.

'The likes of the mashmen and the stillmen, the distillery men, I wouldn't like to say what their wages would have been, but they'd be something like six, seven

Opposite:

*Derek Spark riveting a hoop,
1960s.*

pounds maybe. The coopers were doing well by comparison, but only when they were busy. If you went onto "fallback" rate it was very poor, actually.

'All the cooperages at that time worked on piecework rates. Later on in life when I left and went to Grants it was similar, but it was a basic and bonus. You were guaranteed your basic rate, which was a lot better at the distillery than it was at a private cooperage.

'In actual fact, over the years, proportionally it's gone up a great bit compared to the private cooperages. The last raise they had, since I was made redundant, seems to have gone up and they don't have to do bonus work. I really can't say what their pay is, but what I heard it's well over £20,000. But they've no bonus work to do, they just have to work away, so they don't have to go in and go at it all day. They've got a good pay, without having to do the hard work. Between that and the amount of machinery they've got in now.

'Well, starting when I started my apprenticeship they had machinery; I mean they had jointing machines and they had the bandsaw, we used to cut in the ends of the casks, and you'd to bevel them to fit into what we called the crows and the staves, the top of the staves, and we did all that cutting in by hand. It was quite a number of years before we got a machine to do that job. But nowadays they have a machine, they just put the end in, shut the door, everything's clamped, press the buttons, and that's the job done. That's how they've progressed in nearly every area.

'The jointers are still the same, a jointing machine, a planing machine, they're still the same, but they've hoop-drivers for putting on the hoops, the steel bands. Now they've all these things. Well when I started you'd all that to do by hand. They've got machines for pulling off the hoops now. At one time of day you'd to do all that by hand, knocking them off when you were repairing a cask, opening them up, just the one hoop holding till you put in, replaced, broken staves.

'Then we had to pull them together again, chap on the hoops, turn them over, put on a hoop, maybe sometimes use a chain to pull them in. Aye, they've progressed, they've got a wire puller now, they just loop the wire over the top, pull the handle, it pulls the staves in, and they just drop the hoop on.

'It was very hard physical work when I started. You had to be fit, but it didn't really mean that a bigger boy was a better cooper or anything like that. But I worked with a man when we were doing the bigger casks, it was a bit more awkward for them. You have 40 gallons, that's "Yankee barrel" size, then we used to make them up to 56 gallons, which we called a dump hogshead. You'd traditional hogsheads, that's a variation of sizes and shapes. You can imagine when the traditional hogsheads were made, that would have been in the times when they did them all by hand, and

Hoops at Strathisla
Cooperage, Keith, 2004.

then you got to butts and puncheons, that's the bigger ones, you get short fat ones, and the butts are taller.

'What we called a "new" cask was actually re-assembling American ones, when you got them in from the States in bundles of staves. They used to do a lot of them, and that's what we called a new cask. And they were quite hard to do, I mean they were dried out, and when you went to do them, to raise them up, you held a hoop, and you fixed your first stave in, and held it with your leg, and built the rest into the hoop. And sometimes they were just spread out, the staves were practically straight. So you'd all this hammering, you'd heavy truss hoops as we called them for pulling in, for getting the curves back. You'd to hammer and hammer.

'At one time of day, before my time, they actually did them with braziers, fires, they had the fire going on the inside, hammering and doing, and then turned them over, and at that time they'd a chain and a steel bar, and they just twisted the chain to pull it in enough to get a hoop on, starting at the end, and then get the next hoop on, and that changed when they began to get the machines in. You put a truss hoop on the floor, the heavy hoop, you build your staves in, there's a broad metal band goes round the middle, you pin it, pull it tight, and then you put the wire rope round the top, pull it tight, and put on your end hoop, and then you put on the other hoops, and then you put on a steamer. There's no fires nowadays, just steam, and that closes up all the joints of the staves.

'You'd be putting in maybe four or five staves, depending on the width of the staves, you'd get four or five staves to fill up the gap, to build it up from 40 gallons to 56 gallons. When you were making them up, you started off with the normal end hoop of the barrel, you knocked in the end, and then you just had to work it open a bit, you put on a hoop just down from the top hoop and worked it open, then put in your other staves, and then on your big hoop with the dump size, and just worked it open until you got it filled up to the top, and then the hard work started.

'I started down here 1971, but I was actually in the warehouse for five months till there was an opening in the cooperage, and there would be about six coopers at that time. They had machines for building the casks up, but they were horizontal, and they built the staves into the band in the middle, then put on the two wire ropes on the ends and pulled it in, and they had labourers that did that job, and they built up all these shells, and we got the shells and we had to finish them off. It was like heaven to me when I came down here, somebody else was doing some of the hard work. We were just putting in the ends, and you know how you poke in "flagging", stuff like bulrushes, for sealing, we just did that, on with the hoops, we hammered them tight, and then they'd a hoop-driver. That's the first I'd seen of a hoop-driver. It was like heaven to me, that was a distinct change in coopering to me.

'The first machine we got up at Brown's, for cutting in the ends, that was a local man in Aberlour who made that up. You pushed it in and round, but you had to watch when you pushed it in, because if you pushed it in against the grain it threw the end back out at you, so you had to watch and put it in in the right position, running with the grain, and then you'd to keep it tight all the time. It was quite frightening sometimes, I actually landed on my back on the floor one day, because I'd put it in against the grain and it threw it out and hit me in stomach and I landed on the floor.

'But they progressed with that, they got a swivel thing for a saw. You put in the end, fixed it, and it started going round, and they had this swivel thing with a saw on it, sawed it to the size, they were all made one size usually, and then they had the moulder that went in as the end was going round and cut it, and that saved us all the hand work cutting off the bevel. Everything is changed totally in coopering. There's a lot less physical work.

'The guys that are still in the private cooperages on piece work each time there's a new machine put it, a modern machine, they probably don't get a pay rise, so they've got a bigger volume of work to do to keep the same wage.

'You still need the skill to be able to make sure that your finished article doesn't leak, because they've all to be tested, and we all have our own mark, we've a stamp and we stamp them, and if it leaks the tester puts it back and we have to repair it. It's just steel stamps, an initial usually, you stamp it on the end of the stave, and on the end, so you still need the skill to actually assemble a cask and keep it wind and watertight.

Staves at the former Brown's Cooperage, Balvenie Street, Dufftown, now demolished. In the background are disused casks, converted into garden planting tubs.

'When it came to repairing casks, you might open up a cask and search about looking for a stave to fit exactly the same, but if you couldn't get it, well, you just had to get one, crop off the end, and then shape it yourself.

'We never actually made brand new casks, we've never done that here. The only time you'd have done that would have been with a special order, probably a small cask. But at the same time, you still had the shape of the staves, we've never done them from scratch, shaping the staves. It's all recycled as you would say.

'They're certainly using more bourbon wood just now, but I think they're still trying to keep the sherry casks there because they're very important to a decent malt whisky. They have so many different types of whiskies now have Grants. They've got the Solera. I believe that's in a vat that is never emptied, it's only allowed to go down so far, and then it's topped up with various whiskies. But being a cooper I was never really involved in all that.

'There was a lot of sherry casks still coming in when I was there, up till 1999. They nosed them all to make sure they were in good order. You could have drank the sherry out of the casks that were coming in, you could have drank it out of them, it was perfect. They were coming in complete.

'Our job was to check them for broken staves and leaks and that, they allowed so many broken staves so long as the cracks weren't too big, as long as they could fill it as it was, the less tampering obviously the cask was better. It was best if you didn't have to open it up.

'They had a system of wine treating, with paxarette, but I think they used that more for casks that maybe weren't nosing too well. If they were "tired" casks. I once saw a guy drink an enamel jug full of paxarette, thick horrible stuff. Some of them would do anything for a hit.

'We were slack in the early 1980s, because there was too much whisky around, and we were farmed out to other jobs. To fill in the time. And then they started taking boys up, obviously speculating that it was going to be busy again, and they got a lot of Glasgow boys up and filled up the cooperage, putting in more benches, and we were going flat out a while. I remember that in 1990, I happened to be off work for about five months, and at that time I missed out on a lot of big money. They were really going hammer and tongs, and then things began to wane again, it was up and down. We got shifted out of the one building into a littler building, and they shifted all the spirit handling down into the big building, from Glenfiddich down to Balvenie.

'We were put into this smaller building, the buildings were just beside one another, the idea was to keep everything close together. Your casks arrived down there, the spirit handling's down there. The casks come out of the cooperage ready to be filled with whisky.

'Obviously a cask can only go on so long, and they've got this thing going on with de-charring and re-charring now. All the bourbon casks that come in are burnt. "De-char" and "re-char" means scraping off all the charring, and then burning them again to rejuvenate the wood. The charring is supposed to help the colouring and the maturation. They're coming over complete now. First of all, I think, the boys who are working outside, the labourers, they collect them, and they pick out the best of them for going straight for filling, and they set aside the bad ones, so that the cooperage boys get them in to repair. It can be cracks in the staves, bad ends, buckled ends, you know, maybe rotten hoops, rusted hoops, to be replaced.

'I don't think any other distilleries round about have cooperages like Grants. They'll have coopers on site for dealing with emergencies. Taylors, I'm not sure how many coopers they have now, but it will be twenty-odd or thirty coopers. They had a bad spell earlier this year, and he actually spoke about paying off, but I think they've just been ticking over this year. But he'll try and hang onto his workforce because when they get busy they need them. They seem to experiment a lot with different kinds of casks. They were actually, I believe, experimenting with new wood, and using a sort of laser heat treatment instead of steam. You shape the staves so much with machines, but you have to bend them to get them to make the shape. I never really heard much more about it, whether it was a success or not. They're

Cask stack at the Speyside Cooperage, Craigellachie, 2004.

very go-ahead, I believe they buy the majority of the bourbon barrels in America.

'One of our bosses was in America, and he came back with quite a lot of photographs showing us men working there in the cooperages in America, making the new bourbon barrels, and it didn't look so much different to us. But theirs were machine shops, and they were actually using immigrants as cheap labour. That's one of the things we've tried to avoid in this country, is infiltrating labourers amongst the coopers. At one time the union was very strong. You'd cooperages scattered about all around the North-east. Now you've got Taylors and Glenfiddich, while Browns are finished doing barrels, they only do the washbacks, the vats, there's only two guys there and they've taken over from Arthur Brown. There's a cooperage in Keith, there's not one in Rothes now. There were two in Dufftown at one time, about three in Craigellachie, one in Keith, one across in Insch, and in Elgin, you had cooperages in Elgin.

'Now Taylors do a big production, and there are still a lot of cooperages in the Central Belt, Glasgow area, and there's still some of the smaller cooperages trying to keep going down there. They've still got a cooperage at Girvan now.

'It was always up and down, but over the years they've produced a lot of casks here at Glenfiddich. Unfortunately for the private cooperages, sometimes, when the industry goes down, they can only take it so long. Arthur Brown's the same age as myself, sixty-one, and he'd come to a time where there was nobody to take over the cooperage, so he was just packing it in. But the vat business there now, I think they're the only ones in Scotland that build vats now. Arthur is still there to help them out till they get it properly established. There used to be a place in Glasgow, Lowries, that did vats, but they packed up a few years ago.

'When I left the school it was a five-year apprenticeship, but the year you left the school, from fifteen to sixteen, you were just a "gopher", you didn't start till you were sixteen. Nowadays it's just four years, they don't leave school till they're sixteen, maybe a couple of months they'll get their indentures sorted out, and then they'll be finished by the time they're early twenties.

'A lot of it was "look and learn" in my day. The first year you were running about doing all these odd jobs, doing things for the coopers. It was a case of look and learn, and then when they put you onto the bench they would tell you, "Now there's a 40-gallon barrel, you look round that, see what's wrong with it. Mark all the bad bits." You'd to do this, mark the bad bits, and if you'd done it right, "Aye that's alright." If you'd done it wrong you got a cussing like.

Cask ends at the Speyside Cooperage, 2004.

Cardow (now Cardhu)
cooperage, 1924

'And then they would get you to start knocking the hoops off, and having it prepared for repairing. The guy that was in charge would take out a stave and say, "Now, you go and find staves the same length as that." You cannibalised ones for repairing, you maybe had a few casks all over the cooperage opened up, so you went and looked to find a stave to fit, and you went back and you said, "Is that alright?" "That's right now," he'd say. You'd to joint your staves, each stave. With a broken stave you'd to joint the stave on either side, so if you'd a few broken staves spread round the cask, if you got single staves to fit them fine, put them in, but if you didn't, if the cask you were getting your staves out of to repair had a run of one, two, three, four, five, six, you'd knock round your staves in the cask and you'd just put in the whole piece, which meant that you'd only one stave on either side to joint.

'He'd let you carry on from there. "Now put on the hoops, and make sure that they're all even round the top, no use if they're sitting at an angle. Put in your stave, knock them in, make sure that they're all flush round the top." If they weren't, you'd just slackened it off again and give it a wee shake. You've a top hoop, a quarter hoop and a bulge hoop. The best way to do it was to tighten the quarter hoop, knock off the end hoop, and then tap the staves till they were flush, tap them in the way and tap them down the way, then put on your end hoop, tighten that a good bit, tighten your quarter, tighten your bulge, turn it over, and if you were lucky enough you'd maybe get the hoop on without any bother, so from there on in you just tightened up, keep knocking it out round the bulge, to keep the staves flush on the outside. They didn't want to be shaving off a great bit of wood just because you left it stuck out. You tap them in flush. Then carry on with that, keep putting on your hoops, check your top to check it's alright. If it's alright you can stick it in your end, seal it up, and then tighten the hoops up, and at that time of day you had to drive the hoops the full distance.

'Sometimes your hoops would have to be taken in, knock out the rivets and take it in maybe half an inch, that's to keep it up, because you never allowed hoops down further than a third, the bulge hoops were never allowed to be down more than a third. With experience you learnt just how much you had to take it in, otherwise put it round, line it up with the hole nearest the end of the hoop on the outside, just give it a mark, and then rivet it there.

'It's very surprising that there weren't more injuries, with the dramming that went on. I got a finger cut, down to the cuticle, half the depth of my finger, on a planer, but I hadn't been drinking, there wasn't any drink involved. If it hadn't been that I pulled my finger out with the other hand I might have been up to the knuckle. The bit of wood had a hard knot, it was a piece of end wood, and I was pushing it against the guide, and of course we weren't too brilliant about using the guards and that on the machinery. It had a hard knot and it just stotted right out and my finger went in. And that was a month off work. The doctor wouldn't let me back. Every time I saw him he said, "No, you can't go back till that's healed." So that was my own fault, careless just, if the guard had been on properly it wouldn't have sucked my finger in. After that the boss's son was running round all the machines, making sure the guards were all on.

'Coopering's not a hard job to learn to do, and it doesn't take long to learn to do it, but it takes years of experience to keep doing it properly, wind and watertight. You'd get some boys just didn't seem to be interested, and they thought they'd get off with it, but I've seen some boys having two, three, four casks lying, waiting to be redone, which is a total waste of time. If you do it right first time, that's you finished with that one and on to another one. Especially if you're on piecework, making money.

'In coopering we had this thing about helping one another. I'd a guy working down with us in the cooperage at Balvenie, he was one of the Glasgow guys, and he wasn't really interested in coopering, so why he persisted I don't know. And I used to help him out steady, do my own work and then I'd be across saying, "I'll give you a hand." It was just to give him a chance to keep his numbers up. But in the end he got an outside job.

'That's what I'm saying about the experience. It takes years of experience to actually do the job quickly and still do quality work. To get it right every time. It doesn't take long to learn the job, it takes a long time to be quick and always do it well.

'I don't know if they bother so much now, but when my time was up [completion of apprenticeship] I was lucky, I got married the week before I was twenty-one, and they took pity on me, I think. They had a pick-up and they'd take you all round the town showing you off. I was blackened like, but no tarring, just some mixture of stuff they made up

'And it was freezing, I remember. It was the end of August, and my wife used to work at Glenrinnes Lodge, up on the Tomintoul Road, and they were heading away to go up there and run me round the lodge, and I said, "You're wasting your time, she's not there, she's home this week." I said, "Don't go up there." We'd had a good few drinks in the cooperage first, and then back down into the pubs, round the pubs. It used to be quite desperate, like.

'We did give the young 'uns their initiations down here, but what we did, somebody took down a camera, maybe a cine camera you could video with, and we gave them their blackening down there, and then after we'd all had a drink and everything we hosed them down and put them through the shower, and then we went up the town. A bit more civilised.

'I remember when I got blackened I stayed at the bottom of the town, at the junction for Huntly and Keith, and my parents stayed there in an old house just at the roadside. We'd no inside water facilities, the tap at the front door just, so of course I'm thinking to myself I'm going to have some job getting myself cleaned up the night, but one of my work mates had not long got a council house at the top of York Street, and he said, "You'll come home with me and get a bath," and I remember his wife ran the bath and he gave me a bottle of washing-up liquid, I think it was, to use, so I got myself cleaned up there.

'They used to be quite a thing, the initiations. They'd get an old cask and throw the boy in, inside there, and it full of gunge and everything, and roll them round about. But of course the best part was aye the drams after it.'

8

On Dramming

Of all aspects of whisky-making and distilling life that were discussed with the whisky men, none was the subject of such ardent conversation as the topic of 'dramming'.

Dramming was the semi-official practice of giving measures of whisky to distillery workers during the course of their shifts, and there were several justifications for it. Principally, it was thought to deter workers from helping themselves to whisky.

Sir Robert Bruce Lockhart's family owned Balmenach distillery near Grantown-on-Spey, and in *Scotch* he writes 'When I was a boy, the distillerymen at Balmenach were "drammed" three times a day. In my innocence I assumed that this gift of free whisky came from my uncle's generous heart ... I was of course mistaken. The free "dramming" was instituted for one purpose only; to counteract a temptation which existed then, exists today, and is apparently irresistible.'

Dramming also encouraged men to take on dirty and unpopular jobs with the reward of an extra dram.

According to Ed McAffer of Bowmore, 'I suppose what made the characters in the distilleries was that they were getting their dram. They'd have a dram at six o'clock in the morning, another one at midday, and one at six o'clock at night when they finished if they worked a 12-hour day. And that kept them going, that fired them up, and got the jobs done, because a lot of the jobs were quite dirty and dusty. There was the "dirty dram", as they called it. "Oh, we'll need a dram for that job or we're no' doing it," they'd say. I used to see that and think it was quite hilarious. That was the negotiation, it wasn't about money, it was about having a dram before they'd start and having a dram when they were finished.'

'Big Angus' McAffer of Lagavulin recalls, 'You got a dram handed to you at eight o'clock in the morning, one before you went off shift, and then one at ten o'clock at night if you were on two till ten. It was new stuff, I preferred the new stuff, you always got the new stuff, and you got more than that, of course, you had one on the sly, you know. If you were shouted to go to the warehouse, to stow barrels, to put butts on top of one another, well, the cooper always gave you a dram for giving him a hand. That was an extra. And then a lorry would come in and you'd need to give a hand to load the lorry, well you got a dram for that. And the same with moving casks from the spirit store to the warehouse, you got a dram when you started and another one when you were finished. And then you got a dram for a dirty job, if you were inside the malt bins, it was good for the stour [dust].

'There were no masks or anything in those days, and if you got a dram that cleared the throat. You'd maybe get three or four in a day. You had one in the morning, eight o'clock in the morning, then maybe between eleven and twelve you got another one if you were doing rolling [of casks], you'd get one before you started and another when you were finished rolling. And if you needed to give a hand in the warehouse you'd get one at eleven o'clock. But the person giving you a dram in the warehouse wouldn't know you'd already had one for doing for another job, it was a different person.'

Retired cooper Derek Spark remembers dram-drinking as being commonplace at work. 'One thing about the trade of coopering there was aye a dram on the go. I don't know if I would have been any different through my life if I'd started in another job, but other jobs, most of the jobs, tradesmen, were related to working in distilleries anyway. Dufftown electricians, plumbers, coppersmiths and all that, they all got a drink, they used to give you a dram if you working there. When I started down here they were still dishing out drink. Eight o'clock in the morning and one o'clock dinner time. Then if you were doing a dirty job, you got a "stewie" dram when you were finished the job. This amazed me when I heard it the first time.

'We'd been unloading a lorry with bundles of staves, and they were all dried out, and with the black charring it was really a dirty job, and somebody says, "Right, we'll go and get a stewie dram." I said, "Who the hell wants a stewie dram!" "No, no," they said, "it's because you've been doing a dirty job. It's called a stewie dram." So this was part of the procedure.'

Dramming was the province of the brewer (see Chapter 3, 'On Brewing'), though the head warehouseman would also often dram his workers. The practice was usually undertaken with the tacit approval of, or at least acceptance by, members of HM Customs & Excise.

Archie Ness spent much of his working life at Craigellachie distillery. 'When I started as brewer at Craigellachie we were still dramming, the distillery was dramming right up until the beginning of the '80s. I was dramming when I was brewer. They started with one at nine o'clock. Nine o'clock was dramming time. That was the clearic, the new make. In those days it was 20.8 over proof, so you're talking about something like 68 per cent. We had a horn vessel, made out of deer antlers. We had new make spirit in a jug, and you just filled it into the horn and poured it into a cup. The men all stood in line and were given a cup each, and they went away and drank it. I couldn't drink it at that time in the morning.

'Then you'd what was called a bonding dram, that was after the filling had been done. You got a dram for throwing the draff, which you had to throw from one tun down to the tank to load onto the lorry, and then you got a dram again at four or five o'clock. And the work was always done, you hardly ever saw anyone the worse for wear for drink, and there were never any accidents. And any job you wanted doing no one refused, because there would be a dram in it. Any dirty job I could give them a dram for doing it.'

The frequency, size, and strength of drams dispensed meant that a considerable amount of alcohol was consumed during the course of an average shift.

Ruari MacLeod and Jim McEwan of Bruichladdich on Islay discussed this aspect of dramming:

JM: And were there a few drams going then?

RM: Well, the first dram we had was at seven o'clock.

JM: That was the white stuff?

RM: Oh yes, but that dram was for the maltmen only. Not for the stillman, and then when the manager came in at nine o'clock everybody got a dram.

JM: Well, the stillman would be stealing it anyway. So, that's you had two then?

RM: We'd had two then, yes, and the next one was at twelve o'clock when they were going off. They were 'official' drams. Then, when the shift work men went off, we weren't on shift, they got one. Well, everybody got one then, but it was unofficial for the rest of us. And then you had one at five o'clock when you were going off. And the kilnman had one at six o'clock, he never went off till six o'clock.

JM: So that's six drams a day, and that's full strength. So that was the equivalent to well over a bottle of whisky a day.

RM: Aye, yes it was. You've got the copper here still, but somebody took away the horn they used to use to pour the drams into.

So was dramming a comparatively harmless practice which helped ensure the smooth running of distilleries, or a recipe for accidents waiting to happen and incipient alcoholism? Opinions differ widely.

William Grant & Sons' warehouse team leader Eric Stephen began working for the company in 1962.

'When I started here I think it was five drams a day you got. And they'd find ways to get a drop more too. In those days you had married men going home to their wives, you'd see them crawling up the street there on their hands and knees. Disaster. And if they were working overnight the brewer used to come in and leave the bottle for them. A quarter of a bottle or so each they got. Christ Almighty! Nowadays there are no people bothering to try to get any out. They don't touch it. Job security has a lot to do with it, and the drink-driving thing meant you couldn't have people going home half-cut.

'There were a lot of young people started the same time as me ended up as alcoholics, because of the dramming they got. They got that they couldn't do without it. You get accustomed to it. It was like cutting a kid off sweeties. Some of the old boys, when the brewer paid them Friday night or Saturday dinner time, they would have gone home without their pay, but they wouldn't go home without their dram. They'd wait and wait for him to come with the dram.'

'I remember 2nd of March 1972,' Derek Spark says. 'I'd been across and had my morning dram from the brewer, I'd come back and I'm working away and I said to myself, "What are you doing, you're going to be a bloody heid the ba [literally "head the ball", i.e. be an idiot] before long if you carry on like this," and I stopped drinking whisky. I didn't stop drinking. I still drank beer, but I actually didn't drink any hard spirits for a year after that. I drank sherry and that if we were out socialising, and beer, but then after that I went onto vodka when we were out socialising, the sherry I found gave me an awful headache.

'Actually, I ended up having a bet with one of my workmates. He says to me, "You'll never do it, you'll never stop drinking whisky." I says, "Oh, I bet you I will, but I tell you what, I bet you couldn't do it." "Ach, no bother, no bother," he says. "Right, put your money where your mouth is," I says. He says, "I'll pay you a fiver

I'll stop for a year." I says, "A fiver! Make it twenty and you're on." So we made a bet of twenty pounds, but he didn't make it. But I didn't take his money from him. He was actually in a sorry situation. He left us and went to Mortlach distillery, and he was carrying gin and vodka to his work with him to drink to try and keep this bet going. But he went all to hell and he got back onto the whisky.

'That was one of the things in the trade, that time I was at Brown's cooperage, right up to just after I started at Grant's, when I look back on it in retrospect it's quite sad really to think that we went to work and the first thing we were thinking about was getting a dram. It was all over, all the distilleries did it, all the cooperages that were in existence, they were all among drink. The five months that I was at Speyside cooperage I'd started taking a drink there. The guy in charge there he gave us lemonade with it, but it really didn't make any difference, we were taking alcohol. He poured in the lemonade, he reduced the dram by pouring lemonade into it, but it didn't really make any difference. Theirs was just what was left in the casks that were coming in for repair or whatever.'

Talking to Ruari MacLeod, Jim McEwan notes a sad side to dramming. 'The drink got to a lot of the boys, they got too much. They'd go home at night after a 12-hour shift, they've had six drams, plus what they got in the warehouse, or if there was a puffer in, loading or unloading, there was more then.'

RM: Aye, aye, they got that, they got more if they were working anywhere.

JM: And they'd go home at night, front of a fire, fall asleep, wake up at ten o'clock, go to bed, then up at five, and their children never saw them, their wives never saw them, so it wasn't a great situation.

However, hard physical work did go some way towards minimising the effects of all those drams. Grant Carmichael, formerly general manager for DCL and its successor companies on Islay, says, 'At one time each distillery probably had from eight to twelve people employed in the malt barns, where the malt was turned by hand. Drams were plentiful, but it was hard physical labour, and the effects of the dram were soon worked off, you sweated it out. You couldn't afford nowadays to have the dramming that we had in the old days because people now are sitting at a computer, pressing a button. Press the wrong button and you're in big trouble, so it's not worth it.'

According to 'Big Angus' McAffer, 'You watched yourself, you weren't drunk. You knew the limit generally, but maybe sometimes one of you would have a wee bit too much, but you helped him, you did his work as well as your own, and that covered him before the next shift came in, and nobody knew anything, his work was done. When the next man came in, there was plenty of coal, the boiler was clean, the boiler was going, we were helping one another. He'd do the same for me, that's the way you were working. You watched your jobs, and there were never any accidents due to it.

'There was no such thing as overtime in my day. You'd get a "wee sweetie" for the extra work, a wee dram. A lot of the boys liked the new make better than the mature stuff, it went down nice and easy. The new make was nice, but I won't say no to any of them! I was more or less brought up on the stuff. Everything's bad for you now, whisky's bad for you, they go overboard for you now. I'm still going yet, and I've drank plenty of the new make and the mature stuff too, both, and it didn't do me any harm. If you took your food you were fine. The trick is to eat. We've gone from distillery workers expecting to be drunk to distillery workers expecting to be sober. If you take a drink in a distillery now it's a stigma. You came to your work to get drink and then you went to the pub!'

Dramming became such an integral part of distillery life that if the dramming routine was interrupted for any reason, the effects could be significant, as Ruari MacLeod recalls.

'We had an office cleaner at Bruichladdich, the late Maggie Fletcher, she was always down before seven o'clock, but this morning she wasn't, and I couldn't get into the office for a lemonade bottle full of whisky, this was for the malting floors. So this morning she slept in, and it came to seven o'clock and there was no whisky. Well, I couldn't give them a dram, and the best of it was they went slow.

'The manager came in at nine o'clock and well before eight o'clock the kiln would usually be loaded, because we were stripping number one malt floor and filling the kiln. I said to the manager, "Well you'll have to see the maltman," and he had him up and he says, "What's wrong with you, why is this not on?" And he said, "Well the kiln's not loaded yet." "Oh, you had a breakdown," he said, and off he went. We went one hour late, but we made up for it later. This was because there was no dram at seven o'clock.'

Dramming was a practice that affected more than just the distillery workforce, however, as Grant Carmichael remembers. 'Dramming time. Oban was the place I remember, working in the very early '60s, before I came to Islay. Dramming time in Oban was lunchtime, when the men finished, and people would appear out of the woodwork. The railway lorries, the railway delivery men, always found an excuse to come to the distillery when it was dramming time. The postman always

Stafford Street and M'Caig Towers, Oban   Valentines Series   41612

Oban distillery, c. 1907.

delivered the mail at that time. They had it worked out that they knew exactly when dramming time was. This happened all over, it happened on Islay and it happened on Speyside.'

In some distilleries 'dramming' was done with new spirit, or 'clearic', often colloquially referred to as 'fresh', while in others more mature whisky would be dispensed. It tended to depend largely on the amiability of the Excise officer on the premises, but not everyone thanked him for his benevolence in allowing mature whisky to be given out.

As Jim McEwan notes, 'The great thing was that the shift men loved the white stuff, and come the slack season when we went out to cut the peats or clean the lade, the whitewashing the buildings, whichever one of these three jobs you got, and there was no white stuff, the boys hated it. They hated drinking the warehouse stuff. Jimmy McCall, the manager, would say to me, "Here," and give me a gallon can, and say, "Go and fill that with good sherry cask old stuff for the boys' dram." And it was amazing. Coming towards the end of August, when it was coming close to starting again, the boys would be rubbing their hands and saying, "Oh, next week we'll get some of the white stuff." They preferred the white stuff.'

Ruari Macleod agrees. 'That's right. I was the same too. Even to the present day. Now and again I call in Bowmore distillery, and sometimes the other distilleries as well, if any of my relatives are home and they're wanting to go. I am offered a dram at any time in any of the distilleries. I was over last summer, and I was given a shout by the manager, and he says, "You'd better have a dram," and it was out of a sherry cask. And I said to him, "Any clear stuff?" "Yes," he said, and he went away and came back with quite a big bottle, and he poured one and said, "You'd better have the whole lot," so I had to have the whole lot. Yes, even to the present day I prefer it.'

Derek Spark, however, liked the more mature spirit. 'When they were bonding the whisky [storing the casks of new make in the warehouses], it was aye about half past ten in the morning, and you got a good dram for that, you got a fine old dram for that. It was usually clearic you got, the normal dram, but you got a good dram for the bonding.'

Ian Millar of Dufftown echoes Derek Spark's experiences of being drammed with good, mature whisky, in his case in the warehouses during his early days at Blair Athol distillery in Pitlochry.

'Before dramming was stopped, I worked in the warehouse. I was only nineteen at the time, and not interested in whisky. There were three official drams per day – at 09.50 a.m., 12.20 p.m., and 4.30 p.m. My job was to turn up each time at the appointed time with a bottle of water and a large glass. The warehouseman would then take whisky from one of the best barrels and fill up a large glass tube. All of the guys queuing for their dram would take it straight out of the glass tube and the water and glass were never, or extremely seldom, used. One day I fell on the way up to the warehouse and broke the glass. I presented the bottle at the dramming and even though the glass was not used I got hell from everyone for breaking it.'

In some instances, however, the drams available were much more variable in quality and provenance than those dispensed in distilleries by the brewer or warehouseman. 'In the cooperage when I was a loon [lad],' Derek Spark remembers, 'you'd get in casks from the distilleries, I remember once there was a load came from Glenfiddich. Brown's cooperage used to be down at Parkmore distillery [which closed in 1931, but remains externally intact, with warehousing used by Highland Distillers], it used to be down there, and we got this load of butts and puncheons, and I was at the unloading of them and taking them in. It was a warehouse that the cooperage was in. Double-roofed. One half of it was the cooperage work area, the other half was storage.

'So I was taking in these casks one day and the old guy that was the foreman, *Bowmore distillery, 2004.* I says to him, "You know these things are splashing in there, they're loaded with stuff." He said, "Righto", and he had a kist [chest] and various vessels in it, stain jugs and such like. So he says, "You give me a hand here," and we started emptying them, took the skids we used for rolling barrels, took them and a pan, well, there was no way he'd enough vessels in his kist to hold this, so he says, "Take one of those coopered barrels there" – there was a stock of coopered barrels – "take it round the side there," and we filled it into that barrel, and we stuck it back up where it had come from, because he didn't want any of the boys getting in – you'd maybe get some of them going there helping themselves to bottles out of it.

'He drammed the boys, it was unofficial this, but he drammed the boys three times in the morning and a couple of times in the afternoon if he had the drink. He'd just get it out of empty barrels, well they were classed as empty barrels, but quite often just like this occasion, there was some left in. But actually we found out after that the boys that had been emptying these casks had been leaving them for themselves at Glenfiddich, and they were near crying when they discovered they were put straight over to us for repairing. We got the fruits of their labour.

'But it went on all the time. And actually some of the stuff that we drank

Glenkinchie distillery,
Pencaitland, 1960s.

would have been wood alcohol, the casks would be sitting there if it was fine weath-er, they produced more, it came out of the wood. And later we were up in Balvenie Street [the cooperage moved from Parkmore distillery into the centre of Dufftown], and we used to fill cider flagons in the morning from casks that were coming in, and that should do us all day. A lot of it was good, just newly-emptied and straight over to us, but at times when there were no casks moving from distilleries, we depend-ed on the heat to produce some! It was a bit rough, some of it.

'I came down here in 1971, and moved up to the cooperage in 1972. You mind the time of the power strikes, the lights were all cut short, you didn't have as much light, well I started up in the cooperage just the week before that started, it must have been about February time if I remember properly. And we were doing alright for drink, we got our dram in the morning, that was still going on, and we were getting this buckshee stuff, we were just next door to the filling store, and they just rolled the repair casks right round into the cooperage. Fresh as anything.'

According to Grant Carmichael, it was the early '70s when dramming stopped. 'As in distilleries, traditionally breweries had their "pundie house", where you went in and got a beer, and they have them yet. What stopped dramming was when Edward du Cann [Conservative politician, chairman of the 1922 Committee] stood up in the House of Commons and made such a stushie [commotion] about the amount of money that the Exchequer was losing with all these distillery workers in Scotland drinking so much whisky. It was bloody nonsense, of course. However, he was listened to, and action was taken, and a lot of the distillers, who were getting a bit more modern then, were quite happy to.

'So it suited the industry, and it suited the families, it suited the wives, because a lot of these guys, though not everybody by any means, some lads would get their pay and have a good bumper in the distillery, and on the way home call in at the pub. So when the drams stopped, every distillery, though some more than others, started to issue the men with a bottle every couple of months or whatever. It's pretty generous now, the allocation they get, which is better. They can take the bottle of whisky home, and the bottle of whisky's in the house, and the lady of the house can keep an eye on it.'

Reminiscing with Ruari MacLeod, Jim McEwan says, 'Bowmore was the first distillery to stop dramming and move to bottles. A chap called Alistair F. Ross, who was the manager in the early 1970s, Alistair Ross was the first man to stop drams.'

RM: Oh is that so? At Bowmore?

JM: Aye, and I thought there was going to be a riot. He said, 'You get a bottle of whisky a month and you drink it or save it, but we're stopping drams.' And very quickly others followed. So Alistair Ross at Bowmore was the first man to do it.

RM: Ian Allan was the first one here. He said, 'Anybody wants a dram, come up to the office.' After a week, nobody went. Nobody went.

'There was a story going at Glenkinchie,' notes Grant Carmichael, 'and if you work it out it's absolutely true. This old man retired, after over fifty years in the distillery, and when he first started he was the carter. It was a horse and cart, and there was a little station at Glenkinchie, Saltoun Station, and even when I was there, in 1960, one of my jobs was "second man" on the coal lorry. We didn't have horses then, it was tractors and trailers, and you were left down at the station, and your job was to load the trailer, and help the driver load another one. But this was what happened in the old days. The carter got a bottle in the morning, and that kept him going for the day. And it was calculated out that this old boy by the time he retired must have drank more than the equivalent of a butt of whisky (110 gallons). That's what kept him going. He'd never had a day off work in his life. He was a marvellous character, finished up in the malt barns.'

If dramming is a thing of the past, then so, largely, is the traditional distilling community pastime of 'liberating' whisky from its legal owners. It was but a short step from semi-official dramming to extremely unofficial self-dramming, as we shall see in the next chapter ...

9

On Helping Themselves

As is already evident, 'dramming' provided distillery workers with significant amounts of free whisky, but there was frequently a desire for more. As one retired Dufftown distillery worker puts it, 'Some of it was taken to be sold, but a lot of it was just about beating the system, it was the sport.'

Nevertheless, with wages in the whisky industry comparatively low until recent times, 'liberated' whisky could be an effective and profitable bartering tool, or a source of cash, especially when the relative cost of whisky is considered.

In the mid-1960s, £10 was an above-average weekly wage, and a bottle of blended whisky cost around £2 12s (£2.50).

Talking of the late 1950s, when he was an apprentice cooper, Derek Spark says, 'The coopers at the Speyside Cooperage then, after a while they'd been there, they were quite busy, and they were making £15 a week, which at that time compared with a top footballer in Aberdeen.'

With a bottle of blended whisky costing around £10 today, it is obvious that the percentage of a worker's income required to buy a bottle of whisky has decreased enormously. This makes the whisky men's eagerness to help themselves when the chance presented itself all the more understandable.

Today, pay is better, the penalties for helping yourself are severe, and opportunities for employment in the whisky industry are limited. As Ed McAffer of Bowmore points out, 'It's not worth it nowadays. And in them days there was so much work going about that guys would come in and if they did get the sack they'd probably get a job tomorrow somewhere else, maybe not in a distillery, but maybe two or three years down the line they'd get back in the distillery, but there was that much work going about in them days that it didn't really impact too much. Nowadays it's quite a well-paid job, and it doesn't come around very often, the chance to get into a distillery today. And before you get the job they interview you and you're well screened before you come in.'

Grant Carmichael echoes Ed's observations. 'There's very little whisky comes out of warehouses now, it's not worth it. If you were caught now you'd be instantly dismissed. It's a fairly well-paid job, whereas in the past people weren't paid a lot, though the distilleries were better paid than the farms, but one of the perks of the job was that you had a house rent free. No longer the case, for quite a long number of years now everyone has had to pay rental.'

Some former whisky men delight in telling stories of 'helping themselves', while others become quite indignant at the very idea.

According to 'Big Angus' McAffer of Lagavulin, nothing ever disappeared from the warehouse. 'Everybody was getting their drams in those days. You'd get one in the morning, one at dinner time, and one at night time before you went home. Nobody was pilfering because you got it handed to you. The manager or the brewer gave it to you. If you were caught stealing it there was a great social stigma. But you'd use the foreshots, my mother's generation, you'd rub it into your joints, it was good for bad joints.'

Perhaps the Lagavulin staff were unusually law-abiding. According to Ed McAffer, things were different in his early days at Bowmore:

'In the warehouses there was always pilfering going on. The Customs did what they could do, they were always there, but it went on. The roles are completely reversed now, the traders are in charge, and pilfering, certainly at Bowmore, just doesn't happen at all now. But in them days, when all the casks had cork bungs in them, and quite a lot of guys in, contractors, working on roofs and doing jobs in about, the old "doonker" was on the go, a sauce bottle with a string on. The cork bung came out easy and you just dropped it in. Everything's hard-bunged now, so you can't get the bungs out without making an awful noise. In those days it was just a quick flick of the wrist and it was out.

'The guys didn't go overboard, they'd have just enough to keep them going at home at night. They used to think, a lot of these old guys that worked there, that they were the pillars of the community, they used to think that you would never see them coming out of a pub staggering about, and they went to church every Sunday, and then when I started in the distillery you'd see them having their two or three drams during the day, and maybe a wee sauce bottle away home, they just went home, it was in the privacy of their own home that

Ed McAffer

they'd drink. They didn't need to go to the pub. The pub would just have annoyed them as much as anything.'

Methods of 'helping yourself' were various and ingenious, and the sauce bottle 'dooker' as described by Ed McAffer was just one. Glass bottles certainly seem to have been favoured on Islay, as Jim McEwan confirms.

'The most successful vessel for stealing whisky from a barrel was created by Heinz. Heinz made salad cream, and the very shape of the Heinz glass bottle fitted through any bung hole, and it was designed by Heinz specifically for stealing whisky! The fact that it was good for storing salad cream was neither here nor there. So you could drop your salad cream bottle in there, pull it up, it was perfect. There was no buggering about. There was more salad cream sold in Islay per head of population than any other place, and not a lot of salad was eaten on the island.

'Some places used copper dogs, copper pipes, but we never used them on Islay. In my lifetime I've seen about four casks completely contaminated with the whisky as black as ink. The copper dog had fallen in and totally contaminated the whisky, which was a real tragedy. So we used glass.

'As coopers we used to open up the casks, and you'd find salad cream bottles in them, and that would be fine. And you'd find all sorts of things. What they used to do was get a regular Biro, just take the end off and pull the refill out, and that's you got your sook-through. So what you'd do is move your cask to make sure that all the fusel oil was mixed in. I mean we're connoisseurs, we don't just drink any old shit, and everybody would have a Biro in their pocket, and they'd take the end off, the middle out, you'd rock your cask, and then pull the cask towards them, and then just stand there at the bung hole, sucking away like kids at a mother's tit, You know, sucking away like a man at a pipe.

'I remember in Bowmore, one of the funniest things I ever had to do … one of the guys was sucking away and he had two false teeth at the front, which didn't fit – they didn't fit for years – but he had them anyway, and every time he spoke they fell down. He was sucking away and a wee bit of charcoal came up and choked him, and he coughed and the two teeth went into the cask. Suddenly he realised he'd got no teeth.

'"Christ! What do I do?" So he puts the bung back in the cask, puts the cask back, and he comes and he says to me, "Jim, I've got a problem." I says, "What's your problem?" He says, "You'll no' believe it, I was sooking the cask and my two teeth are in this hoggie [hogshead] there. Can you get them out for me?" I said, "Oh no, no, we don't serve six years apprenticeship to be going playing at dentists. Your teeth are in there, they can bloody stay there." "Oh, I can't go home, what'll my wife say?" I said, "Tell her you were sick, or lost them in a pub." "Oh Christ no, I can't go home, I'm in trouble, I'm in trouble." He was begging and pleading, and I was just keeping him going.

'"Oh, I'll need to go, sorry," and he was begging and pleading. So anyway, I eventually relented, and we tipped the cask up on its head, off with the top hoop, off with the quarter hoop, took the end out of it, and there just going round and round nicely were the two teeth. I think that's why the movie *Jaws* was made, it was based upon that. Into the barrel, out came the teeth, right back into his mouth, right as rain. So I've pulled bottles out of casks, I've taken copper dogs out of casks, and I've taken false teeth out of casks.'

Methods of extraction were clearly quite similar the whisky world over, as Eric Stephen confirms regarding Glenfiddich.

'The men had all sorts of ways of getting stuff out. Sauce bottles, and even taking out the inside of a Biro pen and having a sook. They'd take it from the casks. In them days the casks were all cork-bunged, but nowadays they're all hard-bunged. It would be too obvious now. You'd hear them "howk howking" away. In them days it was all tacketty boots worn in the warehouses, and people would hear you come into the warehouse. But nowadays it's soft boots, so they can't hear you creeping about.'

Grant Carmichael recalls:

'The dodges people had to take whisky out of the warehouses. Sauce bottles were the thing, or World War One or Two shell cases. Some of the coppersmiths and plumbers, including the plumber in Dufftown, did a roaring trade making dogs with these things. All you had to do was get a cork for him, he would put a couple of lugs on the shell case for a strap, and this was carried down the leg of your trousers, your dungarees.'

'When you were working in the warehouse, take the top off and just drop this in a cask, and then drop it back into the trouser leg. And HP sauce bottles were just the right size. And medicine bottles. In fact, you'd get casks that when you were rolling them out you'd hear a noise and you'd think, "Ah, somebody's dropped the bottle in it."

'There was another dodge in the warehouses. You had your allowance for ullage in a cask [the amount of empty space in it] and sometimes your cask looked low on ullage if some had been taken out of it by the men. In those days every cask going out was examined by the Customs and Excise officer, the "gauger". Generally speaking, the Excisemen were very good, they were part of the community. If a cask was low, one way to get the ullage up a bit was to tighten the cask, drive the hoops, and when you made the cask tighter the level of liquid rose and your ullage was less. Another favourite way of getting whisky out of the warehouses would be that people would have wellies on, so they would have their little bottle pushed down the wellies. That was a common one. There were all these ways of doing it

'The other way people were able to get whisky was when the puffers were being discharged in Glasgow, or MacBrayne's cargo boats. The MacBrayne boats had a tie up with Johnnie Walker somewhere, anything going to Kilmarnock [the Johnnie Walker blending and bottling plant] was MacBrayne's. In those days we had the passenger and vehicle ferries and the weekly cargo boat. That went into Bruichladdich, Port Ellen and Port Askaig, and it used to come into Caol Ila and also Bunnahabhain, if they had anything for Johnnie Walker.

'At Caol Ila it was always worth their while coming in, because we always had a lot for Johnnie Walker. Caol Ila is still the base of Johnnie Walker, as it was in those days too, whereas Lagavulin was the base of White Horse.

'The dockers used to "spile" the cask as they called it. They used to bore a hole in the cask, and they were always making tea, so there was always somebody going up and down the ladder into the hold with a teapot or a kettle, and they had these spiles, little conical pieces of wood, which were knocked into the hole.'

Jim McEwan observes, 'They were stealing whisky at the distillery, on board the ship – once you got out of sight, open up the hatches, in you go, get whisky out. The puffer men, they were stealing it; it got to the Clyde and the boys on the Clyde were robbing it, so by the time it got to the bottling plants there was a good glass taken out of it.'

Some of the funniest stories told by the whisky men concern helping themselves. Jim McEwan remembers being in the malt barns at Bowmore. 'I was with Paddy Gillies, who was a good Gaelic singer. I must have been about seventeen or eighteen, and we had just been at a dance in the village hall in Bowmore, and where else would you go late at night except a distillery, where you can get free whisky, have a good heat, and a bit of chat by the fire? A chap called Angus McKechnie and myself we came down, and we were watching Pat, and he's at the fires in the kiln.

'There's a fireplace here and a fireplace there, and in between the two fireplaces is the peats, built up perfectly in a wall, all the way up from the floor to the ceiling. So we're watching "Paki", Peter Gillies, and he's a great Gaelic singer. So we're watching him through the crack in the door. And he's singing away, and then he's counting up the peats out loud, *aon, dà, trì, ceithir, còig, sia, seachd*. One to seven.

Aon, dà, trì, ceithir, cóig, sia, seachd, ochd, naoi. One to nine. So it was seven up and nine along, and then he took the peat out, okay, and then he broke the peat, and he put his half-bottle in the hole behind it, and put the peat at the front of it.

'Unfortunately for him, we watched him, so he came out the kiln, away up to plough the floors, and we were in just like ferrets. One, two, three, four, five, six seven – one, two, three, four, five, six seven, eight, nine. Out comes the half-peat and there's the half-bottle behind, the white stuff, so quickly we emptied the white stuff into another bottle, filled the original with water, and put it back in. Then we thought that's a bit stupid, that's a really mean thing to do. So we put a proper peat in the hole, took the half-peat and put it in the fire, put a full peat in the hole with no bottle behind it.

'So about half an hour, three-quarters of an hour later, Peter comes down, he's sweating and he's ready for his dram now, he's just turned the floor, and he's singing the Gaelic song, and he's counting again, *aon, dà, trì* and so forth, and it's a full peat! And he's half-pissed, and he's trying to remember was it seven up and nine across? or nine down and seven across? and we kept watching him, and at the end of the day the bloody whole peat stack was demolished, because if you pull one out, the rest of them fall down. Peter never discovered our secret, and after that he never did it again. He hid it somewhere else.

'Long after dramming stopped they were still getting their stolen drams; there wasn't a house you went to in the village without a bottle beneath the sink or a bottle in the airing cupboard.

'Old Davy Bell [long-standing Bowmore cooper and Jim McEwan's mentor], he was working at Bunnahabhain. He left Bowmore, he retired, and he went to Bunnahabhain. Davy liked to steal a dram. The Bunnahabhain boys were telling me they were coming from Bunnahabhain one night to Bowmore with a van load of boys from Bowmore, and old Davy had a half-bottle, and they were driving along and it was a hot summer's night, and suddenly there's this "bang". Davy's bottle had burst. Davy never cracked, he just sat there like that and looked around him, and the smell of whisky was everywhere, but he never moved and just sat there, kept the jacket on. Whisky was running down, but he never moved, very, very cool.'

Ian Millar was also privy to some humorous efforts at whisky liberation during his time at Blair Athol distillery.

'Jimmy was helping out in the filling store, and when the filling ended, the Exciseman left the filling store to go up to his office for a few minutes. By this time George was already outside the filling store with his fag in his hand, so Jimmy asked him to stand guard, and if the Exciseman came back George was to signal by whistling.

'Jimmy then picked up the pail of spirit he had just filled after draining the filling heads. As he raised the pail to his head, the handle of the pail dropped over his head and lodged neatly behind the back of his ears. Just at that moment, George started whistling. He wasn't whistling a warning, of course, he was just whistling to himself. George was always whistling. Meanwhile Jimmy was trying to wrench the pail off the back of his ears, but to no avail, and in the background he could still hear George whistling.

'He tilted the bucket up to gain some visibility and darted off in the direction of the large receiver, only to meet a strategically placed barrel head on. He hit the barrel at knee height and at speed, ending up on the other side of the barrel, upside down, coughing and spluttering with the spirit which had shot up his nose, down his throat and into his eyes. As he sat there with the pail on his head he could still hear George whistling at the door.

'Night shift were in charge of stocking up on "white stuff" – new make whisky straight from the still. The method used was a Tupperware box hard up against the dip rod (used to measure the depth of spirit in the spirit receiver). The rod was pulled out of the vessel at high speed and with it came a quantity of spirit. If you kept this going you quickly filled the Tupperware box inside five minutes, and this was the equivalent to a bottle of whisky.'

Jim McEwan describes a very similar process at Bowmore.

'The best way a stillman could get his dram was using the dip rods in the spirit vat. That was called milking the cow. As the dip rod tapers it goes down quickly into the vat, and it comes up quickly. So you'd fire it down into the vat, it comes up full of whisky running right down it, you put a sponge round the bottom of it, the sponge collects it, and it's happy days. Down she goes again, up she comes, and you'd very easily fill a glass just by squeezing the sponge. Called milking the cow. Sometimes when a new dip rod went in it was too stiff and you couldn't get it pulled quickly, so you'd get a bit of glass, just a piece of glass, and scrape the side of it.

'That was one way of doing it. Another thing they used to do, the stillmen, or the mashmen ... the pipe from the spirit safe travelling along the alleyways, the black pipe coming off from the spirit safe, to the intermediate spirit receiver, generally that was underneath, tucked away somewhere. So what they would then do was just drill a little hole in the pipe, and out would come the whisky when they were pumping from the ISR to the spirit vat, out would come the whisky. What they would do was hold their bottles below the pipe, or their glasses, and then get some putty, and in these days the distilleries all had coal, so they'd just mix some coal dust with the putty and just cover the hole over. That was the first place a customs officer visiting a distillery would come. He would always check the undersides of the pipes. Most of the pipes after a few years were like watering cans.'

Ruari MacLeod says, 'Oh aye, yes, it was the same here. And of course we had two brothers, MacLeans they were, and they used to just use cardboard. You'd wrap the cardboard around the dipstick, and then pull the cardboard down and it would run into the glass. You'd fill a glass in about half a minute. They were experts at it.'

Not all stolen spirit came from the stillhouse or the warehouse, however, as Dennis McBain confirms.

'Once a week I was also sent down to the bottling hall at Glenfiddich to push home the corks in the full bottles – there'd be about eight of us doing it, and you'd do it for maybe four hours at a time. The filler was an old six-header, and it's now on display in the reception area at Glenfiddich. It worked on a siphon principle. To start it up you sucked on each of the tubes to get it flowing.

'The work left you with an indentation in your palm from pushing the corks home, but it was a popular job – the lads liked to get their turn at it – and I soon discovered why. Every now and again, the chap operating the filler would send along a half-full bottle, and you could either take your swig from it or ignore it if you wanted, and the bottle just went round and was washed and eventually came back through again.

'When I first joined, the brewer's office was next to the workshop, and every week he'd call me in and there'd be all the pails lined up from which the men had been drammed. He'd hand me one still maybe a quarter full of the new make spirit, and give me a cloth and tell me to go and clean the windows of his house. He also told me the first time I did it that on no account was I to let the pail out of my sight while I was doing the job. Well, I didn't think much of this until one day I was doing it and I needed a clean cloth, so away I went to get one.

'I was only away about three minutes, but when I got back there was only half an inch of spirit left in the pail. I found out after that the boys had been watching my every move, just waiting for their chance, and finally I gave them it! Even though the stuff had been used to clean the windows and had had a dirty cloth in it, it didn't stop them. Out they'd come with sauce bottles and whatever else. Mind you, it made a grand job of cleaning the windows, really put a sparkle into them.'

Archie Ness remembers that during his time as brewer at Craigellachie distillery, 'The empty casks were stored round the back, and they had what you called the "billings" in them, the residue left in the casks after they'd been emptied. After they'd been emptied they came back and sat in the yard. I never bothered with the billings because it was from right at the bottom of the cask and you had all the wee bits of stuff and everything in there. But you'd be up in the tun room at night and you'd hear "clatter clatter", and you'd look out and you'd just see a white light, and hear the men moving around. They'd be up the back draining it out into a pan.

'This morning I was on six to two with the tun room operator, and you had funnels with filter paper for filtering the samples from the washbacks which you took to check the gravities before you brought them across to the stillhouse. This morning we couldn't find the funnels, and by this time it was eight o'clock, and the brewer comes in at eight, looking for his samples. We went through into the stillhouse just before eight o'clock and I said, "Have you seen the funnels?" but the stillman hadn't. We had a coal bunker where the coal came in through the elevators, and I opened the door in there, and right at the front were the two funnels sitting, with billings filtering through the filter paper into two bottles! The brewer came in and I said, "What's this?" He said, "Ach, it must have been night shift." I said, "Well I want these filters quick."

'How much you'd get out of a cask depended on the weather and that. I've seen then come back with a panful sometimes. Some of them didn't filter it at all, and it would have bits of sticks and things like that left in it. It was a thing I never tasted, the billings.'

'At the time they were getting their drams, morning and night, not much whisky ever went missing from the place,' Archie reckons. 'When they cut out the drams it did start going then. One or two were caught, because it starts off with a wee bottle or a dog, but when they start taking a bucket out, that's it.'

'They'd be in the warehouse maybe bonding or storing casks, and they'd take a dog with them, or maybe a sauce bottle on a bit of string. One or two you knew were doing it, but you couldn't do anything about it without being sure. If they were caught it was instant dismissal, but it didn't happen a lot.

'The filling store at Craigellachie was concrete at the front, a concrete floor, and a warehouse all the way back. One day when I was brewer I walked in with the Exciseman, and the men were in before us. As the warehouse boys came through the warehouse this small laddie came through, and as he walked onto the concrete, crash! A lemonade bottle down the leg of the trouser. And I was standing there with the Exciseman. You should have seen the laddie's face. I'll never forget it. It was

instant dismissal, and they were all searched, but he was the only one with anything. I don't know whether when we walked in the door he let go or what. It was harmless really, but then it was all adding up, I suppose. The Excisemen were quite good, a lot of them. You'd get to know them, and at least you knew where you stood with them. They were fair with you.

'One man was caught helping himself to whisky, and he was demoted. He was put to painting, late in the year, and it was frosty, and this day he was painting the coal elevator, from the bottom up. So he's climbing up the stair, painting, and it's going down his hands. I asked him what he was doing, and he said, "You asked me to paint it, so I'm painting it from the bottom up." He was just being awkward. So I just left him to get on with it. Never took any notice of him. But he got back into his job as stillman, he was promoted again after a certain time.'

'On one occasion when I was at Craigellachie we caught somebody trying to get whisky away with him,' remembers Sandy McAdam, 'but it's a case of if you go

The former Knockando railway station, later used for a time as Tamdhu distillery visitor centre.

about things the right way you can deal with it without too much trouble.'

'This last long time there's not been the same amount of that going on, anyway. I'd say that when the drams stopped it fell away to nothing like the same extent it used to be. Jobs were better paid, and the men didn't want to lose them. Also, a lot of them were travelling to work, weren't staying at the places, so they weren't drinking because they had to drive. Over the last few years there are a lot fewer people that would drink the wash, the "Joe", compared to before, too. Never try it, it does terrible things to your stomach, and it's bound to taste horrible.

'This old boy had an illicit still up in the Hill of Dallas, in a peat stack. That's the only one I've heard of around here, but that was years ago. If you go from Knockando over to Forres, it's over there. That'll be going back fifty years or so.'

Dennis McBain of Dufftown declares that despite everything, the actual process of making whisky never changes.

'You make the computer do the same thing that the man did in effect, and it's not rocket science making whisky, it's an easy process. You could do it in your kitchen if you had a mind to.

'The illicit still people made it in various contraptions, though it was probably poisonous with the soot, and they were making it in mild steel, which isn't good. They've got beer kegs and stills that came off ships and all sorts in the Whisky Museum up the road in Dufftown.'

'There used to be illicit distilling on Islay,' recalls 'Big Angus' McAffer, 'and going down to the Mull of Oa there were caves that you could only get into when the tide was out. The shepherd down there was put in the prison at Lochgilphead [on the Argyll mainland] because he wouldn't tell the Excise where the caves were that were being used for distilling, although he knew well enough. McGibbon was his name. He had to walk from Lochgilphead to Tarbert to catch the ferry back to Islay after he'd served his time. It's the hard road. The men at the Oa, they knew the tides of course, and they went down into the caves by rope. They could only get into the caves to make whisky by going down on ropes. That's what I call covering your tracks! Illicit distilling is the hardest thing in the world to keep quiet, because it loosens the tongue.'

Until the decimation of the railway network during the 1960s, many distilleries used trains for their principal transport requirements. Trains brought in coal, barley and even yeast, and took out casks of spirit, destined for bottling plants and blending halls.

Railway workers became adept at 'helping themselves' and the story is told of one Speyside signalbox where a bucket was apparently filled with sawdust, pre-

Opposite:
The 'Whisky Train' at
Craigellachie station, 1959.
At that time it travelled
twice a week from Cromdale
— at the head of Strathspey
— to Keith, where the trucks
joined a train to Glasgow.
The final train might have
included up to 50 wagons
loaded with casks of whisky.

sumably in case of an electrical fire. Scoop the sawdust to one side, however, and the bucket turned out to be filled with clear, new make spirit …

One method of helping themselves devised by railway employees entailed loosening one of the cask hoops, drilling a small hole in the wood where the hoop had been, draining off some spirit, then hammering a peg into the hole to prevent further leakage. When the hoop was replaced, there was no sign that the cask had ever been interfered with.

Sandy McAdam was employed at Cardhu distillery in the days before railways gave way to road transport.

'There was a distillery lorry that drove the coal from the Knockando Station to the distillery, and they took the draff back in the lorry, and it went away by rail as well. All the whisky went out by rail too, from Knockando station, where Tamdhu distillery is. What was later used as Tamdhu visitor centre for a while was Knockando station. That went over to Aviemore. Normally it would go to the south by Aberlour, Knockando, Blacksboat, Ballindalloch, Aviemore, and from there down to Dewar's in Perth or Black & White, or whoever it was going to for blending. Two or three times a week there was the "whisky train", which went up country. It was the LNER, from Craigellachie right up to Keith.

'I think there was a lot of pilfering going on from the trains from what I've heard and read. I remember my father once had to go to a court case at Keith because there had been pilfering from the railway. There had been a Cardhu cask and he had to go and identify the cask in court. Somebody had pinched it off the train and then spiled it [i.e. broached it and pegged it].'

According to retired Chivas blender Jimmy Lang (see Chapter 20, 'The Artist'), the customs people always allowed a tenth of a gallon for loss from casks during transit. 'One story that comes to mind concerns Bowmore. The casks would be loaded onto a lorry at Bowmore, and they would be coming into one of the warehouses on the mainland. The Customs men would dip the casks before they left and dipped again when they arrived, and the Customs men with the warehouse receipt used to complain bitterly that things were always too tight on the gauges, and sometimes they were marginally below what they should have been, but it wasn't big enough to take any action.

'Eventually they discovered what had happened. One particular driver used to stop in a lay by and using his wee drill and his spile [a wooden peg or spigot] he would tap the hoop up a wee bit, drill a hole, drain a tenth of a gallon out of the cask, put in his spile, put the hoop back down, and he would do this to maybe ten or twenty casks every time he moved whisky. Until eventually he got caught. Until the casks went to the cooper, nobody would ever see it. I believe they used to do a similar thing on the railways, moving a hoop, drilling a hole to drain whisky, then putting the hoop back.

'I think they began to suspect something was going on, and they eventually found out who the driver was who was regularly low on the gauges. So they got somebody to follow him and catch him at it with the drill.'

Most Excise officers were diligent in their protection of the whisky in their charge, and with experience, they learnt lots of tricks.

Willie Tait is brand ambassador for the Isle of Jura single malt, having formerly served as manager at the Craighouse distillery. According to Willie, 'We had one little Irish Excise officer, always used to carry a small ball about with him. And he'd throw it when the lads were around, and, of course, they'd dash for it and kick it and so forth. And the reason he did this was so that if any of them had a fly bottle in their jacket pockets, it would fall out when they dashed to kick the ball. That's why he carried it!'

Sometimes, however, members of HM Customs and Excise were not above helping themselves, too, says Eric Stephen, 'When it came to taking the stuff out, the excise were the biggest culprits. They always said it was for testing their instruments, but it never came back.'

While talking to Jim McEwan, Ruari MacLeod says, 'I mind a Customs and Excise officer we had at Bruichladdich, he was caught with a bottle right enough. The bottle was in his trousers and suddenly it went upside down some way or another, and all of a sudden the cork came out the bottle, the bottle didn't burst in any way, and his trousers were soaking. He was an unattached officer right enough. And he had to go in to see Mr Mitchell [the senior Excise officer]. And Mr Mitchell had a look at him, and said, "How did that happen to you?" "Ah well," he says, "it's like this," he says, "I was just sampling a cask like that, he says, and the valinch," [a large 'pipette' used for removing samples from casks] he says, "I just turned it around and I thought it was empty, and the whole lot went from there down to there." And that was the end of it. But it was the other way about. It was the cork that came out of the bottle.'

JM: Customs men were the biggest robbers of the lot.

RM: Oh yes, yes.

JM: I remember every Friday afternoon the Customs officer would give me his briefcase, and in his briefcase would be his bottles, and he would just hand the case to me, not a word was spoken. I would go into the warehouse and fill it up with the best from the sherry casks and hand it back. You can be assured if I was filling his bottles I was filling one for myself as well. There was no bloody way ... if he was robbing the queen then I could certainly rob him!'

It was not only whisky that found its way illegally into the hands of the whisky men, either. Archie Ness remembers, 'When I started at Craigellachie it was all coal, the big lumps of coal, it was by the stillhouse, and it always disappeared. Men would take a lump from a load, so management decided to whitewash it. So they white-washed the front of it so nobody could take it without it being obvious. That didn't stop you though, you just went in the back and took some out of there.'

Grant Carmichael says, 'I can always remember at Glenkinchie, a lot of coal disappeared, and in those days everybody had a haversack for their "piece", for their sandwiches, and none of these haversacks went home empty. There were always a few lumps of coal in each one, and off they went home. So much so that the old manager at the time saw so much coal going missing that around the coal itself was built large blocks of coal to make a wall, and it was whitewashed. So if anybody took coal out of it it was noticeable immediately.

'At one time, coal was generally free for distillery workers, unofficially. People on night shift particularly would carry up a little bag of coal for the house, and it was amazing, it happened at all the distilleries, at Lagavulin and Caol Ila in particular, which I was concerned with, I was always having to order new grates for the fires in the houses, and there were a lot of houses. It was because this small coal, this navigation small coal, was so hot that it burnt the cast iron, while normal house coal wasn't so hot. It just went into a clinker and burnt the grates.

'Nowadays you just couldn't get away with it, because there's so many restrictions and so many accurate costings, they'd know just how much whisky would be produced from each ton of coal used. This is quite critical. But in those days it was accepted, and you just wrote it off.'

Ed McAffer stayed on Islay. 'All the boys had bikes, and if you were on the nightshift you'd take a bag of coal out on the handlebars, two of you would push it home. It would be your turn for the coal one night and someone else's the next. It was pitch dark, there were no street lights in Bowmore in those days, so nobody could see who you were. And you could always tell a distillery worker's house because the back had been burnt out of the fire with the heat of the distillery anthracite. It burnt very hot. And you'd find boys on nightshift slipping over the sea wall from the distillery with a bag of peats. They'd sell them in one of the local hotels for a screw-top [bottle of beer] and a half-bottle.'

10

The Enforcer
IRVINE BUTTERFIELD
Retired Exciseman

'I came from a small village called Farnhill, between Keighley and Skipton in Yorkshire, and worked initially in the post office as a counter clerk in Keighley before transferring to Skipton. I was coming up to twenty-one, when one of the men I worked with indicated that as promotion prospects were dependent upon "waiting for dead men's shoes", a finer career was to be had, and suggested the best prospect was in the Customs & Excise service. It was with this mind that I went along to the local office in Skipton where two officers were based, and talked to them about their work. As it seemed like a good job, I took a correspondence course and attended night school to brush up on my maths and English, and then I sat the open examination for the Customs & Excise in 1957.'

'In those days when you eventually got to the top of a lengthy incremental salary scale in the service it paid the magnificent sum of £600 per year, which was the equivalent to an MP's salary. So in those days employment as an officer in HM Customs and Excise was a career in itself.

'As a trainee, you went on the road for a certain period, before you were appointed to a fixed position. Most of us dreaded the thought of going to London, because in those days London covered such a number of posts, a huge number in the Port of London, which was still a massive and thriving dockland. I got 'fixed' in Manchester, doing Purchase Tax, then I moved across to Burnley. After that I went to Edinburgh and finally Perth, where I was based for twenty-odd years until I retired.

'As an "Unattached Officer" I was in a lot of distilleries, including Cameronbridge grain distillery in Fife, Teaninich at Alness up in Ross-shire, Tomatin near

Inverness, and at Highland Park and Scapa in Orkney. I was only in Orkney for three months but I cried when I left because the people were so wonderful and sociable.

'Here, we're talking about the '60s, when I was on the road – you were known as a "UO" – an unattached officer. I was a UO from 1957 to 1966, when I got fixed. There was a Collection in Elgin, one in Inverness, and one in Aberdeen at one time. The Elgin Collection disappeared, and in my day there was just Aberdeen and Inverness. A "collection" was an Excise administrative region.

'As a UO I obtained a transfer to Inverness Collection, and so worked in most of the distilleries north of the Spey, because the Spey was a kind of dividing line between the Aberdeen and Inverness Collections. Dufftown was in Aberdeen, while Rothes was in the Inverness area. I worked in the Rothes area and was there not long after they re-opened Caperdonich distillery in 1965.

'Basically you were on the road as an assistant to the permanent officers, and if you read *The Whisky Distilleries of the United Kingdom* by Alfred Barnard on his visit to Auchnagie distillery at Ballinluig in Perthshire he described the Exciseman's role as "quite a pastoral life", and there was still this kind of magic about it. The young UOs were in receipt of a subsistence, and the object was to try to move fairly frequently so that you got sufficient additional remuneration to keep a car and enjoy a comprehensive social life.

'In the '60s, the Exciseman was thought of as a man of prospects, and as such as a prospective husband quite a catch. You got into the Excise service by an open exam, and there was a minimum standard. If there weren't enough people of that standard, they just didn't recruit a number looked for. It wasn't a case of saying 500 people sat the exam, there was a requirement for a hundred recruits, so the top 100 were taken on. In my year, insufficient numbers met the required standard, so vacancies still existed.

'The first potential for promotion was to supervisor or surveyor as they were called, and this required that you sat an examination. Beyond that, to become an Assistant Collector or Collector, promotion was by a promotional interview board.

'The beauty of the Excise was that whatever your character, whether you were an eccentric or whatever, you always had to work under a supervisor, and whether you liked him or not you respected him for his position. Some of them were quite eccentric, and they all had very individualistic characters. They all worked in an area, termed a District, that was their responsibility.

'From the point of being an Excise officer in a distillery life was pretty straightforward – the rules didn't change much, it was a fairly set pattern. You still had to attend at certain recognised times to open locks so they could move crans

Exciseman Irvine Butterfield (right) with a gamekeeper at Gairnshiel Lodge during the 'Whisky Smugglers' Challenge', 1983. Butterfield led a party of five men and one woman on a 140-mile trek from the Macallan distillery to Perth, following a network of routes once used by whisky smugglers. The trip was sponsored to raise money for the Erskine Hospital. The participants wore period dress and casks of whisky were carried on Highland garrons.

[valves] and examine locked plant and isolate vessels to take account of spirits or feints. All the spirit vessels were under Excise lock and key.

'In a lot of the distillery offices you would find an old chaise longue. I remember the one at Highland Park in Orkney was big, heavy, and leather covered. At one time, during the working season when the wash vessels were locked up, a lot of the unlocking was done during the night, and the officer attended on notice – as it was called – when the distiller said he wished to open locks or crans at a certain time, and the officer had to attend. The officer in those days was provided with a "bed" on site so that he was readily available.

'Most of the furniture in the various distilleries was either Victorian or very early twentieth century, with chaise longues and beautiful bureaux and so on. I suppose, as with so many other artefacts and furniture, it would all just be discarded at some point. Now a lot of the old items from distilleries would be of real interest. The Excise officers' houses were always on a par with those of the managers. Most of them had a room for a maid, because an Excise officer could afford to employ a maid, just like the local minister. When Glenturret at Crieff opened in the late '50s, the owner, James Fairlie, had to provide a house, which was a serious cost to him. Distilleries have sold off a lot of the workers' cottages in many cases, and the Excise officers' houses, too.

'In a lot of rural areas, unless someone wanted them as country cottages there was not much local demand. There's not the farm labourers any more, and even some of the managers and other staff cover vast distances. Just before he retired recently, the senior warehouseman at Blair Athol distillery told me they were covering movements of whisky from Dalwhinnie, which is more than twenty miles away, and a hellish drive sometimes on the A9 in winter.

'When I was there for a time, most of the workers were housed in a hostel. One of the stillmen was a local, and the manager and the Exciseman had houses, but the rest of the staff was made up of several single men – all the odds and sods that nobody seemed to know quite what to do with. "You'll find some of them somewhat strange," the manager warned me. Basically, these boys lived in the hostel, got their food and their washing done, and they seemed to spend most of their time in the pub playing darts.

'Dalwhinnie was some place. We actually had to chip a cask in the warehouse out of the ice one day. The roof had leaked, and the cask to be got out for delivery just happened to be on the top stow below the leak. The lads had the paperwork telling them which cask numbers were needed, and suddenly the cooper came and told me we needed a pick and shovel. I told him to pull the other one, but then I realised he was serious as he took me in to show me. The cask was literally sheathed in ice, absolutely solid like a miniature iceberg.

'When the lads finally managed to hack it out, the spirit sample was so cold we couldn't get a reading on the thermometer. We carried the sample over to the office and put it on the side of the fireplace during our tea-break, and waited until we could get a reading some twenty minutes later.

'One of the things you should remember is that there was often very little entertainment in these country areas. If you were on Speyside there was always Elgin and the Two Red Shoes dance hall, which was known to everybody, and in Orkney there were dances in local halls. These dance halls were almost always in old huts that had been part of wartime encampments, and every one was identical. When you came out of "the hall" it was often very difficult to remember where you were.

'There would be whist drives in rural areas, and when I was at Talisker on Skye it was the days of the Highlands & Islands Film Guild, where you got to show films in places like Carbost village hall. Carbost was miles and miles from any cinema. The Film Guild van went round the Highlands and Islands, to the halls, with all of the film equipment.

'The Exciseman said to me, "Oh, you're a bright lad, you've been going out with all these nurses to the pictures, you can select the films." Actually, I never went to the pictures, but it became one of my tasks. I was instructed that I could choose pretty much what I liked, detective films and so on, but you always had to select one biblical film, Cecil B. de Mille or similar, and must include *Whisky Galore*. The latter was obligatory, and was regarded as an annual performance.

'Before my time in the service, the distilling season wasn't as long as it later became. Here we are talking pre the Second World War, because by the '60s the industry was gearing up – production was increasing by roughly 10 per cent per annum – the start of the big expansion, when it was realised that Scotch whisky was very important from an export perspective, because it was one of the things that still had that cachet abroad – especially in America.

'Gradually during my time in the service the system for locking was changed until latterly, of course, it was just done by the industry's own management. The old system was based on the idea that there was a potential to produce spirit without anybody knowing – introducing an extra mash, for example, with distillation done undetected, so the control was quite tight. As control tightened up on the books side, where managers at distilleries became progressively more beholden to the major companies, yield figures became more important. The companies looked for maximum production, and as an indicative figure used chemical analysis of the grain which told them what the yield ought to be. If the yield wasn't achieved, there had to be a reason, so managers were increasingly under pressure to extract maximum yield and also reduce losses at the time the spirit was filled into casks.

'Gradually the Excise work became that of auditing working and accounting. The managers now move locks and make a note of what they do. Previously the control was more rigid, and even as late as the '60s, it still operated very much like an agricultural industry.

'Then, the industry still had a strong agricultural base. Most of the distilleries still had maltings, for instance, but this area of operation saw the first major change when production went over first to Saladin boxes and then these huge grain preparation plants for malt at Burghead on the Moray Firth and elsewhere. There were a great number of people employed in the malting process at distilleries. I don't know what loss of jobs there has been, but if you took the maltmen from a reasonable-sized distillery you'd have a dozen men, and warehousemen. A lot of distilleries no longer now retain spirit on the premises because, in the case of Diageo, for example, they've opted for centralisation at Menstrie, near Stirling.

'These also led to a huge social change, as it meant that the men who were still retained in the distilleries became fewer in number. But it also meant that the salary structure improved. In fact, some of the managers are now earning more than the Excisemen, which you couldn't have conceived of in the '60s.

'The Exciseman lost a lot of his status when VAT came in. He became, in the public perception, just another civil servant. When I was on Speyside I met D.K. Johnston, always known as 'D.K.' – the father of Russell Johnston, MP for Inverness-shire and leader of the Scottish Liberals. D.K. used to come and visit me when I was at Glen Elgin, as he'd been the previous officer there, and he was fascinating to talk to, because he'd delivered pension books to the island of St Kilda in the 1920s or early '30s, when he was the officer at Lochmaddy in Uist. He'd also been the officer at Talisker and knew much about the Hebrides.

'A lot of Excisemen were very knowledge people. I was at Invergordon when the new grain distillery opened in 1961, and the supervisor, Alan Brockbank, the supervisor for Tain, had been an engineer. He was very interested in the plans of the new distillery, and as a result, he saved them a problem because he realised

Gauging the first cask to be filled at Invergordon distill-ery, July 1961. Irvine Butterfield is the Excise offi-cer, on the left.

they hadn't put a locking point in a part of the pipework, which technically meant they'd got a siphon system built in!

'Because of his engineering knowledge he picked up the error when we asked for and received a copy of the full diagram of the plant. We did a colour-coding of the pipes on the diagram so that we could understand what was happening and how the liquids would flow, because neither I nor any of my colleagues had ever worked in a grain distillery before. We needed to work out which pipes went where and what purpose they served so that effective control could be applied.

'I liked the idea of them opening a distillery somewhere like Invergordon because it brought employment to an area that badly needed it, and it used the sort of skills that men in the area already had. For a time, the maize for distilling the grain spirit came in by rail, and in the early '60s there was a threat that the line might be closed — it was the line from Inverness to Wick — and having this freight maybe helped to keep it open. What many failed to realise was that the railway had first to close a line to freight before it could close it to passenger trains, too.

'The first stillman at Invergordon had previously been a baker's roundsman. He'd not worked in distilleries before, and when they began to do the first distillation the whole plant shook like crazy. Worried, he asked me what I thought was wrong. I told him I wasn't sure, but that I was going to get off the viewing platform immediately because something was obviously wrong and the whole place might blow up. Eventually I conjectured that there was probably not enough water getting through to "balance" the system. They opened a hatch to the cold feints tank and found the feints were boiling. Steam was obviously coming over the top of the still column and into the feints.

'The stillman closed the still down and we eventually discovered that no water was getting through because a ballcock in the water supply tank was rusted up. We also discovered a slight bend in one of the pipes, and the whole still column had obviously been very close to buckling and imploding at the time we shut down the still.

'Quite early on there was a problem with the distillery discharge, which should have been clear water, but wasn't. The Sunday papers got hold of the story that there were drunk swans around the place! A retraction was duly sent to the media as the story suggested bad management of the plant. In reality, the swans were gorging themselves on spent grain and other minor solids.

'Everything got a lot better after a management buy-out took place. The staff supported it and got shares, and as things went well over the years they became worth quite a bit. One old maltman at Tamnavulin distillery, which was also owned by Invergordon Distillers, wanted to buy a modest cottage when he retired, and as far as he was concerned all he had to his name were several five-shilling shares. When someone looked into it for him it turned out he had accumulated additional shares, and with much enhanced value. He was able to sell them and have enough money to buy a new bungalow in the Spey Valley.

'When I was a UO in the north of Scotland, life was still quite simple to be honest, and the digs were some of the best you could wish for. There was a certain cache attached to the landladies, even. They took Excise officers! One landlady in Dufftown had three daughters, and it is said she managed to get them all married off to Excisemen. I don't know whether that was a good thing or a bad thing … but you were likely to have a small car, where a lot of people didn't.

'An important aspect of your life's pleasantries was due to your landladies. They formed a real part of your life. I still write every Christmas to Mrs Smith who used to be at Birnie, at Glenlossie distillery, where her husband was under-manager. She now lives in Elgin. Her charges were modest, and she even did your washing. She was a great one for tattie drottle soup – made with potatoes and, I think, leeks. You got a big breakfast, then you got a piece of cake and a flask for elevenses in the warehouse during the morning. Then you got lunch and finally high tea. You were fed like a fighting cock. They were more friends than landladies.

'The names of good digs were passed on from one officer to another, and you didn't muck your landlady about, because she was part of the whole welfare scenario, and you were to regard yourself as a 'gentleman of the Excise'. They would take an interest in "their" Excise boys, and would ask you, "How's so and so getting on?", who he was courting, which lassie, and so on.

'I don't know how many Excisemen there are based in Elgin now dealing with distilleries – I should think about four at the most. When I was up there there was one at every distillery, plus the unattached officers. In Rothes, for instance, there were two Excisemen at Glen Grant, and two at Glenrothes, one at Speyburn, one at Glen Spey, and Glenrothes and Glen Grant usually had an unattached officer each during the "season". There was a fixed officiator – who was a semi-fixed unattached officer – who covered the leave for a certain number of officers, and he also lived at Rothes during my time up there.

'There was a semi-permanent staff of unattached officers, because in the '60s with the industry gearing up for increased production there were new warehouses being built. A huge new warehouse went in at Glenlossie, near Elgin, and at one stage we were moving 120 casks a day from Glenlossie. We had to dip all the casks, sample the spirit for strength, and work out on a "head rod", the old slide rule, the liquid quantity and the proof quantity in each cask. We'd do 120 in a morning – that was your day's work. The men liked it because they had them all bunged ready for dispatch, and could busy themselves in the afternoon getting the next load ready to go out the following day. These were casks of maturing or mature whisky ready to be transported to the blenders.

'Then with the advent of the Distillers Company Ltd's massive storage ware-house-building programme in the 1960s at Menstrie, the companies were filling the new spirit into casks at the distillery to be trucked straight through to Menstrie. Now, of course, most of it goes through in tankers to places like Menstrie, and the casks never move off the Menstrie site.

'Basically, the control by the distillers was the manager, sometimes with an under-manager who ran the whole show. Under him there were brewers, who saw to the brewing, the mashing. Sometimes they were also nominally in charge of the distillation side, or were linked in to it. There was usually a senior clerk, who took the spirit charges and did the paper work with the Exciseman, and might also check dips and strengths of casks with you.

'The spirit charge is taking the account of the alcoholic strength and the liq-uid amount in the spirit receiver, and computing the total of proof gallons, now litres of alcohol. The distillery manager had to give notice to the Exciseman when he wanted the charge to be taken. When you did a spirit charge you had to lock off and isolate the spirit receiver. You'd lock off the inlet in the closed position, and then after taking account put the outlet on a locking position to allow casks to be filled. The procedure was reversed once the receiver had been emptied.

'The cooper or warehouse foreman was in charge of the warehouse squad, who stored the casks, brought them out ready for delivery, got the samples for the Exciseman, because every cask was dipped and sampled before it moved. Then you'd got the senior maltman on site, with the men under him, responsible for producing the malt.

'Most of these people lived in provided houses, and as a condition of licence the Exciseman also had a house provided by the distiller if the distillery was situat-ed more than three miles outside a market town.

'So within a distillery area you had a sort of self-contained community, where the manager and the Exciseman were the two key people. Obviously, the Exciseman and the manager, if they were sensible, worked hand in hand, so the operation ran smoothly. It suited the Exciseman, because if he could keep the manager's system working he could arrange it so that the men didn't have to go into the warehouse every day, and that on a particular afternoon time could be had to play golf or follow other pursuits.

'By the same token, the Exciseman had to do surveys to cover a full 24-hour

The Glenfarclas Glenlivet Distillery.

cycle during the year – so he'd to go in at two o'clock or three o'clock in the morning at some stage, at random. Although he might get his afternoon off for golf he had to attend at some awkward hours.

'In places on Speyside like Dufftown or Rothes there was quite a community of people attached to this industry, which still had strong connections with the land. I know the grain wasn't usually produced locally by that time – the only distillery I knew that still used local grain was Dalmore, at Alness on the Cromarty Firth — they tended to buy Black Isle grain. The owners of Dalmore were the Mackenzie family, and the director was "HAC" Mackenzie – a senior officer in the Seaforth Highlanders, and as such he had a great authority. Some of the men who worked at the distillery had served in the Seaforths – not necessarily under his command – but there was this family "clan"-type relationship within some of the plants.

'Some distilleries, like Dalmore, were still independently owned – eventually it became part of Whyte & Mackay. There were a few like that, but most even then were owned by the major companies. The Grants of Glenfiddich were always independent of the major groupings, and the Grants of Glenfarclas still are, of course. Bowmore on Islay was still independent, too, and Macallan before it became part of

Glenfarclas distillery, Ballindalloch, early 20th century. Glenfarclas is one of the few remaining Scotch whisky distilleries to be family-owned, having been in the possession of the Grants since 1865.

Highland Distillers. The majority were in the big groups, such as the Distillers Company, with further amalgamations later.

'There was still then, a tendency for quite a few of the distilleries to have a long association with a family or families. There wasn't then the possibility of quite the overall control that there is now. The bigger the groupings, the more control they had to have on their own workforce. There was more independent thought then. People thought, "This is my wee company."

'The distillery I did my training at, Glen Albyn in Inverness, was a twin with Glen Mhor across the road. The Excise officer there was an interesting character. Apparently he'd been a lieutenant colonel in both world wars, so he had a standing other than being an Excise officer. It used to amuse him that the director, Mr Birnie, would introduce visitors to the distillery by using his full title. He'd say something like, 'Oh, we must go and see our Excise officer, Lieutenant Colonel Stanley Hill!' He was well known in and around Inverness, and he drove a white Ford Consul convertible, which was considered very special. He was much liked and well respected by the men.

'They respected him as a person because he had been in the local regiment, and many of the men at the distillery had fought in the war, usually with one of the local regiments, either the Seaforths or the Camerons. Distilling wasn't a reserved occupation, so a lot of them had fought. It added to the aura that attached to the Exciseman, and they attached great store to the fact that they worked at the distillery under his charge.

'They used to say that the three people who made the distillery areas tick were the local minister, the doctor and the Exciseman. That was the kind of social plane he was on. A lot of them played golf and bridge, and some of us went hill walking. Most of them had a talent or interest for which they were known. For example, there was an old bachelor officer in Rothes who used to go off bird-watching at night, and he had a tame pheasant. When you went to act for him when he went on leave the only thing that really mattered were the boxes of seed that were there to feed the pheasant.

'It came to a sad end, however, when an officer who was known as "Bang Bang Willis" came to cover and shot the pheasant. The whole of Rothes was waiting with bated breath for the old officer to come back from leave and discover the pheasant's cause of demise. When he found out what had happened he insisted "that man will never come into this distillery again, I'd rather not go on leave," and neither he did.

'Excisemen were almost always incomers, and often English, but there wasn't usually any resentment, unless they were patronising, and overplayed their hands. Getting drunk was regarded as an occupational hazard – Burns always being cited as an example – but becoming objectionable with it wasn't. You didn't make a nuisance of yourself, and you paid your bills. Not to do so was letting the side down.

'Standard dress for an Exciseman was a Harris tweed jacket and flannels, though some wore plus-fours. Before my time, a lot of even the UOs adopted plus-fours, a tweed jacket, and sometimes a waistcoat. I only met one younger Exciseman who wore plus-fours at times, and there was one Exciseman in Fort William, Charlie Hurry, who worked at Ben Nevis distillery and regularly wore plus-fours and the "fore and aft" cap. He was regarded as being of the old school.

'He commanded respect as the Exciseman because he had quite a difficult job at Ben Nevis. It was one of the distilleries owned by Joe Hobbs, and they were always jumping and changing and on some ploy. He was always looking at ways of saving money and experimenting, and he sold a lot of new spirit to the South Americans. He was likely to turn up and say that he had a client coming and wanted this and that. Charlie Hurry just accommodated him and sorted the paperwork out afterwards, but he was still very much in charge and had to be given respect.

'There wasn't an Excise dress code as such, but there was practicality in that the Harris tweed jacket was very hard wearing, and if you were in a warehouse work-

Glen Albyn distillery, Inverness, 1950s, with the Caledonian Canal in the foreground.

ing you needed to be able to move quite freely. Some officers wore brown or white warehouse coats, but I always found them a bit restrictive, and tended to roll my sleeves up and get on with it. There was no heating in the warehouses, of course, and any heating in the offices was well attended to, because they were paranoid about fire.

'The great thing about the Excise tradition was that setting a precedent was always the point. When, for instance, the Excise service realised that there were a lot of staff tied up in dipping and checking the strength of casks to be sent down to another warehouse, it was a supervisor near Alloa, who was employed at Menstrie, who came up with the idea that if you could get a secure vehicle to transport the casks from warehouse A to warehouse B, you could save all that time dipping and checking strengths. Staffing could be reduced accordingly.

'The vehicles had to be secure, with non-tamper-type seals, and initially they only approved this concession for the conveyance of new spirit, the theory being that people would be less inclined to try to steal the new spirit than the mature stuff.

'A "watcher" [a uniformed officer of minor rank] was set on to check the security of the vehicle. Some of the vehicles had a dual purpose. They went south with whisky and came back north with grain. They were so constructed that they had hoppers in the floor to allow discharge of bulk grain. Having got this facility, the industry was able to go a stage further, and started transporting the mature stuff in the same way.

'Instrumentation such as the rods and the hydrometer had been invented by Excisemen, and the continuous still had been invented by Aeneas Coffey, an Exciseman. There was then a tradition of helping the industry, as well as being a controller of it.

'You were part of an elite group of people and were sometimes seen as such, although you didn't consciously play on it. You were a gentleman of the Excise! You didn't patronise people.

I was a young Exciseman at Hillside distillery, near Montrose, which was silent at the time. I think it had been a small grain still. They had a maltings and also stored grain spirit there.

'From the top warehouse you could see across a field up to the bridge at Kinaber Junction, where the railways used to meet. The LMS route came in from the south by way of Brechin, and the LNER east coast route by Dundee and Montrose. In the days of the "race to Aberdeen" the LMS and LNER trains were timed to arrive at Kinaber about the same time, so the objective was to reach the junction first and secure the priority run forward to Aberdeen.

'From the warehouse door at Hillside you could see the peg on the signals go "off", and the men would have a bet as to which train would get priority clearance. This would be around 1960, and I was then twenty-three or twenty-four years old. One particular day the men were sitting outside the warehouse having a break and a smoke when one peg went up, and then it dropped. Then the other went up, and it dropped. Then it went back up a second time and the train went through. An argument then ensued over the bet, with some of the men saying they'd won because "their" peg had gone up first, and others saying they'd won because "their" train had gone through. It all became quite tense, as there was half a crown at stake.

'The old cooper, Willie Fraser, said, "There's only one way to settle this. We'll ask the Exciseman." I'm sitting there, they were all in their forties or older, but they asked me to be arbiter of the argument, a young and innocent gauger. I said that surely the bet was about the train actually passing the signal, as that was what the race was all about, and so those who'd bet on that were the winners. That was my decision, and to my amazement everybody accepted it. The Exciseman had taken the decision and it had to be right, such was their trust in your judgement.

'You'd do a survey at least once a day during the distilling season. You'd check the gravities of the washbacks to see how the fermentation was going, you'd check mashing times, collection of wash, stills operation and the collection of spirit charge. When the stillman filled the wash still he had to record the quantity of wash going into the still, and you'd check his declaration and the time it was made. As the work followed a pattern you were able to identify if working practices had any abnormal features which could mean problems.

'One of the jobs on a survey was to check the pipe work. You might not check it all, but you'd have to designate on your "line of survey" what you'd done. The sample safe was always recognised as being the most vulnerable, and where you had lengths of pipes joined with flanges, the bolts to the flanges were often burred over so that they could not be opened. Some had a small box fitted round them with a lock on the box, so that if the box was taken off the flanges could be accessed. Some distillers preferred that method of securing flanges because it was easier to deal with in an emergency. When doing a survey you were looking for places where people might interfere with the pipework to try to extract spirit. Obviously you didn't want people drilling holes in the soft copper pipes. You had to look at the plant and think, "If I was going to get spirit out how would I do it?" If anyone could extract spirit in any quantity, they had the potential to sell it, of course, because it was a very marketable commodity, even if it was clearic [new spirit].

'When I went to Talisker on Skye they had just completed refurbishment of the distillery after a fire. The Exciseman there suspected something was going on, because a butt [a cask of approximately 110 gallons content] had disappeared from the cooperage. As the officer knew I'd been involved previously in incidents in Rothes where I'd discovered a way of extracting spirit from the plant, I was the "wee smart guy" who was going to find out what was happening at Talisker.

'The Exciseman said to me, "If they've stolen a butt they're into something big." A butt held 110 gallons, remember! So the challenge was to find where this "leak" was. I looked at the plant and I never did find it, but after I left someone else discovered it. They'd found one of the nuts on a flange slightly different to how it had looked on a previous survey. They thought "the boys" had been disturbed while extracting spirit, and had been in a hurry to put the nut back in the proper position. They'd been collecting spirit in a bucket, and the officer suspected they had probably dumped it in a washback and had just had time to get rid of the evidence. They always had somebody on lookout.

'The ploy I did discover at Talisker was in the filling store, where there was a remnant cask, known as a stock cask. When you filled whisky to casks you never got the last cask completely full, so the stock cask, a butt, held the remnant each time. The quantity in it gradually built up, and at some stage after you'd filled a cask off the vat, it was filled by using a pump from the remnant to top it up. The pump was a barrel on a stand, with a pipe coming out of either end, one to go in the remnant or stock cask, the other to the cask being filled up to full. The pump was operated by a hand lever and was very simple. The operation occurred probably every second filling.

'This particular day casks were being filled, and I was standing outside, watching the men taking the casks out of the filling store down to the warehouses, and I was stood by the hand pump, which they had taken outside. They always took it outside, and I thought this was so that they could get the casks out more easily, but there was actually plenty of room up the side of the vat.

'Then it dawned on me. On the bottom of the barrel on the pump was a nice little brass tap. I stood with my back to it, and reached behind me and twisted it. I heard this trickle of liquid and as that was happening one of the men came past and realised that I'd rumbled their little ploy.

'The men were able to get a good half bottle at least by draining the pump barrel. The warehouse operative didn't say anything, but I said to him,"'Aye, Donald, you've got to be gey old to teach a gauger new tricks." He just looked at me, and after that they very purposefully carried the pump into the corner of the filling store and opened the tap and drained it into the stock cask.

'This sort of trick on the men's part wasn't a major thing. It was a bit of a game of cat and mouse really. There was a challenge for them in getting some of the stuff really. But you have to remember that in those days these people were not paid big wages. You wouldn't bother even thinking about it now because they get good wages.

'I said that when I went to Talisker I'd previously been involved in cases where spirit had been disappearing while I was based in Rothes. One was when I was at Glen Elgin it was just coming up to New Year. The men used to clean the sample safe to remove small solids in the feints coming across. and they used to clean the sight glasses. In the safe there were two compartments. The one where the bowls where, for low wines and feints, and spirit, usually had a big pane of glass.

'Usually the pane of glass sat in a small trough, and was held in a slide on either side. The actual pane of glass itself held at the top immediately under the bottom of the lid. Although you could lift the glass out to wash and clean it, the upper part was obscured behind a large area of brass at the top of the window. The trick was to substitute the glass with a bit that was smaller, so that you could push it up with your hand and get in under the lower part of the raised glass. To disguise any slackness in the glass a couple of matchsticks were placed in the troughs at the sides to jam it in place. The Exciseman would check it by putting the flat of his hand against the glass to check it didn't move. If it rattled you knew something was up.

'On this occasion the men cleaned it and very obligingly shut the lid, put the locking bar in place, and finished it all off while I was finishing up the paperwork in my office. Later on, going round doing a survey, I checked it and the glass moved up. So I was straight into the manager's office and said he'd better come and see for himself. I told him that they'd obviously done it when they'd cleaned the safe, and he said, "Oh God, they're not up to that old trick are they?" They'd obviously got their own piece of glass and put it in.

'The manager then had to put in an Excise notice to open the safe, because a new piece of glass of proper size couldn't be put in without opening the top of the safe, which was locked. To unlock the safe the manager has to give a reason to the Excise for opening it. The "notice" was to advise the officer of a need to open a lock, in this case that to the sample safe.

'You could get a blocked nozzle where the samples came out, and I seem to remember that I was kind to the manager, and we put that down as our reason for opening the safe. But I told him that it really wasn't on, not even at New Year!

'Most distilleries gave the men a dram at least once a day, and a blind eye was certainly turned to the practice. Some gave them cleric, and I never liked that because it did contain impurities that aren't good for you. The old coopers used to "grog" casks, that is put water into them to get the last drop of whisky out, and eventually they tended to go a bit "odd" as a result. I used to prefer to give the men mature stuff. Usually you would get it at the time they drew samples for the dispatches [casks leaving the warehouse]. At most distilleries the men got a dram, it was traditional.

'At Glen Elgin just before New Year one of the lads came to me and said, "Is there any chance of getting a bit of spirit for the pheasant?" I looked at him, and he assured me that it really was for the pheasant, and he only needed a wee drop of clearic. I was intrigued, so I let him take a drop, and later in the day I caught him plucking a brace of pheasants. I asked him what had happened, and he explained that he soaked some grain in the whisky then scattered it behind the distillery. "The pheasants come out and eat it, and they're too drunk to fly. Then 'wallop' with a shovel. Lovely for Hogmanay!"

'Whisky was often a kind of currency, and one fisherman I met on Speyside decided he wanted to get the best fishing on the river. He asked some locals in the pub who would be the right person to ghillie for him, show him the best spots to fish and so forth. They gave him a name and said that if he gave the ghillie a half-

Talisker distillery, Carbost and Loch Harport, with the Cuillin Hills in the background, early 1960s. Photo taken by Irvine Butterfield while serving at Talisker distillery.

bottle of whisky he'd be sure to show him the best pools. The angler thought let's make sure we do really well, and bought a full bottle instead. The ghillie didn't seem too pleased when he handed it over, which surprised him a bit, and he had a very poor afternoon's fishing. That evening he told the locals in the pub about it, and that it hadn't gone well. "We told you to give him a half-bottle," they said. "That's the problem. While you're fishing he goes along to the distillery at Carron after drinking the half-bottle and gets it filled up by one of his pals who works there. A full bottle won't fit through the distillery railings."

'I'd have to say that drink could be a problem for managers and Excisemen alike. You'd often be living in remote areas with not much else to do except work, and you had the ability to get hold of the stuff, let's face it. The best advice I ever had was from an old Exciseman at Teaninich, at Alness on the Cromarty Firth. He used to say never drink before lunchtime and always take water with it.

'Derek Hickman, the Exciseman at Talisker on Skye, was a bit of a wag, and he had the original Board of Excise order from the 1880s, which stated that the men were to be given two wine glasses of the new spirit per day. He had it on display on the mantelpiece in the Excise office, along with something which he used to taunt the manager with. This was an injunction to the Excise officers that they should not consort with brewers and other low-class persons.

'The manager was from Edinburgh, which was a bit unfortunate, because in the islands Edinburgh was seen pretty much the same way that London was. He had very red hair and a distinctive accent that might be regarded as posh. If he and Derek had an argument about anything, Derek always pointed to the notice and reminded him that he shouldn't even be consorting with the likes of "brewers and other low-class persons".

'The men at Talisker had their own way of working, which you just couldn't change. When they took the casks into the warehouse there was a slight incline up to the door. They always stopped at the door, not that there was any real reason to, but they always did. On one occasion the young under-manager came dashing past, and said, "Come on, lads, come on, we must get on," and hurried into the filling store.

'I heard some muttering in Gaelic from the men, and it was clear they weren't very pleased. I told the Exciseman when I went in for coffee and he said that it would be interesting to see what happened, because they would never normally talk in Gaelic if you were stood there.

'The wee bus came up from Glenbrittle to take the boys away to Portnalong, as some of them lived locally, and at four o'clock when they knocked off all the men were stood in the yard, they didn't get into the bus at all. The

Exciseman and I were looking down from our office above the yard, and the men wanted to see the manager. The Exciseman pointed out to me that the boys from Portnalong all had crofts, which provided their bread, and that the distillery was their jam. They could live without jam.

'He said, "You'll notice that the ones standing at the back are mostly from the island of Harris, and they live in the provided houses. They have to be seen to be supporting their mates, but it's a bit dodgy because they are in the tied houses."

'Well, the manager appeared, and they told him they weren't happy that the under-manager had been up rushing them around, and was he not happy with what they were doing? In their eyes the under-manager was only doing what the manager had told him, so they were really having a go at him.

'He did a bit of a grovelling act, blaming it all on head office, saying they didn't understand how things worked there, don't take it too much to heart. He then suggested they go into the cooperage where they had their dram, and they all got another dram to keep them happy.

'They had the manager tied up a bit, because Derek said that if it was harvest time they would sometimes play up a bit because they wanted to get the harvest in, and they knew that the distillery couldn't operate without them. Skye was exceptional. Talisker was kept going in part I believe because it had a name, because it was certainly a remote location.

'I was at Talisker as an unattached officer, during the winter, in the early '60s, and I stayed in digs on a croft at Drynoch. Normally you'd have stayed in the local pub, probably, but I couldn't stay in the wee inn at Carbost because Excisemen were persona non grata. The reason was that the Irishman Maurice Walsh had written the popular novel *The Key Above the Door* during the 1930s, and he was an Exciseman. He had links with Talisker, and he'd stayed at the inn, and in the story there was an Irishman, who was based on a real Irishman who had been an Exciseman at Talisker and had bottled a grass snake and an adder in whisky.

'They were on the mantelpiece still in the office at Talisker when I was there. In the book, Maurice Walsh made some derogatory remark about the table linen in the inn, and although he didn't say it was Carbost, people knew it was Carbost, and for that reason the Excisemen were not welcome to stay there. By the time I was there, the Excise supervisor was allowed to stay at the inn, because so much time had passed since the book was written, but Excise officers still weren't accepted.

'Maurice Walsh and Neil Gunn were the best-known Excisemen in the north, because of the books they'd written. Neil Gunn was a real connoisseur of whisky as well as an Exciseman, and wrote a book called *Whisky & Scotland*, which is still in print today. Maurice Walsh, at the time of the split when they set up the Free State in 1921, went back to Ireland. Officers were given the option of staying on in the Free State if they wanted, and he stayed in Dublin.

'When the government introduced non-contributary pensions in the 1920s, it was the Excisemen who were involved, because in many areas of the Highlands and islands they were the only people on the ground. I mentioned D.K. Johnston and St Kilda. They did dog, gun and game licences, too. The Excisemen was the only government official in many places. They even did port work in places like Stornoway on behalf of the Board of Trade. If there was new legislation to be introduced, then the Excise officers were often the only government officials in many of the remoter locations, and were best able to implement it.

'In the days when there were more people employed in distilleries and few people had cars, the communities around distilleries were very strong. They relied on each other, and when they did get cars they learnt how to service them and work on them themselves, because they were often a long way from any garage. Just as they would be able to fix pieces of agricultural machinery with anything to hand.

'There are still a lot of Ferguson tractors in the Highlands that are operational. Some of the cars were very old, but then they did very small mileages really. We did what were considered big mileages in those days. You could be in Wick, then move across to Skye or down Inverness way, or Fort William, and then right across east to Elgin.

'Elgin was quite a centre for us, because you'd got several distilleries near Elgin, as well as all the rest of the Speyside distilleries round about. You had Miltonduff, Glen Moray, Linkwood, then Coleburn, Glenlossie, Glen Elgin, and the Rothes foursome.

'And you'd be in touch with your mates across in Dufftown, and all up the Spey valley. Socially there used to be a meeting every Thursday night at the Fiddichside Inn, near Craigellachie, and one of the boys would play piano and you'd sing and have a pint or two.

'The first distillery I ever worked at was Edradour, near Pitlochry, and that was a special place for me, I suppose. Geordie Warren was the manager, and he was a gem of a man. When you were at Edradour you were assisting the officer in Pitlochry, who was based at Blair Athol distillery. Edradour operated on such a small scale that if you forgot to put the sample back into the cask when you were taking the account you'd end up with what was technically a chargeable loss, because the amount of whisky being made was so small.

Edradour distillery, 1980s.

'You could see everything at a glance at Edradour, and Geordie Warren took the time and the patience to explain what was happening. There were just three operatives, and the skill was that they used to have fires under the stills then, and they would damp the fires down at night. They would be running on spirit, and it would just be dribbling through, and the vapours were just coming over the top. It should have been very good whisky when it matured because distillation certainly wasn't a hurried business.

'You knew you were good at your job when you could calculate what the dip should be in the spirit receiver and what should be happening at any given time of night. Then you'd go in and do your night survey, and it was quite satisfying if you'd calculated it right, because you were talking about being to within about a tenth of an inch on the dip in the spirit receiver.

'Being small the place had a bit of magic about it, with the romance of it having the smallest still in Scotland, and even the question of whether it was really legal. The minimum content, I seem to remember, had to be 500 gallons. If you filled the Edradour low wines and spirit still right up to the hatch it would just about be 500, but it was pretty close.

'On Wednesday when they did the filling [of casks] you were invited down to the manager's house and his wife made tea and home-made scones, and gave you all the local gossip. Some of the boys used to have fishing rods and would go out and catch wee trout in the burn that runs through the distillery.

'From the Exciseman's point of view it was an easier place to work things out than in somewhere larger, particularly somewhere with banks of stills like Tomatin in Inverness-shire, which had 10 or 11 stills in the 1960s, and eventually 23 in 1974.

'You learnt a lot about how whisky-making actually worked at Edradour, which was a very valuable grounding. Geordie Warren must, I think, have taught more Excisemen how a distillery worked in practice than anybody else I've ever met. He was from a proper distilling family – one of his brothers was at Ben Nevis in Fort William and the other at Lochside in Montrose.

'At Edradour they had a wee chap called Jock McArthur who was the only one who could really get into the spirit still properly to clean it. Kenny, the other lad, was too tall. It worked like clockwork, and you learnt about the potential problems, what could go wrong with the wash, for example, if you got wild yeast.

'I was sent to Dewar's in Perth in the mid '70s. There were seven officers when I first went there, two clerks and seven "watchers", and in the end staffing was just myself as senior officer, an executive officer, and a clerk. That was at Inveralmond, and the company also had warehousing in Glover Street in Perth which was used for cask storage. Eventually they sold it to the town for a pound and it got knocked down and the site was redeveloped.

'The chap who got the demolition contract made a fortune. The old warehouse had a slated roof, and the floor was thick pitch pine, which was worth a lot of money too. They reckon he made as much out of that wood as he got paid for the demolition.

'I retired just before they closed Inveralmond in 1990. The place was a blending and bottling plant, and was designed to handle three and a half million cases of whisky per year, and sometimes it was doing 4.2 million. Latterly, it was bottling Claymore and all sorts of other things besides the Dewar's brands.

'At one time, of course, part of the Excise officer's work was trying to catch illicit distillers. Even as late as the 1930s, one of the Perthshire Excise officers was still allowed time to look for illicit stills. Surprisingly, there was no such work allocated to Speyside and Glenlivet. Who knows, there might still be a drop or two of the stuff being made even to this day.'

I I

The Rebel
'D'
Illicit Distiller

'D' is a retired farmer and former distillery worker, now in his late seventies. He is one of the last illicit distillers in north-east Scotland. A senior figure in the distilling industry on Speyside, a distant relation, offered the following anecdote about him.

'"D" worked at ———— distillery and had a croft. He took clearic when he was working on the night shift and dark grains for his cattle. He reckoned three drums of clearic would last him four weeks. One morning he was leaving the distillery at the end of the night shift when Jimmy, who drove the draff wagon, came back in and said, "Don't go round by such and such road, the bobbies have got a roadblock up, a full roadblock, there must be a prisoner escaped from Peterhead jail or some such."

'Well "D" had had a few drams at work like, and he'd face anything, so off he goes, his usual way home to his croft, along the road, and he comes to the roadblock. And Alistair, the local bobby, puts his hand up to stop the van. Now here's "D", way over the limit, no licence, no tax, no insurance, probably a couple of bald tyres, two squash containers full of clearic, and stolen dark grains in the back of the van. Then Alistair sees who it is, and he says, "Ach, it's you "D", on you go." Now that's what I call community policing!'

'I use four stone of malt, which I steep in an oak barrel which I use as a mash tun. First I use 40 gallons of water at 140 degrees and leave it to steep for one hour, then I draw off the sweet worts and put it into another tub, while I fill the mash tun again with another 40 gallons of water, this time at 180 degrees. Again I leave it to steep for an hour, draw it off and add a final 40 gallons of water – this last lot of water has to be boiling like mad before it is added, then it is left to steep for another hour. Then I add 10 tins of baker's yeast and leave it for 48 hours before putting the mash into my still.

'I use a copper water tank with a pipe at the top, which is attached to a copper coil with about four rounds in it, kept in a tank of cold water, as the worm. I put the still inside an old-fashioned boiler to lift it off the ground so you can get a fire underneath. I burn anything on the fire, but nowadays I suppose you could do it better with gas, because you'd have more control.

'Next I bring the stuff in the still to the boil – you have to watch the fire carefully and as soon as it comes to the boil I shut the fire down until the spirit starts to run through the worm, which can take around an hour. If it boils too hard, the spirit comes off black – the slower it is boiled the better the whisky. After the spirit is running, you can start up the fire again slowly. As the spirit comes out, it comes in small bursts – it's a bit like a man having a pee.

'The worm is kept in a tank of cold water that is always flowing in and out at the same rate to keep it cool – and the worm has to be at least a foot away from

the still to stop it getting heated by the fire, and it has to be lower than the still.

'What I take off is about four gallons of feints. Then I empty the still and put the feints back into it and bring it back to the boil, which takes about half an hour as it boils real quickly with only the four gallons in it. You need to make the second lot run slowly too. When it starts dripping away I catch the drips in a plastic bowl. Then I take the strength by putting some in a plastic tube and using a hydrometer. The first wee while it comes off at 120 degrees, then it goes to 100 degrees and then it goes down to 70 degrees – then after that it is spent lees, which you have to throw away as it's poisonous.

'Unless I want to keep some to drink myself at 100 degrees, I mix the spirit up at about 80 degrees, which is a fine dram. When at 100 degrees it is real strong – I can drink it but most people put a suppy water in it as it is too strong. I usually drink it as it is and take a drink of water after to cool the throat a bitty.

'I bottle the whisky in lemonade bottles as plastic containers may taste it a bit – and it might melt them. I drink it straight away and never put it in a cask as there's not enough for that. The most I can make is around two gallons of whisky which equals about twelve bottles from the four stone of malt. I put the spent lees down the burn. At one time of day I would make a batch during the winter and another batch in springtime – but it has been four years since I made any.

'I learned to make the whisky myself – when I was working at the stills. I asked the mashman how much malt, how much water, what temperatures he used and then worked it out on a scaled down version for the four stone of malt.

'It takes about a week from the start of getting ready and mashing. I bruise the malt using an old-fashioned agricultural bruiser to grind the malt before it goes into the mashtun. I got the malt from the stills where I worked by telling them it was for my hens. The stills now can't make whisky like I do – it is better than any of their clairich [new make spirit].

'When I was working at the stills, you got drams given to you when you went to work each day, and at other times if there was any hard job that needed doing. But we also tapped into the still's pipes where the clairich came off and I would fill up a plastic container for myself and one for the man who supervised me while he kept a look out.

'Once a delivery boy came to the still to warn me not to set off on the road home as I was taking a container of spirit with me, and I had a van full of cattle pellets which I'd taken for my cattle. He said the police were waiting for me on the road just outside town. But I'd had a few drammies at work that day so I said to hell with them, they won't stop me. And sure enough I passed the police car waiting at the end of the road, and I was driving with the spirit held between my feet, but I just waved at them and drove passed and they didn't stop me – they were waiting for someone else.

'My sister-in-law was married to a policeman and one time they came to stay with us and I was in full production. I told him to come outside to the shed as I'd something to show him, and he was amazed and said I could be done just for having a still, never mind making the whisky. But he said he wouldn't say anything – and he took a bottle of it home with him.

'One of my neighbours knows I can make whisky and he's always asking me to show him before it's too late and I'm too old. He's seen my set-up and offered to make some refinements as it's hard work how I do it, with pails and that. He wants to put in some more bits of pipe so there won't be so much lifting. But we can't get the malt so easy now and my wife doesn't like me making it in case I get into trouble.'

12

On Distilling Communities

Due to the factors that influence their location, including a plentiful supply of pure water, many malt whisky distilleries are to be found in comparatively isolated places. In the days when distilleries employed substantial numbers of staff and personal transport for distillery workers was limited to bicycles, true communities grew up around distilleries.

Today, there are fewer members of staff in distilleries to create a community, and with almost every one of the whisky men owning a car, they and their families do not always want to live onsite in remote places, often too far from shops, schools, and other services.

One of the more remote Speyside distilleries is Cardhu, situated on the slopes of Mannoch Hill at Upper Knockando. Sandy McAdam was born in Cardhu.

'My father had 44 years with SMD [Scottish Malt Distillers, the malt distillery operating subsidiary of DCL]. He lived in a house at the distillery, so I was born to the business. I started in 1948, just before my sixteenth birthday at Cardhu, in the cooperage. My father was cooper and warehouseman.

'I lived at the distillery, and it was a community in itself. Everybody in the houses was at the distilling. We had a good relationship, everybody worked together and was close. Everybody had their gardens, grew their own produce. There were ten cottages at that time, and in 1948 the council built some more houses on the road up to Cardhu. They were supposed to be for agricultural workers, but there wasn't the call for so many by that time with farming getting more mechanised, so they started to let them out to other people, and some distillery workers got some of them.

'In the late '40s they did build what we called "The Bothy" at Cardhu, which was a lodging house for single men, with a woman cooking for them and that. It's still there, it's a house now. It was never really used much at Cardhu, and after a time an employee went into it as a house.

'Cardhu was quite remote. Employees used to cycle quite a bit before we got distillery transport, maybe from Archiestown to Cardhu [about three miles]. They'd to be there for six o'clock in the morning, summer or winter. The snow never stopped you from getting to work the way it seems to now. And you got a lot of snow in those days up around Cardhu. It blocked the roads but it never stopped you getting to work, and it never stopped the whisky getting out.'

Even more remote than Cardhu is Tomatin distillery, which stands close to the A9 Perth – Inverness road, 16 miles south of Inverness. According to assistant manager Sean Smith, the distillery still owns 30 houses on site, and most of the 44 current staff members live in the company houses. 'There's still a real sense of community here, of family, and there are family connections, with fathers and sons working in the distillery, and so on.'

Cardow (Cardhu) distillery staff, 19th century.

Ian Millar

Stuart Duffy is a former Tomatin worker.

'I started off at Tomatin distillery, I was there for about five years. I started off in the warehouse and then moved into the tun room and mashing. My family's from Aberdeenshire, so there wasn't any local connection, it was just a job. I started about 1967, thereabouts.

'At Tomatin I lived in one of the houses. There were twenty-something houses in a row. Tomatin was so isolated you were only there to make money, on a seven days a week thing. So as soon as they cut you down to five days, it wasn't worth it, and I left. I used to work seven days a week, fifty-two weeks a year. You never even stopped for Christmas. You'd only do that for the money. Grantown-on-Spey, Aviemore, Inverness, they were your nearest towns. At that time my family was young, and it was just a case of trying to make a bit of money.

'It was a close-knit community. All you had was a pub at the end of the road, and there was a big party there usually every Saturday night, and then back to somebody's house. They didn't have that many staff, because Tomatin was automated even then.'

Although many distilleries are situated in comparatively isolated locations, certain towns and villages developed into centres for distilling, such as Dufftown and Rothes on Speyside, which still boast ten working distilleries between them. In places like Dufftown and Rothes there was a common working experience, and a valuable pool of knowledge and expertise.

According to Dufftown-based malt distilleries manager Ian Millar, 'Speyside is *the* centre of Scotch malt whisky. All the "greats" are in Speyside – Glenfiddich, Glenlivet, Glen Grant, Macallan, Glenfarclas, Balvenie. The concentration of whisky distilleries in one area is hugely important to the local economy. In Dufftown you still have six working distilleries in a small town of 1,700 inhabitants. You could say that whisky is "in their blood", and you would be right, literally.

'Pittyvaich, Parkmore and Convalmore are now closed, but Dufftown, Mortlach, Glendullan, Glenfiddich, Balvenie and Kininvie are all still prospering. The industry is less labour-intensive nowadays, with developments in technology through the years, but the whisky industry remains a source of employment for many families.

'Dufftown has successfully fought off many young pretenders to the title of "whisky capital". New Year is always "toasted in" with a dram supplied by Glenfiddich at the Square. The folk in Speyside are very positive, outgoing and humorous, generous with their time and always happy to share a dram with you. As I've said, it's in their blood.'

Ian Millar is a comparative newcomer to Dufftown, but fellow Grants employee Dennis McBain is a true native of the place.

The oldest surviving part of Tomatin distillery, with the stillhouse on the extreme left, the mash house in the centre, and the malt barn to the right.

'I've lived in Dufftown all my life, and I really don't think it has changed all that much. Glenfiddich made a big difference when they opened the visitor facilities. A lot of people now visit Dufftown, it's gained a lot of publicity, which I'm sure has helped the shopkeepers and other local businesses as well. Should the stills close for any reason it would just be a ghost town. They employ a lot of people still really, and they employ a lot of local tradespeople as well. Dufftown's got a bit bigger, there are more houses, but it's still a quaint little town.

'There's still plenty of talk about distilling in the place, and there's a bit of rivalry, because we have Diageo with stills in Dufftown, and Chivas are just up Glenlivet and in Keith. Willie Grant's lads say they make the best whisky and Chivas' lads say they do, and Diageo's lads disagree with them both. There used to be some quite heated arguments in the pubs as to who was making the best. Theirs was rubbish and yours was the best, and that still goes on in the pubs in the town. But it's all friendly enough really.

'In the old days, visitors would be amazed how quickly the distillery lads got drunk in the pubs, but they'd maybe had five drams during their shift, particularly if they'd been doing dirty jobs, and it didn't take much beer after that to get them drunk. I don't think there were any accidents due to dramming, but you'd find a bicycle in the bushes sometimes. A lad could get his body home, but not the bike and his body!'

Contrary to what Dennis McBain says about Dufftown remaining largely unaltered, his former Grants colleague Derek Spark thinks that Dufftown's changed a lot since he was young. 'For a start I can say I used to know everybody, but now I don't ken everybody, it's grown quite a bit, new houses being built, and with regionalisation, people apply for a council house in Rothes and they'll maybe get one in Dufftown.

'The distilleries themselves have cut the staff, compared to Grants. The other distilleries, there's very few work at them now compared to the old days. The likes of Mortlach distillery, somebody commented the other month that there used to be something like 53 worked there and there's only three now on a shift.

'There's been quite a lot of times that the shopkeepers in the town have been very worried, but with this influx of folk it's not so bad. The population used to be between 1,500 and 2,000, just. I wouldn't imagine it would be that much different, the population, because when I was young there were big families. Now there's certainly none of the big families that there was. When I was young they had the Territorials, they haven't got that now. I was never in the army, but I did three years in the Territorials, just for my own benefit.

'There's not maybe a lot to do for youngsters, but that's not much of a change. Though there used to be quite a prominent youth club in Dufftown, the local minister at that time, Dr Steven, he and his wife were very good and kept the youth club going for years. They still have dancing, old-time dancing and Scottish country dancing. They come from all over the North-east to go to the dancing, and they have the whisky festivals, of course.

'The atmosphere isn't the same. This element of drugs creeps in, creeps in everywhere. And the pubs in my day were all busy, you had live music every week. We had dances nearly every weekend at the British Legion Club, in my young days. We had variety clubs came to give concerts and that, the likes of Sydney Devine and Joe Gordon and Sally Logan would perform, but we still go down to the Legion on a Saturday night and it's dead now. At one time of day you'd to fight to get a seat. The Masons Arms up in Conval Street, aye had live music. If you didn't go down about half-past seven you were standing like. There's none of that now. It's certainly a different lifestyle now. I've a tin of beer in the house every night, at one time of day when I was making money I was going down the town every night for a couple of pints or maybe more.

'At that time of day a lot of the guys in the pubs had the whisky industry in common, but now such a lot of the youngsters have to go out of the town looking for work. Some of them work in Aberdeen and that. My own son-in-law works in Aberdeen, and he gets up at five, he leaves before six, and he's never home till about quarter to eight at night, so he's no social life through the week.

'There's no darts league now, at one time of day they were producing teams no problem. Now they can't even get one team out of each pub. What Dufftown seems to have lost over the years is the community spirit. If the old-timers that were in the pubs when I was young were to see them now they'd see an awful change.'

Dufftown, from East

Valentines

If places such as Dufftown are sometimes thought to have lost much of their community spirit, even in these days of satellite television and internet communications, islands tend to engender a special sense of community.

The largest and most southerly of the Inner Hebrides, Islay has been settled since the Middle Stone Age, and whisky made on the island has been noted since at least the late eighteenth century for its individuality of flavour.

Islay produces the most distinctive of all single malts, and currently boasts eight working distilleries. The 'make' of the Islay distilleries is in great demand by

Dufftown from the east, with Dufftown and Mortlach distilleries on the left, undated.

blenders, but the last couple of decades have also seen a dramatic increase of interest in the island's single malts.

Although the eight distilleries of Islay are scattered remotely around its shoreline, there remains a sense of camaraderie between both members of staff and members of management on the island that is more elusive on the mainland.

Grant Carmichael is a former DCL Islay general manager. 'There's always a tremendous atmosphere amongst the distillery workers here. There was no rivalry. There was a rivalry in the marketplace, but on the production side, living in the islands, it was different. And it's still the same. Everyone will promote everybody else's whisky for them. As long as it's Islay whisky people go for, we are quite happy.

'It's not the same among the marketing guys, but on the island it's always been a very relaxed atmosphere, and we'll help each other out. There's a relaxed relationship between distillers on the island, they're all in the same position. I always say if you can run a distillery on Islay you can run one anywhere.

'We used to take yeast in liquid form from the mainland, though nowadays the breweries all compress their yeast, and the different distilleries would all take their turn at sending a lorry down to the pier to pick up the yeast when it came in, and then drop it off at the various distilleries around the island. That sort of thing. Women would come in when they knew the yeast had just arrived at the distilleries, and would come get a handful, just a few ounces, for making bread.'

The Isle of Jura distillery was originally established around 1810, but fell silent little more than a century later. It was rebuilt between 1960 and 1963, and is now owned by Whyte & Mackay Ltd. Manager Mickey Heads notes, 'All the managers of the Islay and Jura distilleries are automatically members of the "Condenser Club", which meets for dinner once a year. If any of us have a problem with a piece of plant or whatever, the others are always very good at helping out, loaning equipment until we get it fixed, or whatever.

Grant Carmichael came to Islay in 1962, as assistant manager at Lagavulin and Caol Ila.

'I was based at Caol Ila. The distilling industry then employed, or was responsible for feeding and clothing, about a quarter of the population of the island. Each distillery would employ between 30 and 40 people, because in those days you turned the malt by hand. All of the stills were hand-fired, and you also needed men, of course, for emptying the "puffers".

'So distilling employed a lot of people. The population of the island at that time would be about 4,000. It's down to 3,000 now. That's the difference of 40 years. I reckon the whisky industry employed directly 250 people in distilleries, and

The Tower from Conval Street, Dufftown.

A.2472.

given an average family of four that's a thousand people, a quarter of the population, not taking into consideration the number of people who were employed as drivers, in maintenance, and even supplying the distilleries with all the services. So distilling at that time was really responsible for at least 50 per cent of the economy of Islay.

'Historically, the island's economy has always been based on agriculture and whisky, but whisky at that time was on the up. It's a different kettle of fish nowadays. The distilleries employ so few people that they are not contributing to the economy to the same extent. They are in as much as people are paid more, and have got more disposable income, but the population has gone down accordingly. The same has happened in agriculture. There are far fewer people employed, and farmers now have to have two or three farms to be viable.

'Fishing boats came in to Islay, and all the distilleries had piers, there was a pier at Ardbeg, at Lagavulin, a pier at Bruichladdich, and one at Bunnahabhain. A lot of the fishing boats would come in, and it was the old barter system, they would tie up, and the crew would have a dram, of course, and a lot of the boats had the equivalent of a Rayburn on board, it was coal-fired. So they would get a few bags of coal to keep the stove going, and in return they would put a box of fish ashore, and this would happen in the middle of the night. They might just call in and see the stillman

The clock tower, Conval Street, Dufftown, c. 1936. Formerly a jail, the clock tower was also reputedly at one time the audacious location of an illicit still.

and leave this box of fish. And it was the night shift's job when they finished at six in the morning to take that fish round every house in the village, so when people got up in the morning there was fish lying at the door for them.

'And we used to get great scallops the same way, when the Isle of Man boats started coming over in the '60s to get scallops they would work in threes, and when they had a load, one of them would go back with it to the Isle of Man. The Isle of Man boats would come in and tie up at the distillery, use the showers there and have a dram as well, then come in with a bucket of scallops.

'It was then that a lot of the local people saw the opening, and with the help of an HIDB grant – the old Highlands & Islands Development Board – there were a lot of boats bought. It was the Isle of Man boats coming in that started the industry off. Before that it had all been line fishing in the lochs as a hobby or lobster fishing. It doesn't employ a lot of people, but it does employ people who might have been employed in distilling, so it's taken up some of the slack.'

Former Caol Ila stillman Neil Ferguson obseves, 'Some of the guys still have boats, though nobody's fishing seriously. As everywhere else, fishing changes as well, but there's still quite a few boats fishing lobsters down the Sound [of Islay] here.

'Originally all these houses in the village of Caol Ila belonged to the distill-ery, with the exception of a little house up there, and there was another one, a very small shack belonging to a fisherman, people who were not involved with the dis-

Neil Ferguson

tillery, who fished from the pier down here.

'But over the years other houses have been built, and as a matter of fact all the houses are privately owned now anyway. The company sold us all the houses. I think there were about twenty original distillery houses altogether, built at the time when the distillery was built, to house the workers. This house has been here since at least 1910. Some of the houses have no numbers, the ones that didn't belong to the distillery have no numbers, so it can be confusing trying to find a house at Caol Ila!

'There was a taxi service here, if they wanted to go down to the pub, or be collected from the pub, they could phone for a taxi. We used to get vans that came round as well, travelling shops selling groceries and meat, on certain days they came round.

'And that's all gone now, apart from the fish van which still comes round. Everybody's got a car now. At one stage everybody had a bicycle. A lot of people had boats, a lot of people fished on the side, and in the distillery there's even a photo of Caol Ila regatta.

'Islay's always Islay, but it has changed quite a lot, the population's gone down considerably. People always managed to get around, one way or another, cars or motor bicycles or bicycles or something, nobody was ever stuck. I used to live over in the western side of the island, and we had a bus service a couple of days a week, way back in the '50s. It allowed people to go shopping into Bowmore in the afternoon, that was on a Wednesday and a Saturday.

'The children nowadays get bussed to school, all the children from Bunnahabhain, Caol Ila and round about, and Islay High School, they even come across from Jura on the ferry to it. It's a long day. But it's a good school, and when you're finished in Islay High you can go straight into university.

'We're very lucky living here. We're only 35 minutes from Glasgow by air. It takes you longer to get over to the airport from here, say, than it takes to fly to Glasgow. It's surprising how you can get around from here. I remember years ago we left here at eight o'clock in the morning, and we went over to Port Ellen, and we went by bus and boat and train, and we were down in London approximately twelve hours later. You wouldn't think you could do that from Caol Ila.'

Ed McAffer of Bowmore says, 'There's a lot of what we call "white settlers" in the island now. At one time you knew everybody by sight, even if you didn't actually know the person, you knew who they were. Now I can walk down into our own local village down there, and you can feel like a stranger yourself.'

Neil Ferguson echoes this point. 'There's a lot more incomers than there used to be. I was in Bowmore with my wife on Wednesday, and we were in the Co-op, and I met a man who used to work with me, a fellow retiree like myself, he lives just down in the village here, and we started talking. And we were talking away in Gaelic, which is our native language, and it's amazing the people who were looking at us as if we were talking in a strange language. And yet a lot of these people had been born on the island, but they still couldn't understand us. There are still a fair number of Gaelic speakers on the island. There's a Gaelic college as well now, just this side of Bowmore. There's quite a bit of interest in the Gaelic language.'

'The opportunities for young ones are few and far between,' observes Ed McAffer.

'The ones that all want to get themselves educated are away and don't bother coming back. Which is the thing to do, of course. But it's a shame for the island. But the way the whisky industry's going, the way they're automating everything, as time goes on I'm sure there's going to be even less guys employed, because they'll end up there'll be two or three people running them, they'll just be whisky factories then, they'll lose the character completely. Bruichladdich is the exception, they've still got the old-fashioned distillery with quite a lot of people employed for what they do, and they've got the bottling.'

Neil Ferguson says, 'We have a lot more going for us in the way of distilleries, eight working distilleries here, which other islands just don't have. So that does affect our economy on the island. There's so many jobs connected with it; lorries for hauling malt from Port Ellen, not just to Caol Ila, but to other distilleries as well. They supply other distilleries too.'

'It's healthy on the island at the moment, the whisky industry,' declares Ed McAffer, 'although it doesn't employ as many men as it used to, it's still pretty healthy. It's great to see the likes of Bruichladdich up and running again. Burn Stewart have bought Bunnahabhain, and they've kept that going, so that's great for the island, and Ardbeg's going from strength to strength now. Port Ellen distillery shut a few years ago, and they trimmed the sails at Lagavulin, a lot of boys got made redundant, and there's a smaller staff, but it's starting to pick up again. The distilleries are going hard at it, and the maltings as well.

'There's nothing worse than looking at a distillery that's "silent", as we would say. It looks exactly what it is, dead, you know. There's something different when a distillery's bristling with life, when there's steam coming out here and smoke coming out there. As long as the steam's going about it looks alive, and guys going around, it makes an awful difference to the whole thing, the place is alive when that's happening.'

The Isle of Jura is separated from Islay by just the narrow Sound of Islay, with a small car ferry making the crossing between Port Askaig and Feolin. However, with just a single shop and one hotel to serve the 150-strong population, Jura has a much greater sense of remoteness than its comparatively cosmopolitan neighbour.

Mickey Heads is one of ten people employed at Jura distillery, and he recalls his early days on the island, to which he moved in 1990. Although being an Ileach from the Oa peninsula, he wasn't prepared for his first Sunday in his new home.

'I didn't know anybody, and I walked down into the village [Craighouse] and went to the shop for a Sunday newspaper. "There's no Sunday papers," the assistant announced. "Welcome to Jura!" Some of the guys were sitting outside the pub drinking their pints, and they bought me one. So I didn't get a Sunday paper but I did get a pint.'

Inevitably, some people love the isolation of Jura, but for others it is just too much to take. As Mickey says, 'When they rebuilt the distillery in the early 1960s [it commenced production in 1963] they brought people in from off the island to

Mickey Heads samples Jura single malt from a Matusalem sherry cask.

help build up the community. They built a row of new houses for the workers, but some only lasted a few months here, they couldn't cope with island life, with being in such a small, remote community.

'Jura distillery is crucial to the island, it's the focal point of the island. People have an identity with it. The distillery is the island and the island is the distillery. I'm passionate about Jura – my life now is in the community here.

Grant Carmichael speaks for island communities in general when he says of Islay, 'There's nobody can come here and try to be what they are not, try to be above their station. People are judged on their deeds rather than their reputation. Islay people are very kind, but very sharp too, so anyone coming here, don't try to be what you're not. They'll soon suss you out. Islay's a great leveller.'

13

On Puffers

In the days before 'roll-on/roll-off' ferries revolutionised transport between the mainland and Hebridean islands during the 1960s, small coasters, popularly known as 'puffers', provided lifeline services to island communities.

Isle of Jura brand ambassador and former manager Willie Tait remembers when the coal for the island used to come in on the 'puffer' to the pier at Craighouse. 'It was divided up into tons, and then was delivered by Islay Farmers to your house – just tipped out at the door and you had to deal with it then. It was noticeable if you went down to the pier that the heaps for the locals were always bigger than those supposedly of the same measure for the incomers!'

In addition to transporting general supplies, puffers were vital to the functioning of island distilleries and others in remote, coastal locations. In the case of Campbeltown on the Kintyre peninsula in Argyllshire, their existence made distilling viable, since moving whisky to the bottling and blending halls of Glasgow and the industrialised markets of the west of Scotland was impossible using the primitive and extraordinarily lengthy road routes available.

By contrast, the sea passage across the Firth of Clyde was comparatively quick, and without the puffers Campbeltown could never have become the major distilling centre that it did in Victorian times.

To many people, the world of the puffers was brought alive by Inveraray-born writer Neil Munro, whose comic *Para Handy* stories first appeared in the *Glasgow Evening News* a century ago. The stories featured the *Vital Spark*, a Clyde-based puffer, and its hapless crew. In 1959/60 the BBC brought *Para Handy* to television screens for the first time, with the Clyde puffer *Saxon* doubling for the *Vital Spark*. Duncan

Macrae played the title role, reprised during 1994–95 by Gregor Fisher.

Although not spoken of with quite such affection as dramming, the puffers are a recurring and fond memory for the whisky men of Islay.

Grant Carmichael observes that the puffer trade traditionally grew up along with the whisky trade.

'Everything came in by those little boats. Puffers would bring in coal, empty casks, and malt, because we couldn't make sufficient malt on the island for our own needs, and of course they would take out whisky and dark grains, dried draff, because there was a glut of that on the island.

'The puffers bred their own characters. Puffers were full of characters. *Para Handy* is absolutely true! Some of these characters would come in when they were doing what we called "self discharges", which meant they would empty a boat of, say, coal themselves, shovelling it into big buckets which were winched up and tipped onto lorries at the pierhead.

The Saint Angus *'puffer'*
delivering bricks at
Craighouse pier, Jura, 1962.

'The guys doing this were black as the Earl of Hell's waistcoat from the coal, and in those days the drams were flowing freely. This was in the days when distillery men would get a dram in the morning, get a dram at lunchtime, get a dram at teatime, and for any filthy job there was always a dram going. What we used to call a "stourie" [dusty] dram. Any time casks were being rolled out of the warehouse, that was worth a dram.

'What was very noticeable when I came across to Islay was that Speyside men would stop work in the rain. Islaymen didn't. They were used to the rain, and of course what kept them going was that everybody just had a dram. We would work on boats in terrible weather, because these boats had to be unloaded and got away if the weather was closing in, so we just carried on. Rain, it didn't matter. And what happened was that nobody was ever off with the cold, because we had our own "cough mixture".

'I can always remember an old pufferman coming into the brewer's office at Caol Ila one morning where we used to pour the drams out when they came in. This was the morning after. He was still black from the previous day's unloading, and he was shaking, until he got a dram. "Boy," he said as it went down, "that's good, but it's no' your frien's that gies ye drink." That's the puffers.'

Jim McEwan adds, 'The puffers had rough crews. Anybody that was on the run from the law was on a puffer. Scars across their faces, bolts in their necks, one eye missing, oh terrible people, but great fun, really great fun. And there were quite a few of these boats sunk actually.'

'The *Limelight* sank off Port Ellen, full of coal,' remembers Ruari MacLeod. 'And one day they were loading at the pier over here, one of the "Lights", of Ross & Marshall, and they were loading two casks at a time. With the swell over at the pier the boat went away and then came back, but the winchman misjudged it, and the casks ended up in the water. One cask was never retrieved.

'But it was 1970-odd, I don't mind what year it was, and the late John Calderwood who was the blacksmith in Kennacraig over there at the head of the loch, he saw something rolling back and for'ard at low tide, and he went down, and there was a cask of whisky. It had come off the puffer. It took all that time before it arrived there. It had taken ten years, anyhow. I don't know if the whisky was still good in it or not, but there wasn't a drop out of it when they dipped the cask. It took all that time.'

JM: Ten years to travel such a short distance, it must have been moving back and forward, a metre a year or something.

RM: I was always just wondering was the whisky good in it or not.

'Most of the puffers were independently operated,' says Grant Carmichael, 'though DCL had their own. It was called The *Pibroch*, and unlike most of the others it was more like a yacht. It was an absolutely beautiful vessel and the skipper of The *Pibroch* was John Ross, who kept his boat immaculate. You could eat your meals off the engine room floor. Five on the crew, and they were all officers! There was the skipper, the chief engineer, the second engineer, the chief officer, that was the mate, and there was the chief steward. So they were all officers.

'The other puffers, originally there were Hay's puffers, they were the *Spartan*, the *Anzac*, the *Alaska*, a lot of them were named after African tribes. Then there were Hamiltons, they were the "Glen" boats, *Gleneyrie*, the *Glenshira,* the *Glencloy*, and then there was Ross & Marshall, that was the "Lights", the *Moonlight*, the *Dawnlight* and the *Polarlight,* but then they all amalgamated, and it became what they called the Glenlight Shipping Company latterly. I don't know if they are still in operation.

'When the roll-on/roll-off ferries came on, in the late '60s, that was the death knell for the puffers. They were all based on the Clyde, Glasgow and Greenock and that sort of area. They did all the islands, they did a lot to Arran, a lot to Islay, Jura, Colonsay, Skye – no bridge in those days of course – and a bit less to the Uists, though there were the seaweed factories at Lochboisdale. They used to go up there with a cargo of coal, probably, and come back with a cargo of seaweed concentrate for fertiliser. Great for the garden, I remember I used to get bags of the stuff when they came in, and it did a great job for the garden.

'So it was sad seeing the puffers go, but when the roll-on/roll-off ferries came in we started bringing stuff in by road transport. The *Pibroch* was sold, and for many years she was working on the Clyde as a sort of tender or depot ship to the American ships in the Holy Loch, and latterly used to carry out the garbage. An inglorious end for her. I think she's still working in the South of Ireland somewhere. She was a beautiful little puffer.'

Working at Caol Ila, Neil Ferguson was also familiar with the DCL's *Pibroch,* but adds, 'Then other boats also used to come in, with barley, boats came in with coal for the boilers, and coke, and so on. So there was always a stir of some kind down there. These boats could be Danish perhaps, or Dutch, as well as British. It was very much a fact that Danish and Dutch predominated latterly, because the British Merchant Navy is virtually non-existent anyway nowadays. They are crewed by Lithuanians and Latvians and Czechs and whatever. It was starting to get like that

even back in the '60s. The Danish boats were different, they were mostly crewed by Danes, because they have a very strong seamen's union there. They make sure they're manned by Danes. The casks went out by puffer too, but with the advent of the roll-on/roll-off ferries they went out on articulated lorries. Usually it was already in barrels.'

Unloading sacks of barley from the Pibroch *at Port Ellen, c.1967.*

'Big Angus' McAffer of Lagavulin, was another of the whisky men who regularly saw DCL's *Pibroch* in service.

'All the barley was English,' he recalls, 'and it came in by boat. All the barley came in railway bags, big railway bags, heavy bags to work with. Most of the whisky we kept, it matured here at the distillery. It was for White Horse going away, or Johnnie Walker, or John Dewar, for blending. It went out in the puffer or it went in the *Loch Broom* or the *Loch Ard*, MacBrayne's boats at that time, but they're all away now, the *Loch Broom* and the *Loch Ard*. They don't have them at all now. They were cargo boats.

'They went to Bruichladdich first, and emptied whatever they had to at the pier, then they came over here on the Sunday, and started on the Monday empty

whatever they had to empty, and loaded it up with whisky. MacBrayne brought the empty casks back in and we delivered them. Sometimes the *Pibroch* brought in some too, but MacBrayne brought in most of them.'

'All the materials we used like barley came in by them,' notes Ed McAffer. 'And they transferred from places like Port Ellen or Port Askaig or Bruichladdich to Bowmore by lorry. There were guys doing docking jobs when we sent our whisky out in the puffers. They brought the grain in and took the whisky out. Now we just bang everything onto a lorry and it's away.

'In the days when the materials came in by puffer the manager of the distillery would go down to the corner and see who was hanging about, and then he would take on what he called casuals, and they would come up and empty the lorries, and they would get whatever the payment was and a dram to sweeten it up, and these guys just came in for the hours to do that job, because obviously the operators in the distillery were too busy doing the distillery work.'

'One company that had the puffers then was Ross & Marshall,' says Jim McEwan, 'and Magnus Vass, he was the shipping agent. One day they'd dropped a cask on the pier and it was damaged, so I came down and worked on it, I did bits and pieces of work for them like that. Interesting that I worked here as a cooper part-time many years ago and I've come back now. I was only here Saturdays and in the evening. It was just money for beer. And I used to go to the hotel in Bruichladdich and get drunk there.

'The puffers came in to Bruichladdich pier, because Bowmore harbour sanded up. I can remember just when I was a kid, puffers at Bowmore, probably the last puffer came into Bowmore around 1960. And then Bowmore would transfer, its puffers would come in to Bruichladdich. But it was not a good port for discharging, there was too much rise and fall, there's no shelter. So we would be going to Ardbeg or Port Ellen. The biggest load of casks ever to leave Islay was 666 casks, on board the *Pibroch*, come out of Caol Ila. And that was the last puffer to leave Islay. What was significant about that was the number, 666 – the mark of the devil!

'It was dangerous, dangerous work on the puffers. The whole shape of the casks was designed to interlock, the elongated shape, which is fine, that's easy loading, in the open area, but the hard bit was underneath, in the hold, in the covered bows and stern of the ship. What you had to do there was get the cask and swing it like a pendulum. So you were young kids, fast on your feet, and this is dangerous, because it's just held with hooks, you're in danger of losing your hand. So you would get your cask moving back and forwards, you had to get right under the hold, and you'd run and push as fast as you could, and shout, "Right!" and you'd

Opposite:

Loading the Pibroch *with casks, Caol Ila distillery, c. 1967.*

hope one of the other boys would shout to the winchman "drop it", because otherwise it came back at you.

'But as the day progressed, the guy on the winch got drunker and drunker, so what you did was fill the stern and the bow first, underneath, and then as you started to build up, and depending on where the tide was, you were lifting casks off the side and dropping them down into the hold, and suddenly you'd look up, and there's the two casks going away over the side of the boat on the winch, and you'd say, "Christ, they've got to come back!" And then they'd come swinging back, and that was a real nightmare situation. How there was not more people lost hands I don't know.

'What they would do they would drop a cask on its head, just the chain on it, they'd drop it about nine inches, and then the head of the cask would shift, the "devils" would shift, and the cask would start leaking. And that was the signal. Teapots, Wellington boots, jars, anything, fill anything, and that was their supply for the day. The crew of the boat, plus the guys working on the boat. Great little boats. You'd see them setting off on a wild night round the Mull of Oa, and you had a high sea, they'd disappear from sight, you'd stop seeing the light, and you'd say, "Christ, I wonder …" and then suddenly the wee light would come twinkling up again. Great wee boats.'

The Lochard *'puffer' conveying sections of stills to Jura distillery, 1962.*

14

On Peat

In *Harpers Wine & Spirit Gazette* for 18 June 1948 'Caledonia' wrote, 'The convenient proximity of a peat bog is an economic necessity for a Highland distillery.'

With the demise of distillery maltings (see Chapter 2, 'On Malting') this is no longer the case, yet peat continues to influence the nature of many single malt Scotch whiskies, and in particular is a key characteristic of most Islay malts.

According to 'Caledonia', 'Peat is regarded as an essential to the formation of character in whisky, the empyreumatic aroma of burnt peat, which is character-istic of all Scotch malts, being introduced through the drying of the malts over peat fires in the pagoda-like kilns. Though the smoke does no more than pass through the grain which is being dried in the kiln, yet it contrives to impart a peaty fragrance which persists throughout all the processes of fermentation and distillation. It can, in fact, be detected after the cask has been 15 to 20 years in bond.'

'There are, of course, peats and peats; good whiskies are fastidious in their tastes, and demand peats which are wholly free from mineral impregnation. The flora of peat mosses vary according to locality. On the north shore of Scapa Flow is Hobister Moor which supplies peat for the Orkney stills and which contributes to the distinctive flavour of these northern malts [i.e. Highland Park and Scapa]. The unique quality of Glenlivet is said to be largely due to the inexhaustible peat deposits, the Falmussach moss, adjacent to the distillery.'

Today, the Falmussach moss is redundant for distillery purposes, yet Glenlivet thrives on malt brought in from commercial maltings, though perhaps a direct comparison between Glenlivet distilled with malt dried with Falmussach peat and that distilled from externally sourced malt would yield a number of differences.

Loading a horse and cart with peats for Cardhu distillery, probably 1950s.

Whether they would be attributable to the peat alone or to other variables is, of course, open to question.

Peat is vegetable matter decomposed by water and partially carbonised by chemical change, often forming 'bogs' or 'mosses' from which it is cut, or 'won'. Island and coastal peat is generally accepted to produce a more pungently aromatic smoke than peat found further inland.

A peat bog may be 10,000 years old and up to 30 feet (approximately 9 metres) in depth. The optimum peat for malting is found close to the surface, where it is comparatively crumbly and rooty. The best peats for domestic fires are found much deeper in the bogs.

Conservation issues being dear to the hearts of modern distillers, peat 'caff' (powdered peat) is now frequently used in kilns rather than whole peats, as this reduces the overall consumption significantly.

Additionally, as former Islay stillman 'Big Angus' McAffer points out, 'The maltings in Port Ellen use a lot of peat, but it's all cut by machine these days, not by hand as it used to be. They don't use as much as the distilleries did, though, because it's all blown through and re-circulated, it's used again.

'We got our peat from over the low road to Machrie, but there's not much peat cut now. Laphroaig is only using it as a show, for visitors coming round, it's only for show that they use the maltings, so they can see how they did it in the old days.'

Modern whisky men only rarely have any contact with peat, but in the days of distillery maltings, peat played an important part in the cycle of distilling life.

The Dufftown distilling brothers Dennis and Bill McBain both recall working with peat, and the Balvenie maltings of Dennis' employer William Grant still require peats, particularly as a new peat kiln was installed in 2004, and a more heavily peated version of Balvenie has subsequently been produced for future blending purposes.

'There's a big peat moss just this side of Tomintoul, beyond Glenlivet,' says Dennis, 'and we buy peat from there and from New Pitsligo [between Fraserburgh and Banff], but they do that by machine now, and it's not the old slabs like it used to be when it was all cut by hand.

'One of the jobs that they did when they shut down in the summer time was to go up the hill and get the long heather, we needed it long to tie it onto the pole, [to scrub the mash tuns – see 'Chapter 3, On Brewing'] and also we went up and cut the peats as well, up the Cabrach [south-east of Dufftown]. All the distilleries must have had their own peat lots at that time.

Bill McBain echoes this, saying, 'In the close season you were up at Ballach in the Cabrach carting down peats for the kiln or you were up there pulling the heather out by the root to make the besoms. You put it into bundles and tied them. There'd be four or five of you up there sometimes for a whole day, and you put it into bundles, and that kept you going more or less for a season.'

Dalmore distillery manager Drew Sinclair says, 'You used to have your silent season, and it used to be quite a long silent season at times, depending on orders, plus the silent season was used as a time for collecting peats and collecting heather. We collected heather as well as peats, and we still have a wee "heather house" at Dalmore. The heather was used for making besoms to clean out the washbacks.

'Our peat came from a bog up at Strath Morie, which is in Ardross, about five miles away. That was strictly Dalmore's peat bog. The other local distilleries like Teaninich and Balblair and Glenmorangie all had their own.'

'In them days we had a longer shut-down period during the summer,' recalls Bowmore's head brewer, Ed McAffer. 'And a big squad would go away out and clean our lade, which runs seven miles down into the village. We used to go out there to

Cutting peat for Dalmore distillery, Ardross, 1970s

clean that, and it was like getting a break away out into the hills after being cooped up all winter. The older men that were there would be right crabbit [irritable] because they weren't getting their dram. Their character changed completely, we couldn't understand how this jovial old guy suddenly became a cranky old guy you couldn't speak to without getting your face taken off. We were out in the wilds, away in a squad of our own. We cleaned the lade all the way down.

'They also used to cut their own peat. Well, we didn't do so much cutting of our own peat when I started. There was a contractor would come in to cut them, but the distillery squad would go down to do what we called the "fitting". We lifted them off the ground to dry. You were talking hundreds and hundreds of yards of peat. They were cut by hand. They just cut them and we went out as a squad to fit them. We wouldn't go there unless maybe the dram came. So somebody would be given the job of pilfering a good dram from the warehouse. We'd have a dram "out of the moss", as they said.

'We had a lot of fun out there, young guys. One guy, he still works for the company but he's away in Glasgow now, he's been away for twenty years, but he was just a young boy and he got engaged, and we set about him. And we left him lying about the moss, you can imagine out in among the heather, and he had nothing but his boots on. We left him there for two or three hours, with just his boots and socks on. It's pretty rough running about the heather in bare feet. Some of the boys took photographs too, but they've since disappeared, which is a great pity. We wouldn't get away with things like that now, there'd be an enquiry into what had happened.'

Frank McHardy of Springbank distillery in Campbeltown explains, 'It's moss peat we use, and you get what they call the "fog", the top layer. We only use about 40 tonnes a year. It's cut with a machine into long 'sausages', and the machine will take it from about five feet down. The arm of the machine extends, comes off the back and extends down and brings it up the conveyor and squeezes it, compressing the peat into a tube which then brings it out.

'The guy who operates the machine, and the farmer seconds this, reckons cutting the peat helps drainage, but we don't really want that too much, you don't want to drain a peat bog completely, you want to keep it wet.

'We cut peat as soon as the weather is suitable, usually May, then we leave it in the moss until it's dry, then we bring it in. Last year we left it, what was it, about four to five weeks, it wasn't too much. Of course it was very dry last year, it's been much wetter this year, and the peat's still out there.'

Frank McHardy and the peat cutters of the Orkney islands, too, refer to the upper layer of peat suitable for malting purposes as 'fog', while on Islay cutters talk about the 'top', 'second' and 'third' peats.

You really cannot get away from peat on the island of Islay. A quarter of the land mass is covered in it, and it inevitably finds its way into burns and rivers, though the amount of influence the peaty water gives to Islay whisky is hotly debated.

Visitors to Islay often complain that there is something wrong with the water supply when they see how brown it is, due to the peat, but even an Ileach like

Cutting peat for Lagavulin
distillery, undated.

Mickey Heads was somewhat taken aback by the water on Jura when he first arrived as manager of the distillery at Craighouse in 1990.

'Just after I'd come to Jura and we'd been moving in furniture I went and ran a bath,' he remembers. 'And it was so peaty you couldn't see the bottom of the bath. Anything could have been in there!'

'The peat cutters were characters,' says Grant Carmichael. 'There was always a peat-cutting squad, and the peat-cutting squad would set off in the morning up to the moss, and whoever was in charge of the squad had a lemonade bottle of whisky with him. That was to keep them going for the day.

'Peat cutting was a big operation then. It's all done by machines now. Mainly it's just done for the big maltings in Port Ellen, and very few people nowadays cut peat for their own domestic use. The modern houses often still have fires, but peat is messy and dusty and smoky, and you get the dust everywhere when you come to clean the fire out. The modern housewife doesn't want to be bothered with that. People don't have the time and they're better off financially, they can afford to pay for oil or electricity or gas.

'Sometimes it was distillery people who did the peat cutting, sometimes it was the same people who emptied the puffers that cut the peat. That was quite often the case. The peat was measured, each bank was measured, and the cutters would be paid on what they cut. The distillery manager had to go out on a weekly basis and measure the peat banks to make sure that he was getting his full measure. Then the cutters would come along and just put the peats on the bank, the way that they cut the peats was different from the north, the peats on Islay were cut by the Irish method, with a "tusker", a long cutting iron, which you lifted the peat with and just slung it on top of the bank.

'Then very often it was women and children who would come along, and they would be paid for this, of course, and "fit" the peats, build them up to let the wind blow through them so that they would dry. Then it was time for the peats to come home, and usually the same men who had cut the peats would come up and they would load the tractors and trailers off the moss. So it provided quite a bit of employment. Again, they supported a big population in those days, the distilleries.

'Each distillery had its own peat banks, paid for in different ways. Sometimes the agreement would be with whichever estate you'd got the banks from, sometimes just a plain, simple rent, in other cases the agreement was that this was in with the rent of the distillery. Bunnahabhain at one time used to give a hogshead a year to Lord Margadale for the peat, and I can remember many, many years ago going along to Islay House with instruments [to gauge the spirit strength] and helping to reduce this whisky down before it was bottled. Other places the rent for the peat banks was that the estate had to get two or three trailer-loads of peat for their use. That was quite a common one, and a pretty reasonable one.'

Jim McEwan, inevitably, has anecdotes about Islay and peat.

'Norrie Campbell's the great peat cutter on Islay, and there's lots of stories about Norrie. I remember once he'd got a croft up on the [peat] lots, and it needed a new roof and work doing to it, so he got a council house in Port Ellen while the work was being done. He took his peats with him and built a peat stack beside the house. But his neighbours kept stealing the peats. So Norrie built the peat stack in the living room instead. You went in and all around the walls were lined with peats, the space you could fit in was quite small as a result. "Ach," he said, "it's awful handy too," reaching up from his chair to take a peat from the indoor stack and throw it on the fire.

'Another time, it was when I was working for Bowmore in Glasgow, there was an American film crew came over to Islay to make a film about whisky, and I came across with them, I was involved in it. I told them they had to see Norrie

Peat cutting the modern way, near Port Ellen, 1990s.

Campbell, the greatest peat cutter in the world. Well, Norrie was off the island, in Glasgow, so it didn't happen.

'But on the way back to Glasgow with the film crew we stopped for a drink in a hotel in Inveraray. It was Sunday lunchtime, and the place was full of families having Sunday lunch. We're sitting there when in walks Norrie, obviously on his way back to the island from Glasgow. Now he's looking rough as a badger's bum, he's obviously had a rough time of it, and he walks up to the bar, orders a nip and a pint. His hands are shaking, but down goes the nip which steadies him a bit for the pint. He drinks that, orders the same again, and after that he's feeling a bit better, so he starts to look around him. He hasn't seen me, so I'm hiding away, and I tell the crew to go up to him, tell him they've been tracking him by satellite through NASA, and they've finally caught up with him. So they do that. They go up to him, camera rolling, and say, "Are you Norrie Campbell, the greatest peat cutter in the world, as Jim McEwan says?" He says, "Well, I suppose I might be." They say to him that they're making a film about Scotch whisky and Jim McEwan says they must talk to him.

'He says, "So how did you find me?" And they tell him the story about the satellite and NASA. So he's looking up at the ceiling, taking all this in. And they say, "Will you demonstrate peat cutting for us now, Norrie?" "Well," he replies, "with what?" It so happens we'd taken down the set of old peat cutting equipment we had in the offices in Glasgow, so they went and got that out of the van. So he stands in the bar, demonstrating peat cutting, throwing up the imaginary peats and all the rest of it, while people sat around having their Sunday lunches and so forth, very perplexed. And all the while he keeps glancing up, looking for the satellite. Then suddenly he spots me and realises I've set him up, and the expletives he comes out with are absolutely amazing.'

15

On Change

Ask whisky men about the most significant changes that have taken place during their working lifetimes, and they will, almost without exception, mention increased automation and centralisation, and the consequent downsizing of work-forces. The apparently ever-growing 'globalisation' of the Scotch whisky industry, its consolidation into the hands of a small number of international operators, is rarely mentioned.

According to Dennis McBain of William Grant & Sons Ltd in Dufftown, 'The biggest change I've seen in the whisky industry has been increasing automation. At Willie Grant's we're a little bit behind other people, the likes of Diageo, as far as automation goes, but we're into it now. When I started you never envisaged a computer or any machine doing what I see them doing now. You press a button and it does the whole operation. One of the main pluses for people going for automation is that you get consistency with your product.'

Inevitably, the increase in distillery automation has led many of the older whisky men to believe there has been a decrease in personal skill and initiative.

As former Mortlach stillman Bill McBain puts it:
'The like of this generation today, they don't know the first thing about making whisky. They've never seen the malt being turned or in the kiln, and they don't know about yeast. It was all work at that time of day, and now it's all automated. It's all computers. At Mortlach there's just one man per shift now, he works the mash house, the tun room and the mill from down in the stillhouse. He doesn't need to come out of there at all.

'I'd like to get a few of the young still boys now and talk to them, see what

they do know about making whisky. Just before I finished down at Mortlach me and another boy started questioning a couple of them, and they weren't happy. One of them turned round and said, "Well, we're not here to make whisky, we're here for the money," and I thought that was an awful attitude to have. He'd no interest in the work, which I thought was bad.'

Tun room control console, Glenfarclas distillery, 2004.

Craigellachie's Archie Ness details just how modernisation and centralisation have affected distilleries.

'When I started at Craigellachie you had 50 staff. You had the maltings, the cooperage, the drying plant for drying the draff and such like. Then they cut out the drying plant, that was transferred away, and then you'd be down to 20-odd. Then the cooperage was finished, with bulk tankering, that cut out the warehousing side of it. I think that was a big loss, for a distillery, even for tourists. We had a lot of Japanese visitors would come to Craigellachie. It cut out another part of the whisky-making process that you could show them.

'You had no maltings, because they went out in the 1960s, you'd only malt coming in, so you just had the mill room, mash tun, tun room, distillation, and then across to the bulk tankering. How do you explain to the tourists that now it goes to be tankered away down south?

'I think it was a big thing when they cut out the warehouses, because you cut out just about half the distillery, the most important part of how you explain whisky-making. With that gone and malting gone, you'd lost the beginning and the ending of the story really. Now you've only seven staff at Craigellachie, with just two on a shift. It's taken out all the pleasure from the job.

'Before I left they started cutting back on staff duties. We went down at night at ten o'clock to walk round the distillery, and you'd sit down and have a talk with whoever was on duty. Then they cut that out. They said you didn't need to go down at ten o'clock at night, just do it at five o'clock and then away home. If there's anything goes wrong, they know where to get you. Now that man's in the stillhouse on his own, he's a mashman through the house, and they keep in contact once in a while, but the two of them on together, it must get boring. And that's what I was getting back. "We miss having a talk with the brewer and a talk with you." They said they missed that.

'I used to sit and talk to them and I used to learn a lot of things from the men. They'd say, "Why don't you try this or that out?" and I'd go back to my office and work it out, and think that might work. And you'd go back and discuss it with them again, and say, "Well, we'll try it." The men that's there now just do the work, nobody speaks to you, so it must be a long night. I had a dog, and I always used to take it for a walk round the distillery at night, it was a fine place to walk it, and I always used to call in and say hello. When I left they missed that. Once they brought in computers, that's it. You can leave it, and it'll just run through its programme. And if you're on with the same mate all the time it must get stale, because you're bound to run out of conversation some time.

'It's changed a lot, and I don't know whether it's for better or worse, but it's certainly different. In the end I was glad to get out. I liked the practical side and I liked mixing with the men. When they stopped all that it took all the feeling out, you lost contact. You were pushed into an office, to a computer. I thought, I didn't come in for all this, I came in to make whisky. I liked being on the floor, and I liked showing visitors round, but that's how the industry goes now. I left in 1997 and I haven't been in a still since.'

Former Mortlach employee Stuart Duffy reckons, 'The biggest change has been in manpower. I was at Mortlach in the office in about '93, and that's where the big changes started there and we went from a good twenty-odd workers. Seven

The staff of Mortlach distillery, 1921.

A maltman sits astride the horse on the left, while a railway employee stands beside the horse on the right.

in the stillhouse, four in the mash house, and there was the tun room as well, so that's another four.

'When I left there, when I retired, there were only five. There were no warehousemen, there was only myself in the office and one clerkess. Whereas there used to be a manager, an assistant manager, two brewers, and about three clerkesses. There was no manager, Steve McGingle was manager after Ian [Millar, current malt distilleries manager for William Grant & Sons Ltd] left, and he was at Dufftown distillery, he ran three, he ran that, Mortlach and Glendullan. There was just like a production manager at each one, and then the overall manager.

'At Mortlach I took a wee bit of interest in the warehousing as well as the production, and in the mornings you went out and took a charge, reduced the whisky, and then you went back and took a remnant and things like that, but at the end of the day that was all passed, it was nothing to do with me, the only thing that I had was production.

'I'd been a supervisor at Mortlach for so long, and then the production manager got his books [i.e., dismissed] and I was stuck into the job just temporary, but I was left there until I finally took retirement.

'I was brewer at Mortlach before that. In the end you were too busy with health and safety and things like that, that took up all your time. I found paperwork bogged you down. You felt as though you'd be more good being out looking after the job than you were signing a bit of paper, writing out a permit, "There you go, go and do the job." You'd have been better off if you'd been watching it.'

'When I was fifteen or sixteen years old,' explains Dennis McBain, 'the brewers were probably only in their forties and fifties, but they were old men to me. As you get older you struggle to grasp new technology, and some of the old brewers would have found it difficult to adapt to the keyboards and pcs and so forth that are in use today, having done it for so long manually, and a lot of it was just up in their heads anyway. It wasn't written down on paper or programmed into computers like it is now. I don't think they'd have coped with the amount of paperwork involved now, with all the legislation that there is.

'In days gone by it was purely a question of doing your job, getting the whisky run into the safe, get it into the barrel, get it down to the warehouse, and that was that. There was very little paperwork, except for the Customs and Excise side of it. We are now more or less detailing on paper every action that we take. A lot of that's because there's not the excise supervision that there was, of course, they're not doing it for the company any more.

'There are fewer people now, of course, but Grants has a no-redundancy policy, we just don't replace people as they retire. About 90 per cent of the cottages you see around here used to be occupied by distillery workers, with one or two for people who worked on the railway. Over the years, Willie Grant bought all the ground from the village of Dufftown up there right down the valley here, and a bit of the hill to protect our water rights.'

Fellow Grant's employee Eric Stephen agrees with Dennis's views on change.

'It's a different ball game now, with meetings and sitting around a table and all that. I don't know what the old boys would think about all this stuff. When I started I was just made to work. That was the older generation. Now it's all boys with degrees and that kind of stuff coming in.

'Little did I think when I came here that I'd still be working here in 41 years time, controlling all the warehousing. But I've enjoyed working for Willie Grant & Sons. I've got a good squad of people working with me, and I know if I ask for an extra push they'll not be short in coming forward.

'There's been a lot of laughs over the years, and everybody was the same. There was none of this back-stabbing kind of stuff. There wasn't the same amount of money going about for one thing. When I started here I was getting about six

pounds, I was a single boy, but the married boys got an extra penny!

'That was a good bit better than many jobs round about. I left a farm to come here and I was getting more pay. You had young boys in here on shifts were going home with about £35 to £40, which was a lot of money then.'

'Sandy McAdam recalls that 'When I started [at Cardhu] I was getting maybe 30 shillings a fortnight, we were fortnightly paid. With shift work you could make bigger money than that, because the work then was seven days a week. Up until the middle '60s you never even got Christmas Day off, or New Year's Day. All you got on Christmas Day was an extra dram and a half an hour extra for your dinner! The whisky-making never stopped, that was just accepted. In the late '50s and early '60s we began to get issued with overalls. That was another big step. You got a couple of pairs, with SMD on them. Before that you just wore your own clothes to work.'

'By the time I finished as manager [at Craigellachie] the paperwork was beginning to increase, and the computer work too, and that was something I knew nothing about then, but I enjoyed my time in the whisky industry, and I enjoyed managing the distillery.

Retirement presentation, Cardow distillery, undated. thirty-five staff members are present, including Sandy McAdam's father, fifth from left, rear row.

'Just about everybody that was in the industry in the old days was more or less brought up to it, and they knew the job and just did it. There's nothing like the characters in distilleries now. From the late '80s onwards it faded out, I'd say. Apart from anything else, if there's only one or two men per shift there's far less chance of you getting a character like you would if there were twenty or thirty there. Some of the changes over the years were for the better, and some for the worse. The working conditions now must be a lot better, but I think it must be more tedious than it used to be for the men.

In the days after railways were used by distillers and before whisky began to be moved by bulk tanker, Sandy McAdam recalls that 'The whisky from Cardhu for blending went onto lorries, it was open trucks then. There were no containers. The lorries just had nets or sheets over them. That happened in the late 1950s, early '60s, and was a big change. One of the main hauliers was Thomas Smith from Newhaven at Edinburgh, and he had a lot of lorries. Haig had their own wagons that used to come up and take casks away.'

Islay's 'Big Angus' McAffer declares:

'There would be friendly rivalry in the pubs between the boys – "We make the best whisky" – and all that sort of thing. And I was better paid here than I was at Laphroaig. These days the individuality has gone, the competitiveness that there used to be between distilleries has gone, they're all working for a common aim, for Diageo. These days they are encouraged to be interchangeable with people in the other distilleries in the company, they have league tables and such like, but in my day you never left the island. It was friendly rivalry, there was no badness.'

Retired Bruichladdich mashman Ruari MacLeod is emphatic that increasing automation has been the greatest change for of the whisky men during his lifetime. 'The work for you now is pressing buttons. On the island, Bruichladdich distillery is the only one, and Ardbeg, Ardbeg the same, where the mashman still has to do the mashing manually. It makes no difference for a stillman, he can press as many buttons as he wants, as long as he runs the whisky very slow, and then to spirit very slow. I'm not very sure about automation. Maybe Jim [McEwan] here can help me out. Is this automation that came in, is it as good as, say, Bruichladdich distillery is at the present, at making whisky?'

For Jim, greater consistency has come at a high price.

'My own feeling is that while there has to be progress and quality control, it's always at the cost of people, always at the cost of people. The first thing accountants do is remove jobs, put in automation. These same people, the marketing people talk about the heritage and the history and how proud we are of our spirit, yet

they've removed the most important ingredient, totally, which is the people like yourself, who have left their legacy behind. And we are extremely proud of Ruari's work. I mean, the 1970 whisky that was voted best single malt of the year, this is the man who made it. We recognise his skills. So it's really a baton race, Ruari's done his bit, he's handed on to Duncan McGillivray, and now it's my turn to run my race, and I'll leave a legacy hopefully for the next guy.

Laphroaig distillery, 1980s.

'So I don't believe the quality is as good, you've not got the same complexity. A good stillman, a good mashman, could just nurse it. You're draining your mash tun, you're looking are your worts clear, so I think it was better quality in the old days. People would disagree with that, but I think it was better. Just because of the hands-on approach. I'm not being sentimental, because I've worked for a large company and I know how it works, I've been in every distillery in Scotland at least twice, I just feel that this important ingredient, this human part, is missing. That is the cornerstone, you understand, it could just be gin, it could just be vodka, we're missing that cornerstone.'

RM: At the present time that's all set, all automated, and you have no control of it. It's a lot easier for any mashman today, it's a lot easier, and they can't make a mistake.

JM: That's right, they can't make a mistake. If you make a mistake, Ruari, this is what happens. Let's say I make a mistake, I'm trying to open a valve, and if I have not opened this other valve first, and I try to open this one, it will not open. A warning light will come on, and that warning light will stay on until I go back to the other valve, and only then can I open the second valve.

It's like if you took a monkey, and you gave the monkey a banana and it's got six boxes, coming down the way, and you give the monkey half an hour it will figure out the sequence to get the banana, we're almost at that stage. But that's progress, we've got to accept that. We've got to move on, and we can't stay like that forever.

The barleys we're making now give much higher yields, and the barley strains are grown specifically for the distiller. In the old days it was Golden Promise, and Golden Promise only, now we've got half a dozen strains of barley. But the greatest whiskies I've tasted are what are now some of the old Rare Malts from United Distillers, the Glenugies and the Clynelishes, great old traditional styles. I feel that, having seen in my lifetime in whisky 46 distilleries die. When I started there were 125 malt distilleries, today we're down to 79.

One positive recent change in the Scotch whisky industry, however, has been the re-opening of a number of formerly silent distilleries, including Glencadam at Brechin, Tullibardine in Perthshire, Benriach near Elgin, and, of course, Bruichladdich, which started distilling again under the auspices of the Bruichladdich Distillery Co. Ltd in 2001, after being mothballed since 1994.

Jim McEwan thinks that 'It's just great to have Bruichladdich open again. When we were opening Bruichladdich, Ruari was invaluable to me because this was a Victorian distillery which I had never worked in before, so the first man I asked for advice was Ruari MacLeod. And he willingly gave it. Which has been great. But characters like Ruari are very, very few and far between. People like Ruari are the heart and the soul of this place, and of the whisky that's been made here. It's fantastic that people like Ruari are interested in and approve of what we are doing here now.'

RM: Oh yes, yes, I'm happy with what you're doing, and I'm happy that you're experimenting with different malts. This is going to be very interesting in eight, ten years time. The different peating levels (see Chapter 2, 'On Malting.'). It's very good for the island to have Bruichladdich open again, particularly for this part, for the Rhinns, and it's good as well that they have their own bottling plant here. My daughter works in the bottling hall, it's the first time there's really been bottling on the island. Having the bottling hall's a great thing.

JM: We're employing twenty-four people here, including a number of disabled people, and long before I ever came to Bruichladdich, this was the islanders' favourite dram.

RM: It was, oh aye, always was. Bruichladdich always seemed to have what people

Hauling sacks of barley to the barley loft, Bruichladdich distillery, c. 1950s. Bill Macgregor is holding the horse. Left to right: Neil McLachlan, Jim Ferguson and Chris Campbell.

wanted, the blenders and that. And that is good.

JM: It put the malts together. I remember that as a kid, working in Bowmore, Bruichladdich was the most popular malt on the island. It still is. It outsells anything else. It's my dream now to get the malt barns up and running. That would be fantastic, to reinstate the malt barns at the back side there. That would be my next dream Ruari, but whether we can afford it …

RM: Well it all takes time, too.

JM: We are contracting a farmer this year to grow barley for us, we'll take it off the island and get it malted off the island, because Port Ellen maltings are too busy to do it. But the next thing would be to get the malt barns going. I've opened my own cooperage now, I've got the cooperage going, I've got young Peter Mactaggart as an apprentice cooper to John Rennie. That's the first apprentice cooper since Ian Gillies was apprenticed to Donald McAffer at Bunnahabhain.

RM: Oh, is that so?

JM: Aye, Ian Gillies was the last one. So I'm very happy to have an apprentice cooper again. We're down to 134 coopers in Scotland now. When I was coopering there was about 1,500 coopers, and they're down to 134 coopers.

RM: Why now is it? Is it that the distillers don't want coopers?

JM: It's cheaper just to scrap casks than it is to repair them.

RM: Well, I can quite believe that.

JM: American casks are very, very cheap just now. Also, Ruari, casks are not given the same harsh treatment that they were. They're on pallets now, so it's pallets and fork trucks, they don't get rolled the same. So it's on a fork truck, on a pallet, build it, build it, build it to the sky. I don't agree with that. I'm delighted that we've got a young apprentice started now, the first apprentice since 1966.

RM: It's all good for the island.

Islay's Grant Carmichael considers the move towards distillery 'self-policing' to be a highly significant change.

'In the old days each distillery had its resident exciseman, sometimes two, and they've all gone now. The industry is self-policing. There are no Excisemen based on the island now, they come across from the mainland. Even before I retired, we had to provide a clear audit trail, if you like, right back from the whisky to the malt we started with.

'The Excisemen had a very high station in life. They had a wonderful status; the distillery companies had to supply a house for the excise, and office facilities. Most Excisemen were decent people, though you'd get some awkward sods, but there were always ways and means of sorting them out. If an Exciseman was awkward, he had to be present every time an account of spirits was taken, and if you had awkward people, you could make it a habit of having to call the Exciseman out during the night to open up a safe, which was probably quite unnecessary, or you'd contrive

Restored 'puggie' engine at Aberfeldy distillery, 1990s. 'Puggies' were widely used to connect distilleries to commercial railway lines until the 1960s. This example was formerly employed at Dailuaine.

to choke something so that he had to come and open the locks to let you clear it. Give that a few times and people got the message.

'Nowadays, it's all self-policing, and we're now looking not so much for manual labour as in the old days. Distillery workers started usually as the labourers, in the malt barns, still fireman, boilerman, tun room man, and you reached the pinnacle as a mashman or a stillman. Or you might take a different direction and move on to the warehouse. Nowadays, most distilleries are looking for people who are much more academically-inclined, which they have to be, in most cases they've got to be computer-literate, as most youngsters are. It's not the same hard physical labour, nothing like it. In the warehouse there's a bit of physical labour, having to roll casks, but there's more and more bulk tankers moving around, and fork-lifts in warehouses, too.

'The major changes in the forty years since I started in the industry are in labour. Distilleries now employ a fraction of what they did. There are less than a hundred people employed in the Islay distilleries now. There's more people employed on the visitor scene [at distilleries] than are actually employed in the distilleries. On a seasonal basis, many of them. Christine [Logan, visitor centre manager] in Bowmore probably has two full-time girls with her and some part-time girls, and the distillery itself will probably employ half a dozen. That side of it has become very important, and the whole economy of the island has gone on to that. No longer is it whisky and agriculture, though Islay is still famous for the quality of its beef cattle, a lot of that due to the wonderful feeding they get from the distillery draff. Very, very high quality cattle.'

'Big Angus' McAffer says, 'At one time the draff here at Lagavulin went up to the farm for cattle feed, and everything else went straight into the sea. But they take the pot ale by tanker to Port Askaig, to near Caol Ila distillery, to discharge it now. The tide at Port Askaig is very fierce, and if there's a high tide the pot ale is back in Lagavulin before the tanker is back! Everything went straight into the sea here, and we were eating the crabs and all sorts. The best place to set the pots was round the distilleries. For hundreds of years Lagavulin was putting it out into the sea. We never came to any harm. But then we were drinking peaty water, boiling it in syrup cans, too, and we're still here now.'

Neil Ferguson of Caol Ila reflects on the changes in waste disposal.

'There's the effluent disposal up the road, the new outlet for that. The articulated tankers come in there, and there's just a little pipe they connect a hose to, and you don't see anything really above ground until you get down to the distillery, and there's a couple of tanks there. They're more or less for our own effluent from the distillery.

'It goes away out underneath the Sound, underneath the water of the Sound out there, just from the point, and it goes away out about 400 feet along the bed of the Sound. The water's pretty deep out there, there's about 20 fathoms of water, so when it's discharged you don't even notice it, and there's also a very strong tidal flow out there. Generally even during neep tides [the lowest level of high tide] it flows about 5 or 6 knots, so it disperses it very rapidly, and the dilution factor is tremendous anyway. This is new, it's an EU thing, and it had to be done by a certain time, otherwise there was a penalty. It comes up from all the distilleries, they even bring it across from Jura.

'In the old days it was just pumped straight out, but it's not in any way harmful to the environment, if anything at all it's beneficial. It's only yeast and ground malted barley. We always kid people along a bit, about the fish queuing up for their dram when they discharge the stills. If anything it's beneficial to the environment, it's not in any way detrimental. They've been doing it down here for the last 150 years, and it's certainly done no harm.'

'Life on the island has changed a lot,' reckons 'Big Angus' McAffer, 'since all the ferries came in. Now it's all drive on, drive off. Before, when the *Lochiel* was there, you were hoisting the cars onto the boat. It's easy doing it now. There's a lot

The staff of Bowmore distillery, 1928. Jim McEwan's grandfather, John, is the maltman third from the right, back row.

more visitors to the island, and a lot more coming round the distilleries.

'The barley comes in now in bulk, in big boats, and they suck the barley out into big hoppers at Port Ellen pier, and Mundell's lorry takes it over to the maltings, and they get it malted there in big drums. The boat comes in with the barley quite often, because they go through a lot of barley, because all the distilleries take it from the Port Ellen maltings now.

'A lot of the people who worked here lived round about. There were two lots of company houses, and then they sold them. The workers got the first chance at them. It was a real community of everybody living and working together, and that's the way Ardbeg was too. I went to Ardbeg school from here, there were a lot at Ardbeg school in those days because there were a lot of people working at Ardbeg and Lagavulin. The distillery in Port Ellen was an important employer then. It employed a lot of people. But the last school leavers were taken on here 33 years ago, four of them. What jobs are there in the distilleries now?'

Bowmore's head brewer Ed McAffer points out the growth of interest in single malts as another significant difference to his earlier days in the Scotch whisky business.

'The biggest change in the industry in my time has been in the single malt market. When I started at first single malt was something you didn't really know anything about. We knew we were filling for all these different customers. The company was called SPM [Stanley P. Morrison Ltd] when I started, so we obviously filled for SPM, and we all understood that they were whisky brokers who probably sold it on, but we also filled for all the big companies that made all the really well-known blended whiskies. That to us was what working in a distillery was, we were making the whisky for that industry. Single malt, you'd have heard of Glenfiddich, to us that was the only one you'd maybe heard of.

'Bowmore as a single malt didn't come until into the '70s. That was one of the big changes from the time I started as we've gone through, the way single malt whisky has taken off. And all the different distilleries are bringing out their single malts, all the different years. It's quite a market. All the finishes and expressions.

'I'm glad that I saw what I did over the years, saw these old guys do what they did. The younger ones that are coming in now, it's a different way altogether. A different culture. When I used to listen to them they'd be saying, "Twenty years ago we used to do this and that," and it seemed such a long time. Now I've been in the place almost forty years myself. I've got the memory of one of the guys that came through.

'One of the things that stuck in my mind was the number of years that they were talking about beforehand. Like small disputes, like when there was a better job going in Bruichladdich, and half a dozen of them were going to walk out of Bowmore. It ended up they all went, except the one guy who'd been the first to say he was going to leave stayed in Bowmore. The job fell flat in Bruichladdich after about six months, and this guy was still in Bowmore and they couldn't get back in.

'I remember them having a right ding-dong about it, and the men I'm talking about were all retired, they were sixty-five and they came back in to work as casuals, and it almost came to blows, guys at that age. It must have been about twenty-five years previously. It happened in the '30s and this was in the '60s. It was a bone of contention even then. They started just talking about it, and it ended up more than a heated argument. I always remember it seemed such a long time ago to me, but then you think back and some of the things that we did don't seem that long ago. When you look at the seventeen-year-old whisky now, you're thinking that's really 1986–87, it doesn't seem so long ago since we were putting that stuff away. We were taking it out of the warehouse and looking at the date, and saying, "I remember when we put them in there."'

16

On Characters

As we have seen, increased automation in distilleries and centralisation of functions such as malting has resulted in fewer workers, and consequently fewer 'characters'. The end of 'dramming' may well have had something to do with the decline of characters, too …

'There was much more fun,' thinks Grant Carmichael. 'There was *time* to have more fun then. Life's much more serious now, and people have got to be much more serious-minded, because there's so much depending on the push of a button. Whereas the old days were much more relaxed. There were more capers, more jokes played on people.

'There was the story of Billy Graham, for instance. Billy Graham was a ram, a Leicester ram, and he had no teeth because he ate the distillery draff, he was fed on the draff, and there was this one wee chap had a good dram in him this day, and he was staggering down the road. What the boys did was they got a set of antlers, deer antlers, that were lying in the distillery, and tied them to Billy Graham. They gave him a dram and then let him off at the end of the distillery road, heading off after this little fellow. Billy Graham went charging down, and he got him alright. That was in Caol Ila.

'Everybody had nicknames, Port Ellen is the worst place imaginable for giving people nicknames. There was a chap there who worked called "Hughie the Loaf", why they called him that I don't know. Everybody had nicknames, families had nicknames, so that if, let's say, you had a lot of Mackays, they would be given a nickname, and you'd know immediately which one it was. Everybody had nicknames, and they still do.'

'The characters that were there then,' reminisces Neil Ferguson of Caol Ila. 'When you're on shift down there now, there's only two of you on, and you're in the stillhouse, the other feller's up in the mash house, you don't see much of each other at all. In the old days there were always a whole lot of people there.

'We did have our characters here at Caol Ila. If you go down to the distillery you'll see some pictures of a gentleman that used to work there [the brewer, "Dolly" McNiven]. He used to have a few drams and he always fancied himself as a piper, but he'd never really got round to learning how to play the bagpipes. When he used to go down to the pub in Port Askaig he'd get a brush, a floor brush, and he used to take the head of the brush, and put the shaft over his shoulder, tuck the head of the brush under his arm, and he used to go around making sounds as if he was playing the bagpipes when he had a few jars.

'He used to go down in the pub and march up and down, playing away at his imaginary bagpipes. We all used to go down there at one time. There was one evening he was in there playing his brush and he came to the end of whatever he had been playing, put the brush carefully aside, and I said, "That was well done, Donald, just one thing," kidding, you know. "What was that?" he said. "Well, I think about the second verse," I said, "when you were doing the grace notes, I'm sure I detected a slight hiccup then." He said, "Did you notice that?" I said "Yes, I'm sure there was." "That was tonight's deliberate mistake," he said!

'I would go back and do it all tomorrow given the chance. It wasn't always

Caol Ila distillery, 2004. The original warehouse in on the left, the stillhouse on the extreme right.

easy, there was a lot of hard work involved, but it didn't bother me, I was fit then. Long hours, and sometimes it could be dusty and sometimes it could be dirty, but the people who worked there, they were really amazing.

'When I worked in the malt barns it was like being in a madhouse. First thing every morning an argument would start. It was never bad-tempered or anything like that, things would get a bit heated. Nobody ever came to blows, but every morning there was an argument started, and kept on during the day. Everything under the sun, the stupidest possible things. But it was great, it was an amazing place to work in.

'You always had the dodgers. In the mornings especially. You see you had to go into the kilns and turn the malt that was drying in there. There was a fire lit underneath and the smoke came up through, and you still had to go in there and turn it. Well, somebody would take a fit of coughing, and had to go out. The same person would have a fit of coughing every morning, sort of thing. Everybody knew, nobody bothered. He'd have to go outside, so the rest of you just had to soldier on and get the thing finished.'

Ed McAffer of Bowmore believes the work environment has changed completely. 'It's a happy enough atmosphere in the distillery, but in a different way. You just have to adapt. As we get older we don't have the same energy for these kind of things anyway. We talk about it, and the young guys look at us as if we must have been off our faces half the time, which wasn't the case. Young guys are a wee bit more serious about everything, just because they've got in and they've got to watch after their jobs. They do the job and they have a joke and a laugh, but it's not the same.

'When we were younger, we'd be doing a job and we'd get the job done and we'd be hanging about for maybe twenty minutes or half an hour if we were finished early, and instead of hanging about what we'd do is get up, go in the warehouse, and have a bung fight. Grown men running about with pockets full of cork bungs throwing them at each other. If you hit somebody there was a big cheer, we were all jouking [darting] about all over the place, and then, of course, it would take us two or three days to clean the place up. Bungs everywhere. I can't imagine what would happen now, there'd be a great clearance and everybody would be out the door.

'There was a big, strong young boy here at one time, but he was the nervous type. And we played tricks on him. One Hallowe'en night we were on the night shift, and he would move the forty-footer "artic" for us, he was very happy to do that. So he up into the cab, and we heard the engine revving and revving, then he leapt out and ran – followed by one of the boys in a monkey outfit. He'd been waiting in the cab for him! You'd never get away with daft things like that now.'

Inevitably, Jim McEwan also has plenty of stories about Islay characters, which he shared with Ruari McLeod.

JM: What about the time the Goat was putting the pitch on the warehouse roof, Ruari?

RM: Oh aye. There was an old warehouse where the bottling plant is now.

JM: Who were the men involved?

RM: 'Jim the Goat' and Donald MacLennan in Port Charlotte, and the late Jim McLasidge.

JM: This is a tin roof, it's a hot summer's day, and they're putting pitch on the roof, that's the scene.

RM: Aye, aye. They were working on number one warehouse and they were walking across the roof, coming down the stair, and going into number one warehouse when the custom and excise [officer] wasn't there, and they were filling a bottle and walking back up, and the manager saw them, right enough, and he shouted to them …

JM: They were covered in tar, they were so drunk, there was tar everywhere, it was like the Black and White Minstrel Show.

RM: And at the end of day they just came down, and there was the bucket of tar down below, and Jim planted his foot in it, and he had to walk all the way trying to get it off.

JM: He came down the ladder, and the one who had come before had left the bucket, so he came down, put his foot in the bucket, and the manager says, 'Right, you, are you drunk?' And he says, 'No, me no,' and the manager says, 'Right, you, across to that office,' and he was walking across the yard with the bucket stuck to his foot, trying to deny he was drunk.

JM: Did I ever tell you the story of Big Donald McAffer and the haircut, Ruari?

RM: No, no, you didn't.

JM: Right. Donald McAffer, Donald Mor, remember Donald Mor, the cooper?

RM: Yes, yes, I know him very well. The cooper.

JM: He was a cooper at Bowmore, Donald had long white hair, very unusual. A big built man. And on a Saturday morning, before the filling, Donald and myself or who-ever was around would go down, and the Customs man would measure the strength of the alcohol, and then would empty the water in, using five gallon jugs. So Donald was a big, strong man, he was perfect to lift the five gallon jugs and tip them in. Once we got the water in the vat, we would start to mix the vat, rouse the vat up, and while we were doing that, the Customs officer would go downstairs and get his paperwork ready. And when the Customs officer was downstairs Donald put his hand in the vat, the white whisky over his head like that, his hair was as white as that, beautiful silver hair, long.

RM: Oh aye, it was.

JM: He said, 'Keep your eye on that Customs man,' and there was a wee horn in there, dramming away, eight o'clock in the morning, dramming away, and mixing away, and the whisky over the head. There was no hairdressers in Bowmore, and on a Saturday morning the cooperage became the hairdressing shop. So at ten o'clock Donald and I go up, the vat's ready, and Donald's hair is shining. Angus McNiven was cutting hair in the cooperage, and Donald says to him, 'Here Angus, take a bit off my hair. But remember, I'm like Samson, you cut the hair, I lose the strength.' 'Don't worry' says Angus, 'sit down, sit down.' So Donald sits down in the chair, and Angus gets a yeast bag, an old yeast bag, puts the yeast bag round Donald, tucks it in, and then he gets the old clippers, remember the old clippers?

RM: Oh yes, aye, aye.

JM: Starts clipping away at Donald's hair. 'Ho, be careful, watch you don't take too much off, because you'll lose the strength, right.' Cutting away, cutting away, bloody clippers, like a dog with distemper, there's holes all over your head. And he goes

round the back of Donald, he puts the clipper down, and he takes out his pipe, puts the pipe in his mouth, and he takes out the Swan Vestas, strikes the Swan Vesta, and Donald's hair explodes. All the hair disappears, just wee curly black bits, due to all the vapour. McNiven took off, broke the world land speed record, with a cooper behind, throwing hammers at him. So that was what happened to Donald. The whole lot went. Not a mark on his head at all.

Bowmore pier and main street, 1950s.

There was also a time in Bowmore when we got the Customs officer's dog drunk. The Customs officer, who shall remain nameless, was not one of the good customs officers, he liked to steal it himself, but he didn't like anyone else getting it. And every Friday he would always go to the Lochside Hotel and get absolutely drunk with the sanitary inspector, that was the two of them.

They would get drunk on gin and tonics, and then in the afternoon he'd come back and finish the filling. And he'd a dog called Bess, and this dog knew if you had a 'dooker', if you were carrying a bottle, this bugger knew. Like one of these modern dogs that sniff for gunpowder at the airport. This bugger was sniffing like that, but thirty years ago. So if you were carrying a bottle at all, particularly a salad cream bottle, this dog would come up and look at you and sit there and bark and bark and bark. It had one brown eye and one blue eye, a right bloody mongrel. Willie Gilchrist, Archie, my grandfather, and old Sandy were the boys that were doing the filling, and I'm putting the bungs in the casks. And old Davy Bell is weighing the casks.

So this is Friday afternoon, and the Customs man is absolutely as drunk as a skunk on gin and tonic. The word comes down from the office, 'A phone call for Mr So and so,' so he goes staggering up the hill to the office, to the phone. It's the surveyor, so he's going to be on the phone a while, and his dog, Bess, is in the corner, sound asleep. So old Sandy said to me, 'Dùn an doras, dùn an doras.' ('Shut the door, shut the door.') I was wondering why, because it's quite hot, and it's better to let the air in to the filling store. And then once the door was shut, he says in Gaelic, 'Go and get that bloody dog.' I'm thinking, why? but when you're eighteen you don't ask questions or you get a slap, you know, so I dragged the dog over to Sandy, and he says, 'Right, hold the bugger's mouth open.'

'So Sandy's got the gun, full strength, I'm holding the dog's mouth open, and Sandy puts the gun in the dog's mouth – shooooosh! Oh a good half pint. Sixty-eight, sixty-nine per cent. 'Right, hold his mouth closed.' So I'm holding the dog's mouth, the dog's kicking and swallowing, it's like a rodeo rider, you know. So the dog is absolutely drunk as a skunk, she goes round and round and round the room, staggering on two legs, just two legs on one side that go, staggering around the room, and eventually she ends up in the same corner, pissed as a fart. Hand over her head like that.

Then Willie Gilchrist says, 'Christ, what if we've killed the dog? If we've killed the dog we're going to Greenock prison for the rest of our lives. Go and check the dog.' So I'm over looking at the dog, no sign of life at all, no. Hells bells, we've killed the Customs man's dog. It's the West Indies! So anyway I kept working, and eventually the dog kind of looked that way, with that pissed eye. Christ, the dog's sleeping, right, get this filling finished quick and let's get the hell out of here. So we get the filling finished, the Customs man comes back down, he's locking the vats, he's drunk, he's really drunk, he's got the keys and he's signing the book, and he heads out the filling store, and we are like, 'Oh Christ, what's going to happen now when this dog tries to stand?'

Anyway, he shouts on the dog, 'Bess! Bess!', so poor Bess gets up. He shouts, 'Bess!' and he doesn't look behind him. And he goes up the hill from Bowmore, he's staggering, and the dog is exactly the same. The funniest sight you'll see. The Customs man staggering, and the dog staggering. The dog never came near the filling store again. It never ever barked at people carrying bottles, it was cured. The dog was cured. But for a moment in time it was have we killed the dog. But we didn't kill the dog.

Some of these distillery dogs used to get used to the whisky because they'd be in the bungs. The bungs were always full of whisky and the boys would roll the bungs and the dog would go after them and sit there chewing them, and they'd get used to it. So some dogs would drink a lot, and most distilleries always had a dog. Or somebody at the distillery had a dog.

One time, when we were getting a boatload of casks ready at Bowmore I was working with Willie Gilchrist and Sandy McArthur, and you had to sample every cask. The Customs man had to put the thermometer and hydrometer into every cask. So what Sandy and Willie used to do … 600 casks was a lot of walking, walking up and down the warehouse all day … so what they used to do is that they got a sample tube and they would come out to the Customs officer, old Mr McCallum, you remember Mr McCallum, Ruari?

RM: Oh yes, I mind him very well.

JM: They'd say, 'Mr McCallum, cask number 1234 and 1235,' and then they'd come out, and he thought they'd walk away up and into the warehouse, but they were just standing outside the door, and they'd wait a wee while, and then they'd come in, 'Hello, Mr McCallum, 1237.' It was the same sample. And this old guy would say, 'It's amazing just the consistency of the alcohol in this warehouse.' It was the same sample every time. Fun and games.

'Big Angus' McAffer recalls that there was no shortage of characters during his time at Lagavulin.

'You'd get paid on a Thursday, cash, and on Friday there'd be the odd one staggering a bit when he came in, but if he was a good worker Monday to Thursday the manager would let it go. These days there's no Fridays like that, no characters. It's all chemists and engineers. One day I heard the manager saying to one of the boys after a Thursday night, "I saw you had a slight stagger going down the road." And he said to him, "Well, if you'd felt like me you'd be staggering too." You got a good laugh in those days, you looked forward to coming to work. It was a home from home.

'There was this man was at the boilerhouse at that time, he was always opening the valve up at the sluice up at the dams. Well they sent him up to check how the water was at the dams, and then he came back and this inspector that was here, he's retired now, he says to him, "What's the situation with the water?" "Well, my advice is to cut out two mashes right away," he says to him. The inspector says, "I can't do that, because I told head office in Elgin we were carrying on." The man says, "Elgin

Lagavulin distillery, 1960s.

is a terrible long distance from Solan Lochs!"

'The lochs are five miles up the hill, and it's a marathon of a walk. He set off at seven o'clock in the morning. He was going away sober and coming back drunk. Five miles up there and five miles back. And he was to the beak [very drunk].

'Hughie McQueen was the manager, and what he said to Hughie McQueen was, "If I'm going to be the water bailiff here, you do as I tell you!" And Hughie says to me, "I don't know where that man's getting all the drink. He must be taking it out of the stones." Well, the stillman was giving it to him. If you did take a day away like that they gave it to you in a wee bottle. And at nine o'clock he was taking it with his tea and the stillman was filling the bottle again.

'Another time a traveller came, with a fancy car, and there were not many cars coming near the place at that time. I was speaking to him, and he comes out with the briefcase, a real fancy man, and he sees Hughie and he says to him, "I would like to speak to the manager." Hughie looked at him and said, "I'm sorry, you just missed him, he's just away down to the village this minute." He got rid of him that way. And the traveller says to me, "Who was that man?" and I said, "Oh, I don't know, he's a stranger to me."

'Once we had a stillman who was a bit lazy, and the manager thought he wasn't doing everything the way he should be, so before he came on at night, at nine, when the shifts were changing, the manager went over to the stillhouse and put a piece of thread across the heavy swing door on the boiler, which was due to be cleaned. When the manager went back a few hours later to see what had happened the stillman said to him, "Yes, I cleaned the boiler, and I put the effing thread back where you left it!"

'We had a lot of managers when I started, Hughie McQueen, Jack Wilson, Ernie Cattanach. Hughie's brother worked here too. He was doing the Malt Mill sometimes, and he was doing the mill house too, Hughie's brother. They stayed over at Dunyveg, just across the water there. The managers would usually stay for five or six years. They came and went but they never changed the Islay folk. There's an east – west divide really. Every manager we had was east coast. West coast folk are more open.

In case it seems that all the true characters among the whisky men happened to live and work on Islay, let Ian Millar recount some stories of 'personalities' associated with Blair Athol distillery in Pitlochry.

'Jimmy and Tuppence were playing cards in warehouse four one day; they were supposed to be tapping casks. Jimmy got caught short and peed up against an old butt. Then they heard the door opening and the cooper calling them, so they hid in behind a couple of butts. Tom the cooper kept walking in, calling them, but then his attention was caught by the damp patch below one of his beloved butts. He

Blair Athol distillery, 1980s.

looked up to make sure that the leak was not from above before bending down to dip his finger in the liquid sitting in the chime [the end of the cask.] He then stuck his finger in his mouth to see if it was indeed whisky leaking out of the cask …

'Bill Milne used to keep two bottles of water to drink in the upper receiver room, next to the stillhouse, as it was a cooler place to keep them. One day one of the tun room men swapped one of them for a bottle of neat spirit, and poor Bill had a good mouthful over the throat before he knew what he was dealing with. Needless to say, he had words with the offending tun room man.

'Peter was of a nervous disposition, but he was sitting innocently and calmly with the paper beside the mashman's desk at 3 a.m. one night shift. Norrie Campbell, who was a young man with a great sense of fun, stuck a pair of wellies on and walked across the mash inside the open mash tun to the other side and put two hands up over the side of the mash tun. Peter jumped out of his skin, of course, and the two of them had to have a dram to get over it.

'Eddie Rose [well-known as a traditional Scottish entertainer] dozed off one night in the middle of the stillhouse. This was unlike Eddie, but he was doing a fair bit of entertaining at that time, and it must have just caught up with him. Seeing that he was asleep, someone sneaked through to the stillhouse and carefully painted his boots bright yellow. He woke up soon afterwards, and the look on his face was something to behold.'

17

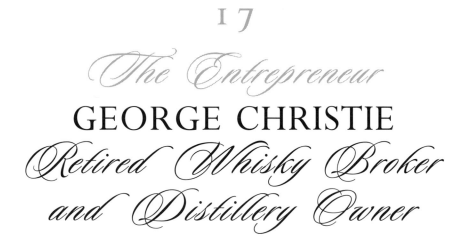

The Entrepreneur
GEORGE CHRISTIE
Retired Whisky Broker and Distillery Owner

'I was born in Troon in Ayrshire, went to school there until I was about eleven. My parents then came up to Glasgow, my father was a butcher, and his father had died in Cambuslang, and things weren't doing so well as far as pop was concerned, so we came up to Glasgow. I was a very keen rugby player, and I went to sea when I was fifteen, and my brother was already there. That was 1935. By the beginning of the war in '39 I was third mate on a Glasgow tanker, and I went into the navy in 1940. I was a sub-lieutenant Royal Navy Reserve, and in late '40 I got into submarines, and I was there till 1945. I was delivering a boat to Russia, so I got back at the beginning of '46. I had command by that time.'

'Gus Paterson, the whisky broker, was in the merchant service too, and he stayed merchant service during the war. All sailors have a "rhythm", there's something that they understand about each other, though they can be completely different. Gus and I were not completely different, cos we liked each other's company, but the long view to Gus was for the birds, which made him more attractive actually, but I couldn't follow that. I would never have been in the whisky business if it hadn't been for Gus.

'In late '46, early '47 I started work in the whisky industry. I started working with Gus. I was sitting for my "Extra Master" certificate which was an examination that only happened every six months. I had a wife and a child to support in the meantime and Gus kept saying, "You should come into the whisky business." His father had been in it before him. I worked for Gus for about five years, and we were always good friends. He was a great guy, and if he had money he spent it, and I was inclined to hang onto it. W.R. Paterson Ltd was one of his father's companies that

George and Ricky Christie,
2004.

Gus took over, and I owned about 20 per cent. Gus was a lovely guy.

'Later I had a half share in Alexander McGavin Ltd's bonded warehouse in Robertson Street, [in Glasgow] and from there I moved on and built the North of Scotland distillery next to DCL's Cambus at Tullibody near Alloa.

'To illustrate how different the trade was, I bought Knox's Brewery with the intention of turning it into a distillery, and it was next door to Cambus. I wasn't going to fight with the DCL, they could have quashed me very easily. So I wrote to them and said I wanted to do this, but would like to discuss it. I had a letter back, saying come through to Torphichen Street [DCL's head offices in Edinburgh], and Sir Henry Ross, who was the boss, was there. He asked what I wanted to do and I told him. I said I didn't want to fight with anybody, and he asked if I was short of whisky. I told him that it wasn't really that, but that I should like to do something myself. He said, "Well, there's no reason why you shouldn't."

'My point is that at that time, a "nobody" like me who had come in could see the head man of the whole bloody industry and he would say, "I don't see why not." Everybody knew everybody in the industry then.

'When we got Knox's Brewery all the brewing plant was still there, but it had to go out. Nothing wrong with it, but once you put in stills, and particularly a patent still, which is a constant-running still, your fermenting vessels have got to match up. In a brewing situation fermenting is in a way the same but it's not really. In the distilling business you have your mash tun, the stuff comes out and goes into your fermenters, and you'll probably run maybe roughly 60 to 70 hours. Then that runs off through your stills and out. Whereas in brewing, it doesn't go through stills, of course, so in actual fact you are running straight off your fermenters. So all the fermenters that they had were far too small.

'We actually put in oak fermenters. It didn't have to be oak in the brewing business, and mostly it was firs, Scotch pine. It was a constant process. You didn't have to recharge your stills every now and again, all you had to do was make sure you had a full load of fermenters all coming to the top at the right time, and they went straight into your patent still, and they were run off down through the still, and you took off all your solids, and you ran the actual spirit, and you could more or less decide where you were going to take it from, into casks.

'We started off with two pot stills as well, but we changed over for all grain in the first 18 months because we knew damn well that we couldn't produce enough. We used the pot stills to produce a single malt we called Strathmore, which we would last make probably in 1958. We traded as the North of Scotland Distillery Co. Ltd.

'We put the two pot stills in first, because we were just thinking we were going to make a malt whisky, and I don't think it ever occurred to us that we might make grain, because at that time all the grain distilleries were quite big. You were talking of probably two or three million gallons a year, and we were probably taking out 200,000 or 300,000.

'Everybody wanted grain, and the space taken up by the pot stills had to make way for grain production. A patent still is probably 30-odd feet high, while a pot is like a medium-sized gentleman, so I had to take the pot stills out and build a long tower and put the patent stills in. But it didn't take long to do, because I had the stills made while we were still working, and we just didn't put the roof on the godamn thing that we were building until such time as we were ready for the change. It's so easy when you've got pressure on, you've got to get off your ass and do it. That's how it was. We were all probably in our thirties and forties, and we thought you could do anything.

'I had been for four or five years in submarines, prior to that I'd been in the merchant service, passed for master, and it's all about engineering, so that's how I was able to do all this. Engineers are the most stupid people in the bloody world. They can only do what they're fucking told. You just get them at the start and say this is what we're going to do. Then they come up with the ideas of how they can do it by themselves.

'It's not a question of being difficult, it's a question of being nearly broke, and knowing that you've got to bloody well do it. Just the same as in the navy, in the wartime, you did things that you'd never have dreamt of doing otherwise, because you were shit scared not to!

'I recollect that at North of Scotland the people there took great pride in what they were doing. We had on the staff probably about 26 guys, and they took pride in the quality of the spirit and in the yield. One day they were putting in a cooling tower, and they'd built this very tall bit on top of the distillery, and it was a case of how the hell are we going to get this in there. It was a heavy stainless steel contraption, and we were scratching our heads, thinking we'd have to get a high-rise crane or goodness knows what, but two of our staff, Bertie and Archie, the two of them, with just a pulley, over a weekend, had it in by Monday morning. We just said, "How the fuck did you do that?" The guys really were passionate about the place and what they did.

'The most grain spirit we ever made was 2.7 million gallons per year. It was bloody good stuff as well. There's still some of it around. When they were doing a review of the description of grain whisky they did a survey of new-fill from all the main distilleries around Scotland to set the parameters of what was designated an "eau de vie" grain Scotch whisky as opposed to just a plain spirit. There were only two distilleries which actually surpassed the criteria that the independent body had set down. One was North British [in Edinburgh] and the other was our North of Scotland.

'We didn't take the last out of it. Your last column, the vapour's coming up, and you can decide at which point in that column you're going to take your spirit. Now you can go up another couple of feet to one of the other trays and draw off there, or you can draw off a little bit further down. We went for character.

'One way to look at it, of course, is that if you've got a lot of malt distilleries and all the rest of it, you're going to get your grain to be as neutral as you can get it, because you can make a killing out of it, but if you've only got one grain distillery you just say, "Alright, I'll draw it off at the point I like," and you always drew it off at the point with a little bit of character. You can drink North of Scotland.

'There was John Agnew who was the goalkeeper for either Rangers or Celtic at that time. He worked for me, and he was a good cooper, and because he was in football, coopers flocked to him. He was known as "Big John", although he wasn't actually very big at all. Coopers are the most appalling characters normally, because

North of Scotland Distilling Co. Ltd's Strathmore distillery, 1960s.

they are completely independent, because they are paid by results. A good cooper can set up seven barrels in a bloody hour, and he's going to get two and three-quarter hours per barrel. So he's going to get [paid for] bloody nearly 20 hours if he can do seven barrels. So what they'd usually do was to do that by lunchtime and then go out and get pissed.

'But with hands-on management, it wasn't difficult, because you were in there and you could swear better than they could hopefully, and John Agnew was such a nice guy. He always used to give his suppliers a turkey for their Christmas, and we could never understand that. You don't give your suppliers a turkey, you give your customers a turkey! But he was that kind of nice guy.

'Once you've started as a distiller you start making more whisky, and where the hell do you put it? So you actually have to find a place. McGavin's in Glasgow could hold about five thousand casks, and that was pushing it, so I bought the United Turkey Red dye factory in Bonhill, which was shut down, with about 50 acres, and I started converting some of their warehouses and building others to store whisky for other people. That made money. I realised that if you were going to be independent you were best to be independent in production, storage, and then the bloody hard thing was to go and sell the goddamn stuff!

'I wanted to expand my business interests, and with three friends I bought a pub in Partick. It was ridiculous, we paid £45,000 for a pub in Partick. That was in

Another view of Strathmore distillery, 1960s, with George Christie's Jaguar XK120 in the foreground.

the 1950s, though it was a good pub! John Scott was one of my friends and partners in North of Scotland Distillery Co Ltd, and he was a prominent publican in Glasgow.

'Things were going well and he bought a Bentley and hired a chauffeur. In 1960 Seager Evans opened Tormore distillery near Grantown-on-Spey, which they had just built, and so John and I were driven up in his new Bentley for the official opening. We went in for lunch, and there was a lot of alcohol around, but we had a chauffeur, so we were able to indulge as much as we wanted to. Well, eventually everybody got up to go, all went out to their cars, where their chauffeurs were waiting, and away they went. Except for John and I. No bloody car and no chauffeur. Some of the older, established whisky people seemed to think it was quite amusing that here we were, a couple of comparative newcomers, without our flash Bentley. Eventually it was tracked down to the Craigellachie Hotel along the road towards Elgin. The chauffeur had gone there for his lunch and had enjoyed himself so much he passed out in the car park. It ended up with John and I sharing the driving home, with the chauffeur still passed out in the back of the car. I think John drove himself a lot after that.

'Around that time they were building Invergordon grain distillery, and they pulled Stanley Morrison back from retirement. [Stanley P. Morrison Ltd was appointed agent for Invergordon grain whisky when production commenced in 1961.] He was disgraced because he had gone broke before the war. If you went broke in the whisky business all it meant was that he hadn't paid other people in the whisky business, and they didn't forgive him. Stanley came back, and Invergordon became quite a big thing.

'Dan Flynn was Stanley Morrison's bookie, and he was well-known in the whisky industry. He would lend money from time to time too, though I never had to avail myself of his services. One day he rang me up and said that he had a punter who had run up £30,000 of debt, and who was offering to settle his account with shares in a whisky company. What did I think? I advised him that this seemed a pretty precarious investment, and not to go along with it. It turned out in the course of time that what he had been offered was a 30 per cent share in the Distillers Company Ltd. Dan was such a lovely bloke though that he still spoke to me after- wards, even when he realised how much money he could have made.

'By now, all the distilleries were getting renewed, and we became agents for Balblair distillery at Evanton, north of Inverness. I started in that with Gus Paterson and then I carried it on with Bertie Cumming, who was the County Clerk of Banffshire. He had somehow got hold of Balblair. He opened Balblair, which was shut down, and Gus Patterson and I were agents for it. We were involved in Balblair for a long time, and then I went up and worked the first week in Pulteney, in Wick, when Bertie Cumming got that too. The distillery had been shut for a long time.

'Another guy who was very, very helpful and we got on well with was Joe Hobbs in Fort William. Joe Hobbs went to Canada in about 1904, had been in the navy during the First World War, and before the Second World War he was the agent for Peter Dawson whisky in Canada. After the war Joe came over here and worked in London. I don't know what he did there but it was obviously successful, because he bought Inverlochy Estate at Fort William, which was the castle and 15,000 acres, which he bought for about £10,000 or £15,000. He bought Ben Nevis distillery, which was shut down, he opened that up, and took off from there.

'He was a wonderful character. He was in Canada when America was dry, and he got an old "bucket" of about 3,000 tons, an old cargo ship, and he stuck it about five miles off Los Angeles, and they came down in launches and other ships from Canada and they loaded it up with booze. Then they ran cruises from Holywood out there. There was dancing and general jollification, everybody got pissed – the booze was cheap.

'Joe told a lovely story about when the new baseball stadium was built in Los Angeles they got the concession to run the opening, in other words the horses and

The original Speyside dis-
tillery, Kingussie, c.1900.
This distillery had a notably
short existence, opening in
1895 and ceasing produc-
tion between 1905 and
1910.

carts that were pulling all the floats and all the rest of it, and Joe said the base of all these carts, the first three, were filled with cases of whiskey, covered over, and with all the dancing girls on top of them. When the parade was finished the carts were in under the stand of the baseball park, and while everybody was watching the baseball going on, all his chaps were in there, pulling the stuff off and distributing it around the place. He had a great time.

'I made a point of knowing pretty well all there was to know about the industry, and in 1955 I set up the Speyside Distillery and Bonding Company Ltd. At the end of the war, all the people that were in it were old hands. Willie Walker [whisky broker] and people like that had been in the First World War, and they knew what it had been like before the Second.

'You had to see what the industry had been and where it was going to go. As far as I was concerned I automatically thought that production would increase and that you would need a warehouse to put your whisky in, and I certainly had the biggest privately owned whisky warehouse in the country. I could store about 200,000 casks. Which was a lot.

'I called it the Speyside Distillery and Bonding Company because I'd bought this place up here [Old Milton House, close to the River Spey, near Kingussie in Inverness-shire], and the Speyside distillery had been in Kingussie [operational from 1895 to1911]. It was the Macpherson-Grants who started it up, and they owned this place. I bought it from the MacPherson-Grants and I'm told, though I haven't found it, that there was a telephone line from this house right along and across the Spey to the distillery in Kingussie. That's why I put Speyside in the company name.

'I was looking at this area and I always intended to build a distillery. The business of doing it in Cambus first was because I knew Knox and when their brewery went bust I bought it for a figure of about £4,000 or £5,000. That was peanuts.

'But the Spey is the Bond Street as far as distilleries is concerned, and when this place [Old Milton House] came on the market, it was advertised in the *Glasgow Herald*, which is how I saw it. Ballindalloch Estates had sold it on the basis that it was trees. A timber merchant from Inverness had bought it on that basis. He cut all the trees down and all he wanted to do was sell it. The agent said he wanted £5,000 for it, and I said, "I'll give you £4,000," and he said, "If you make it £4,200 I'll take it." That's the kind of money we were talking about. That was 1956.

'I had everything I wanted here for my distillery. I had the Tromie running down into the Spey, and I had plenty of ground, so that at some point we could do something, but I had a lot of things on the boil at the time. It was a nice place, but if my wife had thought I intended to live here permanently she'd have left me!

'Despite all the big companies, there are still a good number of individual distilleries owned and run by individuals. As far as they are concerned there is nothing altruistic about saying. 'I don't want to get tied up with so and so and so and so.' They know it will be, take the money and goodbye. There's still a lot of people who care, and it's a bloody good life. Living in a lovely part of the world, and having a job with good people.

'In terms of jobs, I used to reckon when we had Balblair that we needed a dozen men, that was all. The extra above that was warehouse, because you still had to have guys to run out casks and put them in the warehouse and all the rest of it, and most of that has gone now.

'In other words, when you make your whisky it goes into a bloody big vat, a tanker comes up, you pour it into the tanker and off it goes. I did that at Bonhill. I had 200,000 casks down there which I was taking in from everywhere. I was offering the storage. I was storing for Hiram Walker, the Strathclyde distillery and others. Strathclyde distillery is in the centre of Glasgow, for Christ's sake, they didn't have room to expand, they had to go out. If they had a place only a few miles away where a tanker could go in and pump out 5,000 gallons, it was a good, efficient way of doing it for them. It didn't change anything. The whisky still went into oak casks, and still was put in racked warehouses.

'They said, "Look here, can you take it in in tankers?" because as far as they were concerned, once you got into actually filling the barrels or hogsheads or whatever in their own distillery, they had to have a cooperage, and they had to have all the empty casks ready, and it takes a lot of space. So I did the lot. They just sent the tankers down. There were all the various 5,000 gallon vats, all made of oak, and it went into that, and they sent casks down for us to fill for them.

'I can only remember one or two shits in the whisky business, and they were never big shits. All the others were bloody good blokes. We were friends with the Teacher family, partly because of sailing. Ronald Teacher [chairman of Teachers (Distillers) Ltd from 1949, and later president] was a very keen sailing man. I didn't know Ronald so well, but I knew the Bergiuses and the Dunlops, who were associates of the Teachers by marriage. They were all sailors.

'Teachers did a whisky which was quite different from any other. There's no doubt about that. Teacher's Highland Cream, whether you liked it or you didn't, it was different. They didn't need to make a lot of money because they didn't have a lot of shareholders, and they were all working. Robbie was in the office, Alan was out travelling the bloody world, George was out working distilleries, and Ronald was entertaining people and so forth. They were in St Enoch Square in Glasgow, they had a good set up there that wasn't too expensive, and they only had one distillery [Ardmore, near Huntly], and they got their grain from North British. They were taken over by Hiram Walker either just before or just after Ronald died, but Robbie is still working there, and Adam's son Bill Bergius is still there.

'Walter Bergius was deaf, and could only lip read. He was about the most awkward bugger that you ever met in your life. He could lip read like nobody's business. Remember, during the war Ronald Teacher was in the navy, the other two were in the navy, and so Walter was Teacher's from about 1941 right through until after the war. Not being able to hear, he spoke from his diaphragm, and I had one over on most people, because I could understand him! Most people didn't know what the fucking hell he was talking about.

'He was a good sailor, and I sailed with him because I was the only bugger who could tell what he was wanting. I took him down to Spain in my boat one year, and he said, "You realise I can't keep night watches." I asked why not? He said, "Well, I can't read anybody's lips!" I said, "Alright, I'll get you a fucking torch," and he did night watches all the way to Spain. We liked each other, and Walter kept the company going all during the war. And he did it by just being fucking difficult. And he was naturally difficult. I don't think he could be any different.

'We eventually took the decision to close North of Scotland around 1980 because all the grain distilleries were increasing production, and if you're making malt whisky you can live with a few customers taking maybe fifty or a hundred hogsheads of malt whisky, you don't need many customers, but when you get into the grain business, it's all about volume. There was no way in which we could compete with even North British, which wasn't the biggest by any means. But when you had Cambus next door to us, probably producing 12 to 15 million gallons a year, the market for what we had was gone in the sense that we couldn't sell at a price that was competitive with the other grain distilleries.

'One factor in stopping production at North of Scotland was that there happened to be a big whisky loch. Why did everybody produce twice as much as they needed? Suddenly you could buy three-year old cheaper than we could produce new spirit, and it doesn't make sense. So you start eating up the fat, but you're not actually looking forward, and saying, "Wait a minute, if I don't produce today in three or five years time we'll not have any." There are always surpluses and shortages because of the long-term nature of the business. That's always been the case. All you can say when you've got too much is you've got to get off your ass and try to sell more, and you say, "What's the point of selling more because I'm not making any money?" But it will sort itself out, it always has, all that you actually do in the whisky business is survive, that's the business. If you survive you will live, and if you live you will conquer!

'Whatever was happening with North of Scotland, the Speyside distillery was a project that was ultimately going to come to a head at some stage, but in the years of over-production building a new distillery wasn't a priority. There was lots of access to existing stock and you could trade. Ultimately, though, the distillery was my ambition.

'There was the old farm steading at Tromie Mills where the distillery building is now, and I suppose we were really quite secretive about what we were doing. Alex Fairlie, the drystone dyker, began to construct the sandstone building, which I referred to as the "implement shed".

'It was a sleeping project, which only really gathered steam when I discovered that my son Ricky had made an offer for Tullibardine distillery in Perthshire. He'd done this because we'd gone from one extreme of surpluses in the trade to being a Scotch whisky company without any Scotch whisky. When Saunders put the plug in the Guinness loch it was a case of, "Shit, what are we going to do?" So Ricky

Speyside distillery with the River Tromie in the foreground, 1990s.

put an offer in for Tullibardine, and I wasn't happy, because I didn't honestly think the place was right. They were running all the water off the Ochils, they had no way of getting rid of it. Delmé Evans was a good bloke, but I felt he had a limited knowledge of what he was doing.

'We were all fortunate in the sense that when we were building or rebuilding something, like Delmé-Evans and Jura, the prices were quite fantastically low. Labour and everything else. You didn't go for big architecture, fancy architecture or anything like that.

'Ricky claims that if I hadn't been so annoyed about him putting an offer in for Tullibardine I'd never have got off my backside and finished the distillery. If Ricky had got us involved in Tullibardine it would certainly have postponed and possibly put in doubt the Speyside distillery, which was something I'd worked for for a long time.

'As it was, Chris Greig [managing director of Invergordon Distillers] turned down the offer, and the market for distilleries, because of the shortage of stocks, was very inflatedly high, and twelve months later you couldn't have given Tullibardine away.

'That's the whole story of the Scotch whisky business for as far back as you want to go. The answer in all cases is that if you can limit your advance to the amount that you have built up beforehand, in other words don't go in with a lot of money that you haven't got, you'll probably survive. I think that's the only reason we have managed as we have. We've lost a lot of money in bits and pieces over the years, but it's never affected us too seriously. We've never been "in" the bank.

'The size of the distillery was spaced out by the amount of space I had. The old cattle shed was knocked down, and I worked out what I wanted to make production-wise, which meant the size of the stills was determined. Once you've decided the size of your stills you've set up the size of your fermenter, your mash tun, and so forth. We got a stainless steel mash tun which cost a bloody fortune, but was almost as automatic as you could get.

'You don't know what sort of spirit you're going to get until you've got your stills in. You design your stills to get a clean spirit. Nobody's ever been able to design a pot still to decide how the spirit was going to come off. The taste of the spirit depends on the water, but not a lot, it depends a hell of a lot on the barley, the malted barley, the type, and it depends above all on the temperatures in your mash tun. In other words, the wash that goes into the still is almost vital to what comes off. If you want to mess around with it at that stage you're going to have to change the still. You're never going to know what you'll get until you've been running it for quite a while, so it's a dodgy business.

'Back in the early '70s I got Ricky to go out and buy two copper stills from

Macmillan of Prestonpans, near Edinburgh. They made up the plates, made up the base plates, and eventually they said, "What are we going to do with these?" We said, "Well, we haven't really got the project on the go yet," so they shipped them over to our place at Duchess Road, where we had them stored. When the distillery project came up we said, "Right, we have these stills."

'But Duchess Road being in cowboy country, and copper being quite a valuable commodity, we discovered that we couldn't even have made Swiss cheese with what was left of the stills! It had been pilfered over the years. We gave Forsyth up in Rothes what we had left, and they worked from there.

'It took twenty years from start to finish, because I had other things to do. Everything I was doing was making money, and if what you intend to do is going to cost money, and you happen to be in something that is making money, then the best thing is to make money while you can. I sold the Bonhill place for a million quid, and I still had Cambus and all the rest. I didn't need Bonhill because it was purely storage, but it was the biggest storage area round about, and J&B bought it.

'On the night when the distillery fired up for the first time, I left Ricky to get on with it, because I had had to go to Texas to sort out a problem with a shipment of spirit we had sent out to our main agents in Louisiana. By mistake some poor spirit which we hadn't intended to be sold had been included in the shipment. We heard back from the agents that they had shipped out some bottles to Texas and they had been returned. So I went to Texas and found out what had happened, and sorted it.

'Meanwhile, back at the distillery it was a blizzard, the lade froze over, and so they couldn't get water into the condensers, and they had to go out at two o'clock in the morning with golf clubs to break up the ice so that we could actually get water in.

'They were all waiting to see how much spirit they got off the first run, expecting to get between two and four thousand litres, and when they went to look in the spirit receiver it was empty. It was only because it was being re-distilled, it was going into the low wines, but it was really the last charge that actually brought off the spirit. That was on 12 December 1990.

'It was wonderful because Ricky and the guys saw the place from the ground up to producing spirit, and some of the guys that are down there just now have been there since then. When I came back and sampled the stuff for myself I thought it wasn't bad. I never smell the first run off a still, but when you smell it after it's been running for a week you know if it's saleable. You can't say this is the best, it takes time.

'I reckon it's got to be in wood for a twelvemonth before you really know how good it is. You're going to use it after it's been in cask, so just to take it after it's

Spirit still at Speyside distillery, 2004.

come off a still, you know it's clean, that there are no bad feelings in it, but you don't know much more than that. But I think the whisky from Speyside distillery is excellent, a bloody sight better than I thought it would be. [In 2000 Speyside Distillers Company Ltd was sold to a group of investors, headed by Sir James Aykroyd, though the Christie family continues to own the Speyside distillery.]

'Today you have so many different ages, finishes, it's very confusing, you have so much more choice. In the old days basically it was making a clean spirit, looking after it, and having something that's acceptable to you. But none of us, however knowledgeable you are, can say that will sell. And that's what you make it for. You can say, "I like it, and fuck everybody else," if you want to, but you've got to get it acceptable, and the job that the sales people do decides that.

'I am a blend man. I can check all the malts, and I can appreciate them for what they are, but as far as I'm concerned it's down to what you drink yourself. And I drink a blend I have made up myself. I'm not telling you what's in it, but we're scratching around now to find things for it. I say, "Well, I gave too much away," which is bloody true, but the fact is I didn't expect to live this long anyway! There's nothing in there which you might say, "Oh, you must have this and that. That's Glenlivet, that's Glen Grant, there's this that and the other." But what it has got is a long time lying. The actual malts were put together, and then put with the grain, and that has been in the bottle for fifteen years. It was casked for about a dozen years before that, for Christ's sake.

'Whatever you do in Scotch whisky, you don't cheat, because it comes back on you, not just next year, but for the rest of your goddamn life. Produce something that isn't right, and there'll be some bastard in some corner of the world who says, "Oh, I had some of that, fuckin' awful it was." All the time you're trying to be true. You can't be a genius, you can't make the very best, but you can make something which you're not ashamed of.'

18

On Visitors

There was a time, not that long ago, when the idea of visiting a distillery would have been greeted with incredulity. You might as well have suggested visiting a washing machine factory.

For that is exactly how distilleries were perceived; they were whisky factories, nothing more and nothing less. One old whisky man still working in the industry at a senior level recalls that during the 1960s any curious member of the public asking the manager at one of his company's distilleries if they might look around would be told unceremoniously to 'bugger off'.

Then, William Grant & Sons Ltd broke ranks, deciding that as increasing numbers of the public seemed to be becoming curious about what went on in distilleries, there was surely an excellent opportunity to foster what modern marketing folk would term 'brand loyalty'.

Far from telling visitors to 'bugger off', Grants actually developed dedicated facilities for them in 1969 and began offering distillery tours.

Suffice to say, the venture was sufficiently successful to become much imitated, and today more than one million people visit Scotch whisky distilleries each year. As the ante has been well and truly upped, distilleries have vied with each other to produce increasingly 'high-tech' facilities, such as 'Dewar's World of Whisky' at Aberfeldy and 'The Famous Grouse Experience' at Glenturret in Perthshire. Alternatively, the likes of Aberlour and Balvenie distilleries offer altogether more bespoke 'connoisseurs' tours, with the emphasis on personal attention and exclusive tastings.

'Whisky tourism' has become an important part of the economy in Speyside and Islay in particular, with Islay's Grant Carmichael noting, 'There's much more tourism now, and it's becoming an extended season rather than a short season, because as well as whisky people we get the 'twitchers' coming in too, for the geese over the winter [large numbers of barnacle and white-fronted geese winter on Islay], there's a lot of those, and this tends to help the hotels to keep going through the winter.'

Isle of Jura distillery manager Mickey Heads points out that 'It was only really in the 1980s that visitors started coming over to Islay and Jura distilleries in any numbers, and heavily-peated malts have only really become popular since around 1995. When I was at Laphroaig we were down to doing just nine mashes per week, as heavily peated malts just weren't very popular. Speysides were the "in" whiskies then.'

The development of whisky tourism has largely been fuelled by the increasing interest in single malts. This has been aided by a growing number of publications dedicated to the subject, along with the efforts of whisky companies and their ambassadors to offer the public opportunities to sample whiskies and help them discover a tasting vocabulary.

Bowmore's Ed McAffer notes of his former Bowmore colleague:

'Jim McEwan started off the tasting notes and all that. I find some of the tasting notes people make quite humorous. What people actually think they find on the

Approach to Dufftown, 1990s

nosings and on the palate. In the old days if the old guys were trying a dram which would maybe be about fifteen years old and the one would say, "And what's that like, Billy?" or whatever his name was, and he'd just say, "Aye, it's no' bad." That was enough to say it had passed. If it was "no' bad" it was a good dram.

'Nowadays, they've got all the different things they say. It really sort of surfaced with Jim, or at least that's where I first got it when I read a lot of his stuff, and of course he educated so many of these other people. He was a big part of Bowmore, he worked for this company for 37 years before he went to Bruichladdich. I've known him all my life, and he's done well.

'It's quite good reading the stuff that they come up with for the nosing and the tastings. The sea breezes and the seaweed and the old leather couches and the digestive biscuits and the geraniums. I don't understand how they can smell all that in one wee pot. To me it's quite amazing.

'If you nose a nice malt you definitely get the fruity flavours and the sweet smells coming through. That to me signifies a nice malt. And you get the peatiness of course in Bowmore, from the peated malt. The Islay malts are distinctive from that point of view. Some, like Bunnahabhain, they don't use it, but the other distilleries use it.'

Eric Stephen, warehouse team leader for William Grant & Sons Ltd in Dufftown, offers a succinct comment on the development of whisky tasting vocabulary.

'I like Balvenie myself, but the likes of the old-time brewers, if they heard people today talking about aromas of almonds and such like, they'd say, "Christ, what's he speaking about? God almighty, man, drink it up!"'

Archie Ness enjoyed hands-on experience with distillery visitors during his time as assistant manager at Craigellachie and Cardhu on Speyside. 'Having distilleries open to the public brings a lot of people in, and it's good for the local economy,' he says. 'It gave me great pleasure to be able to send people away knowing how whisky was made, and it also kept me up with my job.

'I landed back at Craigellachie in 1993. They had a shift round, with some of the managers taking on two stills, and I was asked to go to Craigellachie, working as assistant manager for Craigellachie and Cardhu. The "Craig" always made a nice dram. You occupied a distillery house in those days, you had a house on the site, and I had the manager's house at Craigellachie until I retired in 1997.

'At Cardhu I was assistant manager to Evan Cattanach. I was there to assist him because he was much involved in PR work, so he was away a lot, and I was put in to look after production. He was away such a lot that I also had to look after the VIP guests when they were booked in. Well, I'd never shown visitors round a dis-

Part of a decommissioned still and floral display, Dufftown, 2004.

tillery, I was there for production. So I said I'd have a go, and I've never forgotten it, the first day I had a visitor.

'It was a visitor from France, and he was booked into Inverness, and he was arriving at 10.15 on Monday morning. I had butterflies all weekend. What am I going to say to him? How am I going to keep the conversation going? – that sort of thing. Well I was sitting in the office at 10 o'clock on Monday morning when the clerkess came along and said, "That's your visitors, they're down at Tamdhu. They're lost." They'd driven from Inverness and had landed at Tamdhu distillery, a few miles away. Tamdhu were trying to give them directions up to Cardhu. When they arrived there was the man and his wife, and they didn't talk a word of English. It was my first day with VIPs and I had no French. It was October, school holidays, so I asked the clerkess to ring Craigellachie school, where there was a woman, a schoolteacher, who did French. But she was away on holiday. So we tried another from Elgin, but she was away too.

'I didn't know what to do, because I was supposed to be taking them for lunch, and there was another gentleman arriving from New Zealand who was to join us. Then I suddenly thought of my daughter. She was at home, and she had school French, just that, but she's very shy. I rang and asked her to get ready to come up to the distillery, and I sent transport down for her. She came up and I explained to her as I went along, the very basics, and by the time we got started the person from New Zealand had arrived, and joined in with us. I made it as simple as possible for my daughter, and then she joined us for lunch to keep the conversation going. So we got through the day, and the chap from New Zealand said, "Well, I'm very surprised how that tour went. Your first, and it went very well."

'After that I just took them on as I went along, and then Evan asked if I'd do the ceilidhs that we had at Cardhu when he couldn't attend. I went along to one with him and then I was on my own after that. Evan did singing when he was there, but I didn't do any singing.

'When I first started showing visitors around the distillery I was told always be truthful, don't sham because you'll be caught out. Some days you'd start at ten o'clock in the morning with visitors, you'd have your lunch with them up in the visitor centre, then they might go away and see something else, and then you'd a ceilidh in the evening. Not every week, but it kept you going. You were running the distillery at the same time.

'After a while, once I'd got used to it, I found meeting the visitors interesting. It was interesting to see where they had come from. I used to go home and had a big map, and it had what they eat in that country, what employment was and all that, and I used to look at that first before I went to meet them. You had a lot of Italians, because Cardhu is big in Italy, and you had French, and they came from all over. Parties of Italians and Japanese mainly, but single visitors included ambassadors and presidents from abroad.

'If the company had visitors they sent them to Cardhu if there was a Johnnie Walker angle, Red Label and Black Label and all of those brands. In those days Johnnie Walker Red Label was five-years old to ten-years old, the malts used in the blend. It was three to seven before I left, which is going to make a difference, in my experience of distilling. A five- to ten-year-old is a far better blend.

'The visitors tended to be from countries where they were promoting those whiskies, but whether they were VIPs or ordinary tourists I never treated them any different. But the VIPs you had to take more time with. We had a number of tour guides, and if you had too many visitors I'd take some of them round. You had bus parties too, but it was seasonal. By the end of September it had died off, and you paid off your seasonal guides.

'When you were showing visitors round, they liked things like the spirit safe and the tunroom. The fermenting vessels. It just depended what stage you got them at. Sometimes you'd lift the lid and you had to gasp. The lid would be up and you'd

Cardhu distillery, 1961.

warn them, but some of them put their heads right in, and got knocked back by it.

'They're interested in the distillation, at the sample safe. You always tried to get a sample to show them. It depended what stage the stills were at. I'd try to get the still-man to take a sample of spirit for them. I never interfered with the sample safe. The stillman's in charge of that side, and although you're in overall charge, you don't inter-fere. Sometimes, you'd have a still maybe waiting to come in, and the stillman would slow it down and just as you came in and explained it they'd slew it to come into the glass and in it would come. That was great, the visitors loved that. A lot of visitors couldn't understand why it wasn't brown when it came out, why it came out clear, and I'd to tell them about the importance of the casks and maturation.'

Over on Islay, former Caol Ila stillman Neil Ferguson says, 'I work in the summer as a tour guide now, and I was showing visitors around for years before I retired. Believe this or believe it not, when they had a dose of visitors somebody would come along and say, "There's some visitors there, Neil, will you go along and attend to them. I'll get so and so to come and run your stills till you're finished." Other people wouldn't have anything to do with visitors, maybe they're shy, but it certainly never bothered me.

'If you look through the visitors' book down there they've had people here from virtually every country in the world. Vladivostok, places like Slovenia, the Czech Republic, Latvia, Lithuania, the Baltic countries, as well as all the more usual ones. In the last couple of years we've had a tremendous amount of Swedes, they've got very into malt whisky. They all think Islay is a terrific place, because the people are so friendly. I just like being able to tell visitors about whisky, and about the island in general. People say that they've tasted the whisky before but never realised it was made in such a beautiful setting. The Japanese especially seem to have an encyclopaedic knowledge of whisky-making. But people generally are more and more discerning. A lot of people are very knowledgeable about their whiskies. Even the differences between, say, a twelve- and a fifteen-year-old of the same single malt.

'A couple of years ago I went down to work in the morning and Billy [Billy Stitchell, Caol Ila manager and fourth-generation Islay distiller] said, "Ah, you're just in time, can you take these four gentlemen around the distillery." They were four Japanese gentlemen. So I took them round the distillery. There were three younger chaps and an older man. Took them back and gave them a dram of Caol Ila. The older man, he seemed to be the man who was in charge. We talked about all sorts of aspects of whisky-making, and when they were about to go he thanked me very much for the tour and he gave me his business card. He was a master blender with Nikka Distillers. Thank God I didn't try to give him any bullshit. They were over across with Bowmore. You never know who you're taking round. So you can't afford to tell them any rubbish, you have to be sure of your facts.

'Nikka are the biggest producers of whisky in Japan, and along with Suntory they more or less have the market, though there are other companies, but on a much smaller scale. It's amazing how much whisky is actually made in Japan, and how much whisky is made in other countries generally. They make it down in New Zealand, in Tasmania, India. It's amazing the countries that actually make whisky.'

Ed McAffer points out, 'There's more and more interest now, with all the tastings and the people going and talking about it and writing books about it, and people come to Islay to have the "Islay experience".'

'Seven months of the year, from April to October there'll be people in here every day, maybe dribs and drabs to start with, and then big parties right through. It's amazing the amount of people that will come through. When you think of all the distilleries on the island, the amount of people that come to Bowmore, and there's obviously the same amount go to the other distilleries, it gives you an idea of how many people are on the island. They can come in now in the morning on the ferry and go away at night of course, they can leave their cars on the other side or whatever, just come in for the day and maybe get a bus trip.

'In 1974 we built this reception centre. Bowmore was right in there at the beginning with the reception centre and doing the tours. There were some contractors came from Paisley, but in them days the guys that worked in the distillery were either time-served joiners or bricklayers, and a lot of the contracting work was phased out, it was our own boys that did that. That was the idea of the management taking on these guys that had these skills, so the bricklayer and joiner that worked in the distillery for 30 years, they're retired now, they built this place as well. They had pride in that. That's changed in that everything's contracted back out again now, even maintenance, but in them days it was our own boys that did building, a lot of the renovations and stuff were done in-house.

'The visitor side of it is a big, big part of it now. Sales and marketing is big now, that's the main thing. It's a huge part of it. We can produce it, but they've got to go out and sell it. Sales of Bowmore have gone up hugely, I think it's the number one malt in Scotland at the moment, and it's number ten in the world. Good marketing can only go so far, though, you've got to have a good product, and we think that we make a pretty good dram, we pride ourselves on that.'

Speyside and Islay both host whisky festivals, and Dufftown-based Ian Millar says, 'Not only are there two whisky festivals each year, but whisky nosings and tastings take place every Tuesday during the tourist season in one of the local halls, promoting malt whisky.'

Ed McAffer notes, 'They come from all over the world to the Islay whisky festival, and every distillery has its day of doing whatever, and that's a tremendous week for the island. The place is just chock a block, bouncing.'

Bruichladdich's Jim McEwan declares, 'The whisky festival is now the biggest thing, we've been going four years now, and the whisky festival is really quite something. It's just wonderful, that whole week, the island gets about £750,000 out of that week, it brings a lot of people to the island.'

Not all of Bruichladdich's visitors actually make the trip to the distillery, or even to Scotland, however, as Jim McEwan explains.

'We do live web tastings here now, you can hit 1,500, 2,000 people, and they love it, it's good fun. The last one we did we expected 500 people on the web site, and we filled up within two minutes, and we asked for extra space, and the streaming company did a thousand, then after about fifteen minutes we had 1,500, and that was it, it couldn't take any more, it was going to blow the place up. We had an hour talking to 1,500 people, live. There was one guy, a Scottish guy, on a super-tanker in the Indian Ocean, and he was watching us from the satellite coming in. A Scottish guy. And of course there's no drink allowed on the ship. So he's sitting there all that way away in the Indian Ocean, and he's watching this live tasting, and he e-mailed us back, he says, "I'm just about to throw myself off the side of this ship, you guys are driving me crazy. I'm in the Indian Ocean, there's no alcohol, and you're drinking alcohol and I wish I was home.'

Ruari MacLeod recalls, 'I was here one day and all of a sudden the girl came in and she said to me, "Do you know anybody in Bowmore called Alan McCecklich?" and I said, "I do. He's somewhere about 400 miles out in the North Sea." "Oh yes," she says, "he's just after coming off the phone, and he was saying, 'What are you doing standing at the bar having a drink when you should be working?" '

JM: He was watching the web cameras?

RM: Aye, he was. On board the ship, and he phoned up Bruichladdich distillery.

Former Inverleven still on display at Bruichladdich, 2004. Inverleven was a small malt distillery within the Dumbarton grain distillery complex, and production ceased in 1991. The still was transported by sea from the River Clyde directly to Islay.

JM: You forget they're there, they're everywhere.

RM: And I was in once, Duncan [McGillivray, distillery manager] was in as well, I was called down here, it was on a Saturday. And we had a dram, and all of a sudden his phone went. He was talking away, and he put the phone back in, he was talking to his wife, and a wee while after that the phone went again, and she said to him, 'You told me you had only one dram,' and he says, 'Yes' 'That's funny,' she says, 'You've had two since you were talking to me.' The cam was in the corner over, and she was watching him. So you can't get away with anything.

JM: I got caught with a PR woman. I was in the bar having a dram, and the phone went, and she said, 'Can I talk to you for a moment about some PR business?' I said, 'Well, it's a very difficult time, I'm actually having a meeting with the Customs and Excise.' She said, 'No you're not, you're standing at the bar having a dram.'

RM: That's it. You're caught! I retired in 1986. And then I was back three times, just to help out other people, of course. And back once on Jura. They had the flu. But I'm back and for'ard pretty often. On the day the distillery re-opened [in 2001] there was a lecture over in the hall, and there were some visitors who were talking while it was going on, then they went out, they disappeared, the two of them. Then my two daughters came out and said, 'Oh, you've missed something.' I said, 'What?' 'Those two stripped naked and jumped into the sea.' They did, aye. The streakers. If I'd been there, I'd have had the camera.

JM: They'd been to the lecture, they were from Germany, and they were very drunk, and they kept talking as I started speaking, so I said to them, 'Please be quiet,' and they refused, so I said, 'You're going to have to be quiet or I'm going to have to ask you to leave.' They said, 'That's a really strange way to treat guests.' I said, 'Well, you're not the only guests, there's another 98 people here who are guests, and they can't hear me, so I'm going to ask you to leave now.' They said, 'Well, you can't make us leave.' I said, 'Well, yes we can, if you wait one minute I'll be right down beside you and I'll make sure you leave.' So eventually we got them out the door. It was a beautiful, beautiful sunny day.

RM: Oh it was, it was, God, yes.

JM: So, the lecture continued, and I said to a piper from Oregon, a big bagpiper who comes every year to play the bagpipes, I said, 'When the people are leaving the village hall could you stand at the water's edge and play the bagpipes for the people coming out?' He said, 'Hey, Jim, I'd be honoured to do that, my son.' So he goes down, and these two people are out swimming behind him, up to there in the water. So he starts playing, and people come out the hall and they gather round the piper.

The piper has his back to the sea, and suddenly out of the water come these two naked people. And everybody starts clapping and cheering, and the piper thinks they're clapping for him. It's the first time people have really appreciated him. Well, this girl was really well endowed, and he's piping away, the piper thinks this is really great, what a crowd, and suddenly these two people come staggering out the water past him, and the piper went 'eeeowwwww'. Well that was the start of a pantomime. They were trying to put on their clothes, and they couldn't stand, they kept falling back with their bums in the air. Of course, that was like four o'clock, and by five o'clock the story had reached Port Ellen. There were rape scenes on the beaches at Bruichladdich, a sex show, there were streakers everywhere. By Monday the whole place was like Woodstock, except it wasn't Woodstock it was Peatstock.

RM: Well, my daughters saw them, but I didn't see them.

JM: She was like 'wow' … Maybe it's just as well you didn't see them, Ruari!

19

On Distilleries and Single Whiskies

One of the great joys of Scotch whisky is its infinite variety. Even today, after so much consolidation and rationalisation, there are still some 87 malt whisky distilleries operating in Scotland, in locations from Bladnoch in the far south-west to Highland Park and Scapa on Orkney. The stylistic variety of single malts they produce is immense. Here our whisky men recall distilleries at which they have served, and make some observations about the whiskies they produce.

Speyside's Sandy McAdam was born at Cardhu, and was associated with more than half a dozen distilleries and their whiskies during his lengthy career.

'I worked for a while at Imperial [at Carron, close to Dailuaine] when it reopened in 1955,' he says, 'working in the warehouse for a short time. It had been closed for about 30 years before that, and it's closed again now, of course. They're big stills there, four of them, huge, the biggest stills that there were round about. The story was that the water had too much iron in it, that was the problem. It was known as the 'Crown Imperial' for a long time, because it had the big crown on the top of one of the malt kilns. It had been opened in the year of Queen Victoria's Diamond Jubilee, but they took the crown down when they were rebuilding the distillery in 1955.

'In 1961 I got married, and we had a house at Dailuaine, so I went to Daluaine distillery then. I was a van driver there for three years, then I went on to the stills there. Dailuaine was very different then to what it is now, with the big dark grains plant. There was a pot ale plant before the dark grains one, and I think it was the first one there was. They took pot ale in from other distilleries to process.

'In 1968 I came over to Convalmore in Dufftown as brewer. Convalmore was a nice, compact distillery which dated from the 1890s. It was good to work in, and it made a decent single malt. I was there till 1970, when I went onto the company's trainee managers' scheme.

'You had to do so long at the maltings as part of the trainee course which lasted for eighteen months, and then you worked in each department at a distillery. I did my training at Craigellachie distillery, and after the training course I was made assistant manager at Craigellachie.

'In 1975 I went from there up to Benrinnes [near Aberlour] as assistant, then in 1980 I went to Knockdhu near Huntly as manager. It was closed in 1983, when the company shut more than twenty distilleries, and I think that was the worst job I ever had, when we had to close the place down. Some of them got transfers to other distilleries, about three were kept on, and the others were made redundant.

'From Knockdhu I went to Glenury at Stonehaven, and two years later that was closed too, when the company shut another 20-odd distilleries. Glenury was a nice distillery with a great situation and it was a good whisky too, but I don't suppose there's a lot of it on the go now. I was back a couple of years ago, just before they knocked it down to build houses on the site, to have a last look around. It was pathetic to see it derelict like that. It had four stills, four big stills, and the whisky it was making was almost the same as Cardhu, I'd say.

'That was a very different character to Benrinnes, a big whisky which was triple-distilled, the only one around these parts that was. I couldn't tell you why it was triple-distilled, but it was always the way there. After the first distillation in the wash still it went through a small spirit still, and then it went through a normal spirit still. It wasn't particularly heavily peated malt or anything, just the same stuff from Burghead that was going everywhere else, but it's a much heavier whisky than you'd maybe expect from triple-distillation.

'After Glenury I came back to Craigellachie in 1986, and was manager there until I finished in 1993. "The Craig" was a great distillery, it goes like clockwork. The way the four stills work, the balance with the wash and spirit stills, was just right, and it's a good dram. It was always the "White Horse distillery", because it had the White Horse symbol on the stillhouse, and it's funny seeing "Dewar's" up there now, now that the distillery's been sold to them.'

Craigellachie distillery dates from 1891, being founded by a partnership of blenders and whisky merchants, which included Peter Mackie, of White Horse blended Scotch whisky fame. In 1916 Mackie & Co. (Distillers) Ltd acquired the distillery outright, and in 1927 it passed to the Distillers Company Ltd. Following the merger of Guinness and Grand Metropolitan to form Diageo in 1997, Craigellachie

A Glenallachie still, 2005.

was one of four distilleries purchased from Diageo by Bacardi, whose John Dewar & Sons Ltd subsidiary currently operate it.

Like Sandy McAdam, Archie Ness was also associated with Craigellachie and Imperial distilleries.

'Craigellachie was all steam engines and coal fires at one time,' notes Archie Ness.

'And the coal would be brought by lorry from the station at Craigellachie, and the big lumps of coal would be stacked up outside and then taken into the stillhouse. It had two stills in those days, they doubled it in 1964/65 when they rebuilt the stillhouse. In 1972 the distillery was updated again, when they went on to steam boilers, and did away with the coal elevators. When they went on to steam the chimney stack disappeared. There was a square chimney stack in the corner of the stillhouse.

'They took down all the warehouses before I left, too. They were old-fashioned warehouses that needed repairs, and you couldn't update them to take forklift trucks because they were too low. So they decided to demolish them and transport the spirit away in bulk in tankers.

'In 1982 I started a two-year course as a trainee assistant manager. It was actually only a year for me as I didn't need to do all the practical side of it, I already had all that. It was just the theory side of it. So in 1983 I became assistant manager at Imperial, and I was there until it closed in 1985.

'Imperial was a bigger distillery than Craigellachie. It was very big, and because of the sheer size of the place you had to go flat out making whisky. It had four big stills. A lot of people didn't like the whisky much, but I enjoyed the whisky, the dram was quite good. It was closed not because it didn't make good whisky but because of economics. It was a distillery that was spread out, if you wish. It was an expensive place to run. You had the maltings, which were Saladin boxes, and that closed due to costs. They started using the barley store there for all the distilleries in the area. It was a sad day when it closed.'

To the east of the Speyside region, Tomatin is a Highland distillery, founded in 1897. It is now in the ownership of a consortium comprising the Japanese distillers Takara Shuzo and Okura & Co., and currently produces between 1.6 and 2 m litres of spirit per annum.

Stuart Duffy worked at Tomatin for five years before moving to Glenallachie distillery near Aberlour. After a short period there he returned to the recently enlarged Tomatin plant.

'I went back up there and stayed for about two years, until the bottom fell out of the whisky market and Tomatin was doing absolutely nothing. They were living from day to day more or less. When an order came in you were flat out, but when the order dried up you were standing around.

'Glenallachie was just started up when I went there. I didn't like Glenallachie, that's how I went back to Tomatin again. There was no character, nothing, although it was a good wee still, nice and easy to work and everything. It was too new, there was no character about it, everything was spotless, and you were cleaning for ever more, you were Brasso-ing for ever more. It was new and shiny and they wanted to keep it that way.

'At Tomatin they were trying to do 80 mashes a week when I was there. They were speaking about a million gallons a week. They managed it a few weeks, but the timing was so tight sometimes you fell behind and you'd to miss a mash, maybe two mashes, you didn't get them through. You'd only two mash tuns and they were four-hour mashes, so on a shift you did four mashes. One mashman did four complete mashes.

'I don't know if the way they were doing it, rushing it maybe, affected the quality of the whisky. If you went into the warehouses at Tomatin there was some good whisky in the old casks there, but I left just about two years after they went into this, and really the eighty mashes didn't last for long, when the bottom fell out of the whisky market, so it was really a big waste.

'They didn't have that many staff, because Tomatin was automated even then. When I came down to Glenallachie I thought I'd gone back into the Dark Ages, because you were turning every valve and cran by hand, even though it was a new distillery. At Tomatin it was all automated, you pressed a button.

'Then when I came down to Mortlach in Dufftown I found that was just as old-fashioned. Folk didn't believe what you did up at Tomatin. That you worked two mash tuns and you looked after twenty-four washbacks and things like that. One man did that in a shift.

'I didn't mind Tomatin whisky. I think they're picking up a wee bit again, they seem to be doing well again. It had already been doubled up before I went there the first time even. It was quite a modern stillhouse even then. The main Perth–Inverness railway line went past the distillery and I've used the "puggie"

'Mortlach-Glenlivet' distillery and Dufftown, 1868.

[small railway engine] as they called it. We used to take all the coke in from the railway with the puggie when they were using the malt barns. I couldn't really say when they stopped the malt barns there, but the malt barns kept going for quite a while at Tomatin. [Around] 1968, '69, they'd have stopped I think. They stopped just before they did the double up again because they knocked the malt barns into a tun room. And they put a mash tun into where the kiln used to be. They kind of used the old buildings, there wasn't a lot of building attached to it at all.

'We had a siding from the main line, a set of buffers, that was the lot, in case you ran into the stillhouse. They'd just put a wagon of coke into the siding down at Tomatin station, and you just picked it up from there and took it up. That was still working till about 1970, probably.

'Two years back at Tomatin, then I came down to Dufftown, to Mortlach distillery. I was on shifts there, all shifts, then onto stills, then in the early '90s, Ian Millar [Mortlach manager at the time] took me off shifts, and took me into the office, trained me up as a supervisor. So from thereon I was kind of pushed about a bit between Dufftown, Glendullan and Mortlach, covering holidays for the production managers and stuff like that. I had a wee stint at Linkwood, just covering. That's the history until I left two and a half years ago, took early retirement.

'I think I liked Mortlach most of all the distilleries I worked in. It gets a good name, it's a good whisky, it's an old distillery, and there's a bit of character there. It's a good dram, though it can be a wee bit heavy if you've too much.

'At Mortlach, production was cut back in the early '90s, and we kind of lost the character then. Mortlach was a sulphury, meaty character, a heavy character, and that was the time, about 1992-93, they started to develop the place and renew things, put in stainless tanks and took out the old cast iron tanks, and it actually lost its character quite badly. The new make was coming out as cleaner and fruitier. So we tried everything. Running slow, running fast, cooling the worms at the top, I think we tried everything, even putting up stands in the bottom of the tanks to try and keep the sediment in the chargers.

'Then they decided, "Well, it's only four men that's working at Mortlach at the moment, they can work it with four men, and we need Mortlach whisky, 'cos it's a good blending whisky, Mortlach." The like of Glenfiddich and that buys a lot, they get a lot filled at Mortlach. So the United Distillers folk in Elgin decided we'd go seven days at Mortlach, and a couple of weeks into this and the character came back, and it came back steady, so it just shows you. It was just the continuous work seven days a week. I would say that'll eventually come through in the single malt bottlings. Mortlach's a slow maturer, it needs about fifteen, sixteen years to get it to its best.'

St Magdalene distillery, Linlithgow, 1971.

Across on Islay, Ed McAffer explains his role as head brewer at Bowmore.

'When the manager's not there the head brewer takes over his role. I'm answerable to him. I oversee the intake of malt barley, do the spirit charges, and the day-to-day running of the distillery plant, because the managers nowadays are very busy with the commercial side of it, with visitors coming in, and they have to spend a lot of time with them. If people come from the Glasgow office the manager's with them, so my main role is the day to day running of the plant. Making sure it ticks over.

'Bowmore's nowhere near the level of automation that, say, Lagavulin's at, where you've got the one man and his console in the mashing. It's a fantastic thing to see, I suppose, but we're not just at that level. I would say we're semi-automated. We still maintain a lot of the traditional things. In the malt barns, though one man does it machine-wise, we still manually wet the steep, take the wet barley out of the steep in barrows and it's all levelled out with shovels. That still happens, and a lot of the old-fashioned ways of doing things we still maintain in the malt barns.

'In the production side, the mashing and the distilling, it is a wee bit more automated, with air valves and such like, and it makes for better control. But it's not computerised as such, it's very hands-on, and the guys have got to be really good at their jobs. It's not a question of them pushing a button and not knowing what's happening. They follow it right through themselves, manually mash in still, check the temperature, there's a lot where they still manually check everything. The malting, mashing and distillation is much the same as it's always been really.

'There's a lot of long-servers in the distillery, there must be half a dozen guys that have been here for almost thirty years, so we've all worked together from the age of eighteen or early twenties, we've all worked together for the last thirty years. There's a young boy works in the malt barn, well I say a young man, he'll be nearly thirty, and he's been here for the last thirteen or fourteen years, his grandfather worked in here for forty years, so he's carrying on in that respect, and the boy that's on the mash house at the moment, his father worked in here for years as a maltman.

'Lagavulin and Laphroaig and Ardbeg especially, they are heavily peated whiskies, which is a completely different thing altogether from maybe Bruichladdich, who use lightly peated malt. They're an old-fashioned operation, and everything's running dead slow and stop, and it really distills a good whisky. It's so smooth because it runs so slowly and so cold, and it's a completely different taste and smell to, say, Lagavulin. Bowmore's in between, in style, and of course that has to do with the time it sits in the cask as well.'

Rosebank distillery, Carron, near Falkirk, 2004.

Lagavulin distillery, 2004.

Although he spent much of his later working life on Islay, where he gained a great practical knowledge of the local single malts, Grant Carmichael's early distilling experiences were in the Lowlands.

'I was born in Edinburgh, where my father was a banker, but I'd always had a hankering for the whisky business. My grandfather had been in it. My father was born at Lochnagar distillery, and I learnt to walk at Benrinnes distillery, near Aberlour, I understand. But when my father was looking for a job it was in the days of the depression, and he was lucky to get a place in a bank, and that was what he did.

'After my National Service I was taken on as a management trainee by SMD [Scottish Malt Distillers Ltd], and was at Rosebank at Falkirk, St Magdalene in Linlithgow and Glenkinchie, south of Edinburgh. Rosebank was triple-distilled and was a far superior malt to Glenkinchie in my opinion, it was an absolute cracker of a dram. St Magdalene had a poor reputation. "Canal water" we used to call it. I don't think the water was acidic enough. When I was there the canal was smelly, but it's all been cleaned up and tidied and it's very nice there now.

'St Magdalene is still being bottled, in the "Rare Malts" range, and it has its devotees, but it was never a grade one. St Magdalene was quite modern in that it had drum maltings, "Galland drums", they were called. Much smaller than the modern ones, but they worked on the same principle. They used to do experiments on peating there too. It was close to the main DCL labs at Glenochil, so it was easy to supervise experiments there, and it was a small distillery.

'Glenkinchie is a very mild, beginners' dram, fine and floral, and very light

Port Ellen distillery, 1960s.

in texture. It doesn't have the sweetness of Rosebank to my palate. Glenkinchie still had the farm when I was there. It was very well known for its prize Aberdeen-Angus cattle. This was to advertise the draff and the processed pot ale that the cattle were fed on. The farm belonged to DCL. Rosebank was quite strange in that it straddled the canal. The malt barns were on one side and the rest of the distillery on the other side. You had to cross the canal to get to the malt barns.

'Port Ellen is a very, very underrated dram. It's only these last few years that people have discovered what a fine malt whisky it is. It's got a very different character from the others. It's strange that you've got these south coast whiskies, you've got Ardbeg, Lagavulin, Laphroaig, Port Ellen, all distinctly different. They've all got the salty undertone, they've all got the seaweedy, seashore notes. Ardbeg's got the taste of kippers about it sometimes, Laphroaig's medicinal. Lagavulin has this lovely dry flavour to it, and Port Ellen as well has this seashore character, and I get a chocolate note off it, very, very nice. It's there among the best. It's becoming rarer and rarer, and too expensive, but that's the law of supply and demand.

'It's a very fine dram, but my favourite's Lagavulin. The twelve-year-old as opposed to the sixteen-year-old. They have a twelve-year-old there now, cask strength, and I think the twelve is a bit more complex in character than the sixteen. The sixteen's smooth. The Lagavulin twelve is like a rough country wine, as opposed to a very mature, smooth claret, or something like that. You get the complexity of character, you get the flavours coming out that are lost in the four years with the sixteen.

'At Port Ellen distillery there's a lot of history. Ramsay of Shawfield was a

Member of Parliament, and a forward thinker. He owned Port Ellen, and he was instrumental in building the first duty-free warehouses in Scotland. Before that it was the malt that was taxed. They're still there today at Port Ellen, and they are listed. We had to pay a fortune to re-roof them, because there was no way we could knock them down. They are now full of Lagavulin.

'The Exciseman Aeneas Coffey did a lot of his work developing the Coffey still at Port Ellen. As well as the Coffey still, Port Ellen also held the first spirit safe, which had the excise locks on it, that again was designed and used at Port Ellen. It had its own pier, which is just visible now, which the puffers used to come in to and bring stuff ashore.

'The distillery was closed from 1930 until 1967, when it was rebuilt. All of that has been demolished recently, and only the original listed kilns remain. The village of Port Ellen grew up around the distillery really, and all of these communities, like Bruichladdich, grew up in the same way as distilleries developed.

'It was closed in 1983, but we didn't know then what a great dram it would be, or the demand there would eventually be for Islay single malts. It was rebuilt in the '60s to supply the blenders, that was what it was built for. And when one of the Islay distilleries had to go, it was the one. When I had to stand up and tell the men it was closing it was one of the worst days for me in distilling.

Bunnahabhain distillery, 1950s.

Construction work in progress on the new Caol Ila distillery, 1974. Note the 'pots' of the stills in place on the right of the picture.

'Such a lot of history, and it was very sad when we had to close it, but I was very pleased when it was closed that there was nobody went who didn't want to go. We managed to employ everybody who wanted to stay. The package was quite attractive, and it let some of the older hands at Lagavulin and Caol Ila go, and create jobs for some of the younger men who wanted to stay. And one or two of the boys went to the fishing.

'Port Ellen had half the capacity of Caol Ila, and Lagavulin a third of the capacity. It was a very efficient distillery, Caol Ila, and they experimented with making a "Speyside" style of whisky there a few years ago because it is very cost-effective, but I haven't tasted the final product. That was done about seven years ago. There was at the time sufficient stocks of Islay laid down, so it was a case of, "What were we going to do with Caol Ila?" and they said, "Let's make some Speyside."

'When I came back to Islay as general manager I was responsible for the three distilleries, some warehousing in Campbeltown that the company used, and the maltings at Port Ellen. What was quite sad was all these guys in Campbeltown and at Port Charlotte [Lochindaal distillery, which closed in 1929, but continued to be used for its warehousing capacity] were emptying the warehouses and the whisky was going off to the mainland, and they could see they were working themselves out of a job.

'The old Caol Ila whisky was very peaty, because we had our own peat fires, just big braziers, in the old maltings, same as Port Ellen used to be very heavily peated with the old floor maltings. And Lagavulin peated very heavily of course, tradi-tionally always did.

'Nowadays they are more consistent, I would say. In the old days it was more rule of thumb. You'd get one run very, very heavily peated, and about a month later, depending on the wind direction and who was doing it, it might be less peated. You didn't have the same consistency, but for all that, Caol Ila was a very, very fine dram.

'That was why Bunnahabhain distillery was built. Caol Ila was built in 1846 and was very successful, and Bunnahabhain was built in 1881 to try and produce a Caol Ila. That's why it was built up there, that's why it was built where it was built, to try to produce a similar whisky to Caol Ila. To produce as near to Caol Ila as you could get.

'The modern Caol Ila is light, deceptively light, and dry, flinty, peppery, and very smoky, but the smoke's in the aftertaste. Very much in demand with the blenders. At the end of the day, that's what the blenders are getting, because there's so much demand for Lagavulin as a single malt. Caol Ila has a wee touch of seashore, but not as heavy as the south coast whiskies, but using the same specification of malt. Caol Ila uses the same malt spec as does Lagavulin and Laphroaig, but you wouldn't think so. A lot of that is proba-bly due to the shape of the stills. Laphroaig has these small stills, Lagavulin has onions, squat things, while Caol Ila is much more to the Speyside idea of taller stills, which pro-duce a lighter spirit, but very smoky, which is what the blenders want.'

Staying with Caol Ila, Neil Ferguson says, 'It was a lovely place to work. When you're working in the stillhouse, the whole front wall is virtually one great big window, a series of great big windows. A lot of distilleries are nowadays, but Caol Ila's just about the only one with a view like that. You're looking out across the Sound of Islay, looking across at the Paps of Jura, and it's a magnificent view.

'Looking out of the stillhouse window you never know what's going to be passing. You had to have your wits about you, of course, especially if you were charg-ing or whatever, but there were times you could keep an eye on what you were doing, when you were working at the console, you could look over the top of the console straight out the window. You never know what you're going to see. It could be anything. It can be an aircraft carrier, it can be navy ships, or a full-rigged ship passing through. Other distilleries, the stillhouse window looks out onto a blank wall just across the other side of the yard. Down here you're lucky, you've got one of the finest views in Scotland, and it's never the same two days running.

'I was born just down the road from here, a couple of miles, at Finlaggan. I came to live and work here in 1969. I was fortunate, I came to work in Caol Ila in the old distillery. In those days we had coal-fired boilers, and we did our own malting and all that sort of thing by hand, using the wooden shovels and so on, and as I say, I was fortunate because in 1972 they knocked the old distillery down, but I had had the benefit of learning the job right from the very basics, like doing the hand malting part of it, right from the start, right from the grain, from the barley as it arrived and I had been through all the different parts.

'I was a stillman when the place closed, and during the next two years I worked with a nucleus of about eight of us who were to be the nucleus of the new workforce in the new Caol Ila, once it was re-built. We worked with all the different tradesmen that were there, that were working there, we worked with the chaps who actually built the washbacks, literally built them in situ, right from the timber that arrived, and that was quite an experience. It's not everyone who gets the chance to build a distillery.

'It was a firm from Glasgow who did it, and the timber came from Finland. And when we had finished the washbacks we went to work with the engineers and helped to install the new mash tun. It was cast iron sections, which were bolted together, and when we had finished working with the engineers we went to work with the coppersmiths. We were involved with building in the new stills and so forth.

'It was all really planned that way right from the beginning, because as we were working with the actual tradesmen at the time we knew exactly where everything was, of course, and the result was that when we started up we didn't need any period of getting ourselves accustomed to it. We already knew where everything was, we were able, all of us, to just walk in and start pressing the right buttons.

'Before the rebuild the distillery had been kept fairly well up to date in any case, but there was a tremendous difference in the new one, because everything was so much easier to operate, everything was so much cleaner, because we didn't have any coal dust or coke dust or peat dust or whatever, because our malting was done for us over at Port Ellen. Port Ellen Maltings was just newly built as well.

'The same firm that built the maltings also built Caol Ila. So the maltings were almost finished by the time they really started here, and a lot of the workforce that was over there was diverted to Caol Ila. By the time Caol Ila was rebuilt the maltings were ready for us.

'The new boilers were oil-fired, and on the whole much easier to look after. Everything was so much cleaner. As I say, we didn't have coke dust or anything like that to contend with any more. It was much easier to keep the place clean, almost clinical you could say really. A great place to work in.

'The old distillery had two stills, one spirit still and one wash still, and this one has six. It has three times the capacity of the old one. And because the way of working is so much more efficient now the output down here is tremendous. They're making about 3.5 million litres a year, and they become more and more efficient all the time. The throughput of material from the malt arriving to the whisky going away is absolutely amazing. With a greater degree of efficiency now they gain so much, and, of course, there's always the fact that the workforce is now smaller as well, which makes it even more economical. The whisky is produced so much more economically.

'I think every year for the last two or three years they have made unpeated whisky, but it takes two or three weeks to switch over from peated malt to clear it all out, and then when you stop you have the same thing to get back on to peated malt.

'They have a lot of different brands, Diageo, so I suppose they do experiment now and again with different blended whiskies. Now and again you can get some terrific whiskies passing through. But because it's a big firm and they're dealing with tremendous quantities there are some whiskies, perhaps, in individual barrels, which are absolutely terrific whiskies, but unfortunately, they all just get mixed together when you're doing a batch of so many.

'The whisky should be virtually the same as that made when the distillery still had its floor maltings, the peating should be about the same. But it is possible to switch in a matter of two or three weeks to making a more heavily peated whisky. They're doing that at Bruichladdich just now, they're making much more heavily peated whisky, really heavily peated, for a relatively short while then back to the normal one.'

Drew Sinclair of Dalmore makes the point that 'Every person has a different nose. If I say about Dalmore, "Oh, I get chocolate and orange and vanilla" and so forth, then people will say, "Oh, well I don't get that."'

In common with most whisky men, Drew has a great sense of loyalty to 'his' distillery and its whisky. 'Some other whiskies might taste a bit like Dalmore, but none is the same,' he says, 'so I just say it's the best bloody malt whisky in the world.'

20

JIMMY LANG
Retired Blender

Although individual distilleries with their frequently fascinating heritage and single malt whiskies with their unique character and provenance are beloved by connoisseurs the world over, the fact remains that for most people, wherever they live, Scotch whisky means blended whisky. This applies to Scotland just as much as to any other country. More than 90 per cent of all Scotch whisky consumed is drunk in the form of blends.

'Distilling is a science and blending is an art,' Samuel Bronfman famously declared, and the 'artist' most closely associated with his stable of Chivas whiskies is Jimmy Lang.

'I was born in Glasgow. Although the name is Lang, we've no association with the whisky Langs. I started with a company called Robert Brown Ltd, and that was one of the companies that was bought by Mr Sam Bronfman [President of Seagram Co. Ltd]. His contact in Scotland was Jimmy Barclay. Jimmy Barclay owned, in effect, four whisky companies at that time: Chivas Brothers, Robert Brown Ltd, William Walker & Company, and the Highland Bonding Company. They were the four companies that were sold to "Mr Sam".

'"Mr Sam" got involved with Mr Barclay and these companies because he found he couldn't take over DCL. That was his aim to start with, because he was big in America and in Canada. Sam came into the Scotch whisky business in 1949, and 1 February 1952 was the day I started with Robert Brown Ltd, up in an office in Renfield Street. We had no facilities of our own, all we had, basically, was the whisky stocks of these four companies. The Glasgow Bonding Company was where we did all our bottling, until we got our own facilities. They did the first bottling of Royal

Salute. They were based under High Street goods station.

'Sam came over about twice a year. He was a perfect gentleman, but he knew exactly what he wanted and he knew how to get it. Sam Bronfman influenced all sorts of things over here. Even the headquarters building [in Paisley]. He wanted something similar to a Scottish baronial mansion, so there were umpteen pictures sent over, and he got an architect to pick out the best of each style. And once the facade was being put up, he came over when the quoins, the cornerstones, were up about ten feet, and he noticed they were of an alternate pattern, and he said, "That's not what I want." So they'd to take it back down and make it straight again. He was that kind of man, he knew what he wanted, and he got it done.

Jimmy Lang (right) taking a cask sample for evaluation.

'I was taken on as a clerk. The blender at that time was a man called Charles Julian, of Julian & Trower, who were based in London. Charlie Julian was possibly one of the best nosers and tasters that I've ever known. Not only did he work in whisky, but he worked in rums and sherries and everything under the sun. He was based in London, and he was employed by Mr Sam Bronfman to reinvent Chivas Regal as a twelve-year-old, because it hadn't always been a twelve. I think it started

Sam Bronfman (right) examining the presentation of Royal Salute, Glasgow Bonding Company Ltd, c. 1952.

as 25-year-old, going way back, and of course they ran out of stocks, so they changed it to be, in effect, a non-aged, but old blend.

'Now Sam Bronfman, knowing a good bit about whisky in America and the UK, realised that there was a market that had never really been looked at, and that was twelve years old. He actually created the twelve-year-old market by the introduction of Chivas Regal at twelve years of age, and it was Charles Julian who was employed to create this new twelve-year-old.

'Luckily enough, he had sufficient stocks of damn good heavy-bodied, robust whiskies to start him off, and when I started, the total production in the year 1952 was only, by memory, 55,000 cases. That was all that was available, and it all went to the States. It didn't go anywhere else but the USA.

'As a clerk, the job I had to do particularly was to do with Seagram's VO and Captain Morgan Rum imports, checking everything about that situation, which I found I could do in half an hour each morning. That was my day's work.

'Charles Julian, the blender, used to come up every fortnight to look at whisky samples, because at that time you were allowed a tenth of a gallon from each

Jimmy Lang evaluating a sample in the Paisley sample room, 1970s.

cask, and they were taken up to the sample room, and once a fortnight he would come up, and the samples would be arranged out for him. He would examine them and say, "Yes, that one's okay, don't use that one, go ahead with that one," etc. Well one particular day about 1954, '55, he was due and the chap who normally laid out the samples had gone for lunch, and this particular day I didn't go to lunch.

'So having nothing to do, just sitting there, I noticed that the sample room door was open. I thought, "What goes on in there?" I opened the door, looked in, saw all the samples set out, so I started to lift them up and have a wee sniff round about, and then all of a sudden a man came in the door. "What the hell do you think you're doing?" This was Charles Julian. Then all of a sudden his attitude changed. He said, "Are you interested?" I said, "Well, I don't really know what it's all about."

'And from that day, every time he came up, I followed him around, and he commented to me on what he perceived in each and every single cask of whisky that was there. Then after about nine or ten months he turned round and said, "You go in front of me, tell me what you see." And that's how it started, that's how I got into blending.

'In 1956 Charles Julian retired and a man called Alan Baillie became the blender. Alan had been in the whisky business all his life, as a matter of fact he'd been manager at Bowmore distillery for 24, 26 years, so he knew whisky, he knew the smell of whisky, he knew what it should be like. He said he would take over the job of blender for Chivas Regal provided Jimmy Lang was made his assistant, so I became the assistant blender in 1956. Alan Baillie died in 1971, I think it was, and at that point I became chief blender, and stuck with that until the day I retired. That was 31 January 1989. So it was a hell of a long time.

'I think all blenders work similarly, but our inventories are not similar. In terms of the working practices everyone does pretty much the same. You start off with your list of about ten or twelve which we called the first malts, so you create something with them, and that's possibly 50 per cent of your total flavour. And then you used the ones not so powerful, just to sort of pack it in. In a talk I gave way back I compared a blender to a conductor or a musical arranger.

'The arranger will use his stringed instruments for melody, and the blender will use certain flavours such as fruity, floral, nutty, malty, fragrant, honey, for his theme. The arranger will use the woodwind section for his harmonies, and the blender's harmonies will be flavours such as leafy, grassy, spicy. The arranger also has his brass section and percussion to complete the composition. This could be compared to the blender's flavours such as peaty, smoky, medicinal.

'Each arranger has in his own mind what his ear will hear as the finished symphony, so it is with the blender as to how his finished blend will impart aroma and flavour. He gets an idea in his mind what the finished product should look like, and if it doesn't look like that he's got to go back and change a violin for a viola. Or a clarinet for an oboe.

'Everyone's got a sense of smell, but everyone's sense of smell is different. Everybody's eyes are different, everybody's ears are different, they hear different things; your tongue, you perceive different flavours. You can only associate what aromas you see with something you have previously known. You can tell other people that that is your association, but it might not be their association. But at least if he tells you what he thinks it is, you relate the two. He says it's this, but I say it's that. So every time he says it's that, I know it's this. That's the way it works.

'Initially what you're looking for, to start off with, are negative factors. Whisky is a nice aroma on its own, but if there are negative factors such as musty or woody, these are the ones you detect immediately, so you know that these whiskies are not up to standard. So you can remove these out of the system altogether in the first place.

'The next thing you would do with anyone coming in who wants to take part in the blending operation is look at the extremes. You've got, let's say, a nice heavy malt whisky, and even let's take one of the Islays – Laphroaig, very peaty, but sweet. Then take a grain whisky, where there's practically no flavour. Almost 100 per cent of the people nosing these two will differentiate. Even if blindfolded. So you move them up to the next stage. Instead of giving them a Laphroaig you'll maybe give them something that's a bit lighter but still in that style, like a Bowmore, and instead of giving them a grain whisky you'll give them a light Lowland whisky like Auchentoshan. And you see if they can differentiate between these two blindfolded. And you take it from there until you've narrowed everything down.

'Invariably you do this in smoked glasses, so that you're not affected by colour. This is important, because way back they used to show a line of samples and you could tell by the colour, "That one's good, that one's not good," etc. The whisky coming out of every cask can be a slightly different shade, because the colour really comes from the wood. But as you're using casks, each successive filling of a cask you're getting less of a colour, you're getting less maturation potential, because the chemistry is coming out of the cask every time you fill it again. So a cask basically has a finite life.

'Generally speaking, the lighter flavoured whiskies will mature earlier than the more heavily bodied whiskies. Grain whisky, for example, will reach its maturation peak a lot earlier than the gutsy, robust malts. During the maturation period the perceived flavours are under continuous change. The sharp edges, the "spirity" sensations are slowly rounded off. The flavours associated with the cask itself start to come through.

'Among my papers I've still got some notes which Mr Baillie, my predecessor, and I produced in 1966. They're comments on samples of various malts that we had been looking at, in conjunction with a man called Bert Thome who was Mr Sam's contact man between New York and Scotland. These notes only reflected the samples that we saw, they don't reflect what comes out of these distilleries, but it was based on the samples of whiskies we had in inventory at that time. Some of them get reasonable comments and others get not-so-good comments.

'This was what was going on at the time, you were making your comments like this. This was the first time that Bert Thome had taken a hand in this, he was American, and he was "Mr Sam"'s contact man. He was another man that had a tremendous nose.

'The head office is in Renfrew Road, Paisley, at the plant there, it's a beautiful building. We had a directors' dining room there, and any time Bert was over he dined with us in there. He always carried a small bottle of Tabasco sauce with him, and Dijon mustard, and every time he had a meat dish he would use Tabasco sauce on it, and then when he got to his biscuits and cheese he would use the Dijon mustard.

'And then about an hour after that we'd be up in the sample room, and he'd be sniffing whiskies and telling you just exactly what they were all about.

Tremendous! I was a smoker, not a heavy smoker, when I took up blending, and I stopped smoking in 1986, and it took me about a year to get back on the rails. Also you have to be careful of your aftershaves, perfumes, soaps and whatever else – they can all affect it.

'As a blender you work by constantly looking at samples, and Charles Julian, of course, has the blend that's written down, what whiskies he's using. And there were about ten that we classified as first class, robust heavy whiskies. Then there were the second degree which were less robust but fruity, and there were possibly fifteen there. Then down below you had the malts which weren't really doing anything, but they were still usable, and then you had a separate category for the Islays. And then the grain whiskies.

'Out of the top ten you would use a certain percentage, let's put a figure on it, 50 per cent of the malt blend would be out of that top ten. It could be a combination of six of them, and it could be a different combination each time.

'We were looking at the situation that we were increasing sales of Chivas Regal at one point by maybe 10 per cent compound annually, so you're looking at whiskies which you are purchasing initially as new fillings from other distilleries, and you've got to be aware that if you're wanting a 10 per cent increase every year, he's needing some himself. He possibly can't give you an additional 10 per cent every year, so you've got to know alternative whiskies that can be used, that would have roughly the same effect. There may not be just one that's the substitute, it may be a combination of 70 per cent of that one and 30 per cent of that one that makes it up. But you realise which ones you can do that with as you are constantly nosing, and this is how it all works.

'We had a hell of a job at times trying to look for substitutions. We always had Strathisla and then we built Glen Keith, but we did quite a bit of what we called reciprocal exchanges, where we'd swap Strathisla for Glenfarclas, we would swap some maybe for Aultmore, Cragganmore, some of the DCL ones. Sometimes we had three-way switches, and I can remember one in particular. We had Glen Keith that was wanted by the Invergordon people, and Invergordon wanted Aberlour, and there was a three-way switch between Glen Keith, Invergordon and Aberlour. They each wanted a bit of each other. And that went on all the time in the industry, switching with each other.

'But before DCL really got together and on computer I can remember about half a dozen occasions where you could buy a certain parcel of whisky from one DCL company in the morning and sell it back at a profit to another DCL company in the afternoon. Oh, they were the good old days!

'We got to the stage too, with Bert Thome who came over maybe twice a year, that we used to actually pub crawl Glasgow to find pubs that held small casks of whisky, because we were so bloody short. We pub crawled Leith and Edinburgh too.

'Braes of Glenlivet [now re-christened Braeval] and Allt-a' Bhainne distilleries were built in the 1970s for the sheer need for volume. To lead up to this, when I retired we had 150 million gallons of whisky in inventory, and we were producing three and a half million cases of Chivas a year.

'Nobody in marketing would give you a bloody clue what was happening. All you could do was have a feel for the damn thing yourself, for how things were moving, a feel for what other companies were doing, so we were compounding some years at 10 per cent, as I said earlier.

'Unfortunately, everybody in the whisky industry at that time thought that they were going to do better than everybody else, so we all filled too much; this was during the '70s. As a matter of fact in 1972 we laid down enough whisky to do five million cases of Chivas Regal in 1984, and it didn't come to fruition, because it quietened down a bit, things began to slow down. So that period from '84 right up to the early '90s was a great time for whisky drinkers, because everything was over-aged, because there was the excess stock. I remember at some times some seventeen-year-old going into Chivas Regal, and that was before we started really thinking of Royal Salute, which was 21 years old.

'We inherited the Chivas Regal formula from Charlie Julian, but there've been many changes over the years, just because you couldn't get volumes of other people's distillate. You were trying always to maintain your own character but at the same time you were also trying to maintain the differential in flavour from the competition. That was the big secret – what made it exclusive was the differential. Nobody can produce a static flavour year after year after year, it's impossible, but you were trying to maintain continuity of flavour and differential with the competition. That's really what it was about. And invariably you will find that nobody was in a position to compare the bottle they've just finished with the bottle they've just opened.

'One of the first things we used to do if we had a complaint, if somebody was complaining about the flavour – it was never really Chivas, but once you got onto Hundred Pipers and Passport, which we developed in the 1960s – somebody's complaining you've changed the flavour of this, that and the next thing. And we had standard letters that we sent back to them asking what has been changed in their circumstances recently that may have affected their palate. And about 50 per cent of them wrote back and said, "Well, we've started going to the Chinese restaurant," or "We've started going to the Indian restaurant," so they realised themselves what had happened. It was their palates that had changed.

'And one's palate and sense of smell and taste do change over the years. You will invariably find that children like sweet things, but as you get older you begin to look at things that are less than sweet, and some people like things that are sour now. I mean, sweet and sour. My wife used to drink nothing but Martini, white, because it was sweet. Anytime now she's having a Vermouth or something, it's a dry Vermouth she takes. The palate changes.

'I was working initially with Chivas Regal, and then we came on to Hundred Pipers, and a couple of years later we came on to Passport. So from working with twelve-year-olds we were now working with younger whiskies. And you were recycling your casks quicker than you would if it was twelve years old. And we realised fairly quickly that a cask that had been filled and been emptied at three, four, five years old, against casks that were constantly being filled with Chivas, had lost their potential to mature a lot quicker than the twelve years old. So there are a number of fillings that timber can take before it's useless, before it's not doing any maturation.

'The only wood that will really give you flavour which one can relate to Scotch whisky at the moment is oak, preferably American White Oak, possibly the second best is Spanish, possibly the third is an Allier Oak from France. I had experiments going over the years using Yugoslavian, Mexican, Costa Rican, all different oaks, but none of them really worked properly, and American is still the best.

'But you wouldn't use new oak because of the tannins in the wood. The best wood to be used for maturation is a cask that previously held bourbon. Bourbon must be entered into a new charred oak barrel, and can only be used once for that purpose. Once that has been done, Americans can use it for corn whiskey or other whiskeys, but that is the best time to use them for Scotch, because the heavy tannins are taken out, and it's all ready for Scotch.

'Carrying experiments over years we have come to the conclusion that you can mature malt whisky up to about four, sometimes possibly five cycles, and then you would not use that cask again for filling malts, but you could use it for filling grain, because you're not looking for the flavour coming into your grain whisky. You might get another four or five fillings by doing that, because you'll get the spirity sensations taken away from the spirit without adding any flavour. And grain whisky anyway is just a diluting effect on what you've created from your malts.

'So I came to think that I could have casks that have ten cycles for twelve years old, so some of my casks would last 120 years, while other ones, let's say at an average of five, they would only last about 50 years. I think it was 1972 or 1974 I came up with the idea to assist coopers and everybody else that the end of casks should be

Official opening of Chivas
Bros Paisley head office com-
plex, June 1964.

painted different colours, dependent on the number of times they had been filled.

'I created this situation where a new cask, you didn't need to paint the end because you knew it was new, but when that cask was emptied it would go through the cooperage shop and be painted, let's say, a pastel pink.

'Now that told everybody that cask was coming up in effect for its third use, because it had been used for bourbon, used for malt whisky, and used for malt whisky again. And after you had emptied that pink cask it went through the system again and it came out maybe pastel yellow. So that you knew by the colour of a cask sitting in the warehouse how many cycles it had done, and when it came to the end of those four or five malt cycles then you retained it.

'The Chivas colour was always a dark maroon, so at that point these casks had dark maroon painted ends, so you knew that was a cask only to be used for grain purposes. Each of the companies used their own colour coding, but we started it. This, of course, was with the help of the Seagram people, because Seagram were worldwide and had plants all over the place, and we used to have annual conferences at which all these points were discussed.

'Another important thing was that this gave you control of how whisky in a particular coloured cask would mature. So you would use, let's say, your pink colours for your heavier malts, and go down the scale as the colour was changing, on to your lighter flavoured malts. And because they were coloured, everybody in the company knew, the coopers knew and everybody else knew, that this was the sequence.

'What was very important was the fact that 5 or 6 per cent of all the casks being emptied require repair. So it may be half a dozen new staves or a new end, or whatever. You must use new parts out of other casks that are broken down. You maybe have ten casks and two of them are needing repairs, so you would break one down to repair these two. But you would ensure that the ones you have broken down to do your repairs are at least the same or in the higher grade so that you don't put well-used wood into a cask that is not well-used. And this again was all to do with the colour system, it helped you to do this.

'As a matter of fact it was right into the middle '90s that a lot of companies still didn't appreciate that this was happening, because it was only really after the war, let's say in the early 1950s, that the American barrel actually came into the system. Prior to that you were using butts and hogsheads, ex-sherry or port, or whatever else. So none of them really had the experience of having casks that were denuded of their potential to mature.

'The most important thing really is the cask and how it's going to mature from a blender's point of view. Personally, I'm a Chivas Regal drinker, but if you can get a good Longmorn out of an oloroso sherry cask you can't whack it. Sherry casks are not sherry casks nowadays. The sherry casks used up till let's say about twenty years ago were casks of sherry that were shipped into the UK, and the sherry was held in them until such time as it was bottled. And then the casks came up. So the actual timbers themselves, the innermost quarter to half an inch of the timber, was soaked in sherry.

'But subsequently, maybe it was 25 years ago, they started shipping the sherry in tankers, but people still wanted sherry casks. So they would fill casks with sherry for about six months, and send them over as sherry casks, but they weren't nearly the same job as the originals. Very difficult to get a decent sherry cask nowadays that has enough influence on the flavour. But there was nothing nicer than a good twelve-year-old Longmorn out of an oloroso sherry cask.

'People were going over to Spain and they were buying sherry casks, but they never really identified what type of sherry had been in them before. There's a huge difference between, let's say, an oloroso and a fino. But some of them were just using them as "sherry casks", and then when they looked at the sample when it was old enough, "What the hell's happened to this?"

'Fortunately for people nowadays, they don't have to think nearly as much as

Strathisla Distillery, Keith, 1980s. Strathisla dates from 1786, and was known as Milltown and subsequently Milton, with the Strathisla name being used from the 1870s until around 1890, and again from the mid-1950s onwards.

I did, because every cask in effect going way back into the '50s, '60s, '70s, '80s and even the early '90s, every successive cask could be different because they were from different sources, different number of uses, until you get into the swing of the 1974 situation where you had colour-coded casks. So you knew that if you were all in pink they were all going to come out the same. But nobody had ever done that before.

'Now that everybody has got a system such as that, the blender doesn't need to worry too much, he knows how, if he's putting good whisky into these casks, they're going to turn out in three, five, seven, eight, nine, ten years time.

'But you always need a man to look at a batch. Way back in Charles Julian's days, he actually separated his Highland malts from his Lowland malts from his Islay malts, and vatted them separately. He put them back into casks and allowed them to marry for nine months before they were dumped as Chivas Regal malts. We studied that and also looked at a continuity system, which we set up in our warehouses in Keith, where you used 50,000 gallon stainless steel tanks, and you always ensured that you never let them get any less than a third full.

'So you worked a continuity system, batch upon batch upon batch, which was similar to what he was doing, but it was a lot easier and a lot cheaper. So you started a continuity system instead of a re-marrying system. Now some of the whisky boys still advertise that they mature twice, but that's just the same thing happening, if you're using a continuity system you're doing the same thing. You're possibly doing something a wee bit better in a continuity system, because you cannot put it into your continuity system until it's the age you want it. In the marrying system you could have put it away a wee bit earlier, you might have put it in casks that weren't as good as the ones it was originally in.

'It's important to remember that nobody really knows what spirit will be like when you open a new distillery like Glen Keith. You can break it down chemically and say that looks like something similar to whatever else, but until you're running it you don't really know. You pay your money and take your chance to a great extent, because you never know if it's going to be a heavy malt, a light malt, or whatever.

'There was one occasion where I had a complaint, and I phoned up Stuart [McBain] and I said, "What the hell have you done with Strathisla in your last batch?" And eventually he admitted that he had run short of water and he'd taken water

Jimmy Lang (extreme right) with samples of spirit and guests at the official opening of Glen Keith distillery, 1960. John Menzies, managing director of the Glasgow Bonding Company Ltd, is second from the right.

Glen Keith distillery. Glen Keith was constructed on the site of an old oat mill, and was only the second distillery, after Tullibardine, to be established in Scotland during the 20th century.

from the Glen Keith source and used it in Strathisla, and we detected the difference. Although they're fairly close together, they are coming from different areas, through different muddy pools and all the rest, and there was a difference.

'Once we had Glen Keith available we took out some others that had previously been there, which we had been purchasing from somewhere else, and it was the same with Braes of Glenlivet and Allt-a' Bhainne in time.

'I could use Strathisla at 11 per cent of the 50 per cent of the malt blend that would be out of the "top ten" whiskies without it coming through. Beyond that point it came through, it stuck its nose out, beyond that point any one of them would have come through on its own. The others I had to use at less, some maybe at 4, 5, 7, 8 per cent. But you could use 11 per cent Strathisla to help maintain the continuity of Chivas. That was the only one I ever did that experiment on, because I didn't have to do it with the others, because I had so many alternatives. But I had to do it with Strathisla because it was there at the time and it was our mainstay at the very beginning.

'We started off with Strathisla, we built Glen Keith, then Braes of Glenlivet and Allt-a' Bhainne came in during the 1970s. Then, of course, we purchased the Glenlivet mob. They had Glenlivet and Glen Grant, and then they re-opened Caperdonich. They bought Longmorn, from William Longmore and Company, with Benriach. So they had the five distilleries. Glenlivet, Glen Grant and Longmorn were always present in the Chivas inventory.

'What I shall call the Edrington Group had Highland Park, Glenrothes, Tamdhu, Glenglassaugh, Bunnahabhain, and when we bought the Glenlivet people the total capacity of distillation of Edrington was similar to ours with the Glenlivet side fixed up. I thought, wouldn't it be a bloody good idea if we could make an arrangement with them that we could pass a third of our production of each distillery to each other. I thought it was a brilliant idea, but nobody would listen to it. We'd have had guaranteed stocks of Highland Park, Glenrothes and Tamdhu, which were all in our top ten. In return they'd have had Glenlivet, Longmorn and Glen Grant. But it didn't happen.

'When we bought Glenlivet, Glenlivet had a twelve-year-old, and the Seagram company in the States wanted to boost the Glenlivet marketing wise to see just how far they could go with it. Ivan Straker *was* Glenlivet, and Ivan had to report back to the Americans.

'Ivan Straker was a character. He was chief executive of Glenlivet. When he came into the business he started calling himself "Major Straker", and Willie Lundie, the broker, insisted as a result that everyone called him Corporal Lundie, as he had been a corporal.

'I think it was Barton and Company who distributed Glenlivet twelve-year-old in the States, and then Seagram took over and said, "We can do a bloody better job than this," so they applied to Ivan, but he didn't have any older stock because he'd been using it all. But he said, "Contact Jimmy Lang, he's got lots of Glenlivet." So they eventually contacted me and said, "Have you any old Glenlivet?" I said, "Yes, quite a bit." "Any twelve years old?" "Yes, quite a bit." "Any chance we could get some of it?" "Yes, I think you could, possibly, because I can use an alternative to Glenlivet, there's no problem there." They said, "Can you give us something a wee bit older than twelve?" I said, "Yes, as a matter of fact I've got some 20 year-old." "Can we have it?" I said, "No, it's destined for Royal Salute." They said, "We'd like to have it." I said, "You'd maybe like to have it." "In which case then," they said, "we're going to reduce your Royal Salute to so and so if you take away the Glenlivet."

'And once Mr Sam realised what was happening there, that they were going to reduce his Royal Salute for the sake of Glenlivet he said, "No, leave it with Jimmy." Royal Salute was going a bomb at that time. Royal Salute was introduced in 1953, and the principal market for it was the States.

'It was a totally different character to Chivas Regal, because initially it was about 70 per cent malt. Nobody had old grain in those days, anyway. It's possibly still 70 per cent malt, it maybe even higher. There were occasions when it was 100 per cent malt because you didn't have any old enough grains.

'When Braes of Glenlivet and Allt-a' Bhainne came on stream we didn't then use other whiskies which we'd purchase from other distillers, which had a similarity. They're both silent at the moment, of course, but Benriach, which was also closed, has been sold and has re-opened. It's good to see that. Benromach started with Gordon & MacPhail, and then Mr Symington [of Signatory Vintage Scotch Whisky Co.] took over Edradour, and a few of them have got Tullibardine going again, so it's happening. It's happening slowly but surely, looking for niche markets in the future. It's nice to see this happening with some of the wee companies.

'It's been a fascinating industry to be in, and it's changed a lot in my time. The days when we were there, there were an awful lot of independent holders of whisky, there were a lot of brokers of whisky, who would build up stock for you. You'd say, "I'm short of such and such at such and such an age," and he would go round the other distillers and see where they could pick it up.

'The Lundies, the Morrisons, W.&S. Strong, P.J. Russell, they were the principal brokers in my time. Peter J. Russell came along to our place and he would never go away without doing a deal. Peter always clinched a deal before he would leave you. Which was quite different from anybody else.

'I knew George Christie quite well. I met George first of all when he had the grain distillery out in the Campsie Hills, at Cambus. We were actually going to buy their grain distillery at one point, and then we decided not to, because with the strength we had and the volumes we needed we created our own price on grain whisky, we were buying so much. We said, "We want so much, and this is what we're going to pay you," and they took it.

'It was more economical not to have our own grain distillery. We used quite a bit of Girvan, but we had our own Girvan "C" type, which was quite different from the normal Girvan that anybody else got. It was one of the American distillers who created a particular bit of plant down at Girvan that could create the special type that we wanted for Chivas Regal. It had a maltiness that no other grain whisky had. We used quite a lot of that at the time, and we also always filled a certain percentage of North British.

'When we started Hundred Pipers, which was started in 1960-something, the instructions from Edgar Bronfman, [son of Sam] who at that time was beginning to come through, was, "Give me a Scotch that is the equivalent to other Scotches as Seagram's VO is to Canadian whiskies." It was a good bit sweeter and a bit nuttier than most.

'How we were going to get this thing was anybody's guess. I was the assistant blender at that time, and we created six samples and sent them over to let Mr Sam see them, not Mr Edgar. Sam said, "I like number three, but do this …" So we went back and looked at number three and made our changes, sent another six samples over. And this time it was Edgar that got hold of them. He said, "I like your number five, but do this …" And this went on for nine months or something. I've got a copy of a letter that Edgar wrote to Alan Baillie and I was copied on, and it starts off: "To be consistent in the constant changing of our minds, will you now make Hundred Pipers so and so and so and so …" He eventually plumped for a particular blend, and when we looked back at the formulation of that, it was one we had given him about the first month.

'But he wasn't ready to market it, that was the whole thing, he was biding his time till he felt he was ready to move. This went on to the American market and it was going reasonably well, and then word came back from the marketing people that it was too similar to Seagram's VO! So we changed the formula again. We were too successful.'

'Today, of course, it's the French who own Chivas, rather than the Americans, and the boss man of Pernod Ricard, Richard Burrows, way back in the '50s was a Seagram marketing man, who was made manager at Bushmills [in County Antrim, Northern Ireland], when Seagram bought Bushmills from Bass. He reported to the senior people that there was a hell of a mess, that the inventory hadn't been controlled, they couldn't maintain formulation.

'So I was sent over; this must have been late '50s, maybe early '60s, to rehash Black Bush and Bushmills, and that's were I met Richard Burrows first of all. And now Richard Burrows is chief executive of Pernod Ricard. He's come a complete circle.

'At one time the distiller at Strathisla, Jimmy Morrison, had previously

Braes of Glenlivet distillery,
Chapeltown, 1970s. The dis-
tillery was later re-named
Braeval.

worked in Bushmills, and Morrison was the first man to control the distillation at
Glen Keith, and he did it as a triple distillation, because that's what he had done at
Bushmills. The triple distillation was lighter than the normal double distillation. So
we also on a regular basis did double distillation for one month and then did triple
distillation for the next month. That gave us two whiskies to use. There wasn't a difference between the two to any great extent, just one was lighter bodied.

'At that time, and this was at the request of the Americans, they started to
use different yeasts. There was a fruity yeast being used, and there was a particular
batch of Glen Keith produced in 1966, I think, that had a beautiful peach flavour.
But things like that you can milk off gradually, and nobody will detect them, so it
was usable, even though it wasn't standard.'